Praise for *The Magic of Hebrew Chant*

"There are two ways to enter the gates of heaven: storm them from without or be invited in from within. Chanting is the way of invitation, and this book is the invitation to the invitation. I have chanted daily for decades, and Shefa was my teacher. Let her be yours as well."

—**Rabbi Rami Shapiro**, author,
Amazing Chesed: Living a Grace-Filled Judaism

"An incredibly clear, valuable, often transcendent transmission of powerful, readily implementable approaches to Jewish spiritual awakening, growth and healing. This is a sacred book to savor and widely gift to family, students and friends."

—**Rabbi Goldie Milgram**, author, *Meaning & Mitzvah:
Daily Practices for Reclaiming Judaism through Prayer, God,
Torah, Hebrew, Mitzvot and Peoplehood*

"Invites the reader of any spiritual path to enter more deeply into the heart of love. Her contribution to Jewish spirituality in particular is immeasurable. May it endure!"

—**The Rev. Robert Corin Morris, DD**, founder, Interweave, Inc.

"Allows readers to inhabit the immersive, transformative, gently flowering yet powerful world of chant: an indispensable guide for the spiritual seeker of our time. Highly recommended!"

—**Rabbi Nehemia Polen, PhD**, professor of Jewish thought,
Hebrew College

"For those new to these pathways to the Great Mystery (aka God), here is an invitation to a richer and more profound life; for those seasoned in the disciplines of meditation, chant and prayer, it will frame your experience with insight and wisdom. It will deepen your practice; it has deepened mine."

—**Rabbi Anne Brener, LCSW**, director of spiritual development, The Academy for Jewish Religion, California; author, *Mourning and Mitzvah: Walking the Mourners' Path from Grief to Healing*

"Boldly yet gently beckons you inwardly with prescriptions of stirring sacred words, offering a practice of wisdom, a pathway of self-discovery and a yearning to reach expansively toward God and compassionately toward God's creation."

—**Rabbi Elie Kaplan Spitz**, author, *Does the Soul Survive? A Jewish Journey to Belief in Afterlife, Past Lives & Living with Purpose* and *Healing from Despair: Choosing Wholeness in a Broken World*

"Lots of people chant and few become enchanted…. Rabbi Shefa guides her readers past the sentries of the legal/rational border into the sacred space of the charismatic/ecstatic realm."

—**Rabbi Zalman Schachter-Shalomi**, author, *Davening: A Guide to Meaningful Jewish Prayer* and *Jewish with Feeling: A Guide to Meaningful Jewish Practice*

"Shefa has transformed the world of chant, allowing both the chanter and the listener to find personal meaning in Jewish prayer through the mesmerizing repetitions of words and meditative melody."

—**Cantor Linda Hirschhorn**

"As it brings text study, song and contemplative practice together—body, heart and mind acting as one—chant is the ultimate, spiritual practice. Shefa Gold is its prophet."

—**Rabbi Mike Comins**, author, *Making Prayer Real: Leading Jewish Spiritual Voices on Why Prayer Is Difficult and What to Do about It*

"A tour de force.... It integrates the extensive research and teaching Rabbi Gold has pioneered and offers a luminous resource for the renewal of Jewish religious life and contemporary spirituality."

—**Rabbi Sheila Peltz Weinberg**, Institute for Jewish Spirituality

"Wise, warm advice from the foremost expert in this form of Jewish devotional practice. It is encyclopedic, thoughtful, accessible and deep."

—**Jay Michaelson, PhD**, author, *Evolving Dharma: Buddhism, Meditation and the Next Generation of Enlightenment* and *God in Your Body: Kabbalah, Mindfulness & Embodied Spiritual Practice*

"A deeply important contribution to all those interested in contemplative practice. At the same time, Rabbi Gold facilitates a profound connection to the sacred texts of the Jewish tradition illustrating their continued relevance to contemporary Judaism."

—**Rabbi Jeff Roth**, author, *Jewish Meditation Practices for Everyday Life: Awakening Your Heart, Connecting with God*

"A literate, personal, inventive, beautifully written anthology of, and manual for, offering 'musical *kavanot.*' Gold offers American Jews seeking to rediscover the melody of meditation the perfect primer and inspiration."

—**Rabbi Lawrence Kushner**, Emanu-El Scholar at The Congregation Emanu-El of San Francisco; author, *I'm God; You're Not: Observations on Organized Religion & Other Disguises of the Ego*

"Combines the insight of a seeker, the textual knowledge of a rabbi, the clarity of a gifted teacher and the voice of a creative composer.... This moving volume provides sufficient guidance for a beginner while taking more advanced practitioners to new heights."

—**Rabbi David Teutsch**, Wiener Professor of Contemporary Jewish Civilization and director, Levin-Lieber Program in Jewish Ethics, Reconstructionist Rabbinical College; author, *Spiritual Community: The Power to Restore Hope, Commitment and Joy*

"This is the finest flowering of Rabbi Gold's vast experience and deep dedication to working with and understanding the energies of body, soul, voice, intention and consciousness in relation to sacred Jewish text."

—**Rabbi Nancy Flam**, co-director of programs, Institute for Jewish Spirituality; series editor, LifeLights

"One of our great teachers shares her secrets of how to enter the heart, open the mind, stir the spirit and awaken nothing less than a transformation in your self-understanding and love for others. The profound wisdom and amazingly beautiful chants are a gift for human flourishing. Be prepared to be touched by a magician of the soul."

—**Rabbi Irwin Kula**, coeditor, *The Book of Jewish Sacred Practices: Clal's Guide to Everyday & Holiday Rituals & Blessings*

"A treasure of exquisite simplicity, wisdom and love! With mellifluous and stunning beauty … offers a path of awakening through which outworn habits of heart and mind are discarded, core truths rediscovered and ever more expansive capacity for joy is born."

—**Rabbi Marcia Prager**, author, *The Path of Blessing: Experiencing the Energy and Abundance of the Divine*

"Shefa Gold has transcribed the music and meaning of Hebrew chant onto the pages of this book. Yet the experience of these chants flows off the page and connects you to the Jewish past and this very moment."

—**Rabbi Michael Strassfeld**, author, *A Book of Life: Embracing Judaism as a Spiritual Practice*

THE MAGIC OF
HEBREW
CHANT

Healing the Spirit,
Transforming the Mind,
Deepening Love

RABBI SHEFA GOLD

FOREWORD BY SYLVIA BOORSTEIN

For People of All Faiths, All Backgrounds
JEWISH LIGHTS Publishing
Woodstock, Vermont

The Magic of Hebrew Chant:
Healing the Spirit, Transforming the Mind, Deepening Love

2013 Quality Paperback Original, First Printing

© 2013 by Shefa Gold

Foreword © 2013 by Sylvia Boorstein

Grateful acknowledgment is given for permission to use "Chant as a Core Spiritual Practice," originally published in *Torah Journeys: The Inner Path to the Promised Land* by Shefa Gold, © 2006 by Shefa Gold. It is reprinted courtesy of Ben Yehuda Press. A version of "Chant: Transformation, Purification, Healing, and Renewal" appeared in *Seeking and Soaring: Jewish Approaches to Spiritual Direction* by Rabbi Goldie Milgram, © 2009. It is reprinted courtesy of Reclaiming Judaism Press.

Library of Congress Cataloging-in-Publication Data

Gold, Shefa.
  The magic of Hebrew chant : healing the spirit, transforming the mind, deepening love / Rabbi Shefa Gold ; foreword by Sylvia Boorstein.
      pages cm
  Includes bibliographical references and index.
  ISBN 978-1-58023-671-3
  1. Jewish chants—Instruction and study. 2. Cantillation—Instruction and study. 3. Hebrew language—Accents and accentuation. 4. Bible. O.T.—Accents and accentuation. I. Title.
  MT860.G635 2013
  782.3'6043—dc23
                            2013005071

10 9 8 7 6 5 4 3 2 1

Manufactured in the United States of America
Cover Design: Jenny Buono
Interior Design: Heather Pelham
Cover Art: © stereohype/iStockphoto.com

For People of All Faiths, All Backgrounds
Jewish Lights Publishing
A Division of LongHill Partners, Inc.
Sunset Farm Offices, Route 4, P.O. Box 237
Woodstock, VT 05091
Tel: (802) 457-4000   Fax: (802) 457-4004
www.jewishlights.com

For my Kol Zimra spirit buddies,
who have been so willing to play with me.
Your generosity inspires, encourages
and opens me to "a new song."

שִׁירוּ לַיהוה שִׁיר חָדָשׁ תְּהִלָּתוֹ בִּקְהַל חֲסִידִים

Sing to God a new song;
God's praise is found in a community of lovers. (Psalm 149:1)
Halleluyah!

And for Evelyn Katz (1924–2013) my "mother dear," my first teacher.
who encouraged me to be just who I am, and to excel.
Your love, trust, and joy now reside within me.

CONTENTS

*F*UNDAMENTALS OF CHANT   1

*T*HE SECRETS OF CHANT

*T*HE USES OF CHANT

FOREWORD

*W*hen I talk to people about spiritual practice—mine or theirs—what I am most interested in is the "Why?" of their practice, the answer to the question, "What do you hope will happen?" The preamble questions "What do you do?" and "How do you do that?" were fascinating in the 1970s when the very idea of spiritual practice and contemplative techniques for laypeople was new. People said, "I've taken up TM" or "I'm going to a Tai Chi class," and the natural response would be "How do you do that?" We had the idea—at least I did—that we had to get good at an unfamiliar technique—that it would take some time every day, like learning to play a musical instrument—and when we had mastered the technique we would somehow feel better. We used words like "liberated," but I knew even then that I wasn't sure what that meant. I think I assumed I'd find out when I got there. These days I think the important word is "transformational," and I define practice as the attempt to establish clarity in the mind so that habits that create suffering are replaced by habits that lead to peace and express themselves as love.

I believe that rather than thinking of particular activities as prac-tice, we can think of all of life as the arena of practice. Staying still or moving, standing or lying down, doing the entire spectrum of life activities, the intentions to heal the spirit, transform the mind, and deepen love—all together the most divine manifestation of ourselves as human beings—can be the leitmotif of a life. As I read *The Magic of Hebrew Chant* I feel as if I am being gently reminded of the deepest truths of living wisely and that those truths are threaded together through the familiar words of liturgy so that they can become the music of the mind that supports, consoles, directs, and redirects—moment to moment—all our activities. I believe that the mind habituated to singing to itself—whether the words are aloud or internal or even unheard, existing only as grooves established in the patterns of thought—is the mind that feels safe and peaceful and loving.

This book is a wonderful—and truly unique—compendium of Hebrew chant as a specific technique of practice. It is also clearly an invitation to leading a sanctified life, one cleansed of confusion, shining in clarity. And, Rabbi Shefa Gold is the best of teachers, charmingly personal and accessible, generous in her sharing of her own experience, inspiring in her invitation to jump into this precious life with her, wholeheartedly.

Sylvia Boorstein

INTRODUCTION

*D*uring my rabbinical training, I had the opportunity to be at a retreat with Rabbi Lawrence Kushner. At the time, I felt inundated by the sheer volume of texts and teachings, codes and midrash, Talmud, Mishnah, Gemara, commentaries, and then commentaries on those commentaries.

I am drawn toward simplicity in my spiritual practice, and I was struggling each day against what seemed like endless Jewish ramblings, thousands of years of accumulated clutter. I was drowning. And with a bit more drama and desperation than was probably necessary, I begged my teacher to please help.

Rabbi Kushner looked back at me with a combination of amusement and pity and said simply, "You only have to deal with one little bit at a time."

I was half stunned and half relieved. Stunned by the simplicity of his answer, and relieved that it was really OK to follow the path of my heart that led me to receive and cherish "one little bit at a time." I saw that each "little bit" was a microcosm of the whole and held within it the overflowing infinite blessing of my inheritance.

The magic of chant is that just a few short words, simply repeated with sweet passion, deliberate intention, and refined beauty, can unlock treasure upon treasure of healing, wisdom, and love.

Well, if it's that simple, why did I have to write this whole book about chant? Why have I dedicated so much of my life to exploring its mysteries?

The root letters *zayin-mem-reish* have a double meaning: *z-m-r* means "to chant," but it also means "to prune."

Coming to the practice of chant, we are pruning away all that obscures the essential. Chant is about honing in on the vital though often hidden core of truth that might otherwise be overlooked.

And then, the chant itself becomes an act of pruning. Each repetition of the sacred phrase can clear away another layer of extraneous clutter and distraction ... until finally we are stripped clean, fresh and newly awakened to the miracle before us, newly inspired for the joyful task at hand.

Chant is a path for all of us who lead with our hearts, who are determined to seek out the truth that is buried deep beneath the ground of our lives, and who have made a commitment to live that truth, from moment to moment, breath to breath, "one little bit at a time."

Chant has the power to open up our inner spaces, and yet it also creates connection and community. As you read this book and step onto the path of chant, you are stepping into connection with kindred souls, across the world and throughout the ages, whose hearts reverberate with sacred texts. Those kindred souls call to you, as I do, to join us in wholehearted, deeply embodied celebration of life and community.

In the first sections of *The Magic of Hebrew Chant*, you will learn the fundamentals, the secrets, and the uses of chant. What is this practice? How is chanting different from singing? What is the relationship of sound and silence? Is this new? How can we connect with the lineage of chant? What is the power of intention? What happens inside us as we chant? How can we focus and shape the energy of a group through chant? How can we use chant for healing, ritual, soul growth, inquiry, and the cultivation of divine qualities? How can we use this practice to heal the spirit, transform the mind, and deepen love?

Later in this book, I will share with you a sampling of some of the practices that I have developed. In this section I will repeat some of the key concepts of chant as applied to specific practices as we explore those practices further. My own practice is to explore a sacred phrase through study, melody, harmony, rhythm, movement, visualization, meditation, and repetition … until something of its magic, its unique power is revealed. I pray that my interpretations of these sacred phrases give you the inspiration to make them your own and the courage to approach other holy texts with reverence, playfulness, curiosity, and chutzpah.

Finally, I will share with you the musical notations for those practices, so that you can share them with your communities and let them live inside you. (You can also find recordings of these chants—and more—on my website, www.RabbShefaGold.com, or on my CDs.)

My hope is that after reading *The Magic of Hebrew Chant*, you will understand that these melodies are not merely songs to be sung; they are spiritual practices that keep on opening new doors, that will continue to reveal their secrets over a lifetime of exploration and practice.

Everywhere I travel, I meet someone whose heart is stirred by chant.

I see in her eyes that a longing that she didn't know she had has been awakened. And that longing is setting her on a path of love, illuminated by the words of the ancestors.

I see on his face an expression of such surprise. He has glimpsed the face of the Great Mystery. He is shaken. The veneer of his cool cynicism has been shattered.

Everywhere I travel, I meet someone who begins to chant, and his hidden sorrow is released, her joy is unbound, his curiosity is sparked, her passion is revealed.

Perhaps you are that someone.

I invite you to join me on this path of joyful adventure. I welcome you into the truth of who you are becoming and into the magic of Hebrew chant.

ABRACADABRA

In the beginning of God's creating the skies and the earth,
when the earth had been shapeless and formless,
and darkness was on the face of the deep,
and a Divine Breath blew across the face of the water—
God said, "Let there be light!" And there was light.
And God saw the light that it was good.

These words—the first words of Genesis, the beginning of Torah—tell me what it means to chant. I am instructed by the highest authority: Speak the word. Don't talk *about* light. Let the word "light" become itself through your holy speaking. You who are made in the divine image have this power of holy speech. And when the first glimmer of creation appears, remember to notice "it was good," to come into awareness and appreciation of the blessing before you. Before each word, you must face the shapeless, the formless. You must enter the darkness, the void ... and then find your divine breath.

Abracadabra is Aramaic for "I will create as I speak."

It turns out that the magic words of creation, transformation, healing, and the expression of our infinite depths have been hidden in plain sight in the words of our inheritance—words that lie sleeping on the page, just waiting for our love to arouse them. So many words, buried in books, seem all but dead. When I find the divine breath within me and resuscitate those words, they come alive and become a vehicle of power and healing. They become incantations.

FUNDAMENTALS OF
CHANT

Chant

WHAT IT IS

*C*hanting, the musical and rhythmic repetition of a sacred phrase from a holy text, has been the doorway for me ... into the depths of my own heart and into the heart of my inheritance. For as long as I can remember I was fascinated with the sounds of Hebrew prayer, not just for what they meant, but also for where they could take me. I found that if I focused in on one phrase, repeating it with a compelling melody, then that phrase could transport me to expansive heights and fathomless depths.

I grew up in suburban New Jersey and attended a conservative temple with my dad. He loved to sing, and he freely composed harmonies, weaving beautiful and decorative flourishes throughout the Sabbath liturgy, studiously ignoring the cantor's dirty looks. The music gave me a secret sense of what these words really meant. I knew that the English translation given on the left-hand side of the page was either just plain wrong or possibly the faint two-dimensional shadow of a mystery that was promising itself to me. These Hebrew prayers were woven together with the magic of childhood. I knew that there was power here in these sounds. This knowledge was a seed that was buried deep inside me, waiting for just the right time to grow.

I left the synagogue and became a seeker of spiritual experience. I stepped into the world with a great longing to know God. Every spiritual experience helped cultivate the soil of my heart; my longing opened up the flow that would water the seed that had been planted so long ago.

Besides being a spiritual seeker, I knew myself as an artist, and I found my voice through poetry and song. Though I am argumentative by nature, I soon learned that my arguments got me exactly nowhere. They only led me toward grief and separation. In contrast, my poem or my song connected me to others, opened my heart, and opened doors of exploration and adventure. In the early 1970s I was a folksinger. Nearly every week, I composed a new song that expressed the complexity, angst, curiosity, joy, drama, and dilemmas of my emerging independence. Through composing, I learned about the subtle juxtaposition of text and melody. Through performance, I learned how to connect with my audience and feel their hearts open in response to my own vulnerability and bold expression. I learned about energy. I learned that the sound was really just a vehicle for that energy. Sometimes when I performed, it seemed as if the audience and I were all stepping into sacred space together ...

But not quite. All that drinking. All those distractions. And those annoying separations between performer and audience.

I was given a glimpse of what was possible, but I couldn't quite make it work in that setting. It was just a glimpse that would stir my soul and awaken my longing. I yearned for that sacred space that music could engender. And I knew that the sacred space I longed for opened out into a much larger reality, a much larger mystery.

My love and longing led me to study philosophy. As the thoughts of each philosopher were revealed to me, I wanted to understand what engendered these ideas. From what state of consciousness did they emerge? How might I step into that same place so that I could know and perceive the world like this? I wanted to *be* each philosopher, to see from their perspective and tune into the same source of wisdom that had inspired them.

Now, as I develop a spiritual practice from a sacred phrase, I bring those same questions. How do I step into the state of consciousness from which these words emerged? When I embody the truth of this sacred phrase, how might my world be transformed?

My philosophical studies led me to an exploration of consciousness. I practiced astral travel and shamanic journeying. And I cultivated a deep respect for my dreams and the power of imagination. I was drawn to the mystical traditions of Christianity, Islam, and Judaism. I went through a rigorous training to lead sweat lodge from a Native American Lakota teacher. In the sweat lodge I learned how to pray as if my life depended on it.

My explorations of consciousness led me to meditation. I practiced the art of letting go of the content of thoughts so that I might rest in God. My inspirations as I developed my own practice of meditation were Buddhism, centering prayer, and the Hasidic ideal of *d'veikut* (cleaving to God).

One night I had a dream in which I was told explicitly by a booming authoritative voice, "You will create *bhakti* Judaism!" I woke up startled and asked, "What is *bhakti*?" I didn't even know the word but soon found out that it refers to the devotional path within Hinduism, the path of love and complete surrender to the mystery of the Divine.

When I first began chanting, I was in love with sound. I experimented with melody, rhythm, harmony, tone, and pitch. But after a while I began to notice that the silence that followed the chant was simply extraordinary. I just couldn't wait for the chant to end because I knew that I would get to dive into that beautiful silence. It was as if the chant opened a door, and in the silence I could enter and receive the true blessing of my efforts. I fell in love with the silence.

This movement from sound to silence to sound to silence eventually began to reveal the secrets of the silence at the very heart of sound, and the sound at the very heart of silence. And these secrets sent me on a path toward listening ever more deeply.

Sh'ma (listen), *Yisrael* (God-wrestlers). Only then will you know the Oneness, the Unity.

This is considered the central prayer of Judaism, spoken morning and night, calling to us from every doorway, awakening us out of the dream of separation, calling us home to unity consciousness.

Chant is the marriage of sound and silence. In chant, they are joined in love and beauty. That love between sound and silence has the power to open me to this truth of essential unity. And the beauty of chant keeps me totally engaged ... because it is really so much fun.

The Sacred Phrase

OR ... HOW A CHANT IS DIFFERENT FROM A SONG

In acts of genuine expression, what goes on between the soul of man and the word of prayer is more than an act of employment, of using words as if they were tools. Here the soul and the word react upon each other; the word is a creative force.

Words are not made of paper. Words of prayer are repositories of the spirit. It is only after we kindle a light in the words that we are able to behold the riches they contain. It is only after we arrive within a word that we become aware of the riches our own souls contain.

(Abraham Joshua Heschel, *Man's Quest for God*)

This quote from twentieth-century theologian and philosopher Rabbi Abraham Joshua Heschel strikes me as a beautiful description of the practice of chanting. When we chant, we "kindle a light in the words" and use that light as a lantern on our journey through the inner landscape. A chant is different from a song. It is a meditative practice that encompasses and integrates our inner and outer dimensions. When I sing a song, I am communicating meaning and expressing beauty to the listener "out there." But when I chant, I am also communicating with and awakening places inside me that need to hear and be touched by the chant. A song may entertain, but a chant is meant to transform. When you have learned the melody and rhythm of a chant, you've only touched the surface. Then you can begin to explore the inner dimensions of the chant. The practice of chant is simple and accessible to everyone, yet it provides opportunities for a lifetime of fascinating exploration and refinement. Through our use of chant as a spiritual practice, we explore the pathways of divine flow, we learn about ourselves, we connect with each other, we open ourselves to the wisdom of our ancestors, and we heal and nurture ourselves and the world.

There are three phases that transform chant from simple singing into a contemplative, ecstatic meditation practice:

1. Establishing the ground of a chant.
2. As the chant is happening, cultivating an awareness of the components of the chant—variables that affect consciousness.
3. Learning to enter the silence that follows. This is when the transformative power of the chant does its work. It is as if we are building a *Mishkan*, a holy sanctuary with the sound, intention, meaning, and fine attention to detail. Then in the silence afterward we must learn to enter the *Mishkan* and experience God's presence that we have invited in with the chant.

The Ground of a Chant

1. Perceiving the spiritual need or challenge
2. Rising to meet that challenge
3. Perceiving the potential
4. Inviting co-creation of group energy
5. Creating expectancy and the sacred container

The ground of a chant begins with an understanding of why you are chanting. What is the need of the group? Or, if you are chanting alone, what is your own need? What is the spiritual challenge that we are facing at this moment? When that challenge is clearly perceived and articulated, then we can find the power and inspiration to rise to the challenge. The leader of a chant must learn to perceive the potential of the group that she's working with, create a strong and safe container for practice, and communicate an enthusiastic expectation of what's possible. All participants must surrender themselves in service to the group and to the sacred purpose of the chant. Before you open your mouth to chant, it's important to formulate a clear intention and direct your heart toward that purpose.

Components of a Chant

1. Meaning of the sacred phrase
2. Breath
3. Intention
4. Sound—vowel and consonant
5. Melodic story and harmonic intervals
6. Tone and rhythm
7. Visualization—imposed or discovered
8. Context from which the sacred phrase is drawn
9. Balance of will and surrender
10. Vertical and horizontal axis
11. Stereoscopic consciousness

The chant begins with a piece of text. The sacred phrase, drawn from liturgy or scripture, becomes a doorway. We enter through that doorway by using each of the components of the chant as variables that have an effect on our state of consciousness. By becoming aware of those effects, we can use these components with more and more awareness and skill. By bringing attention to the rhythm of breath, to the sounds of the words, to the many layers of intention that evolve with the chant, we transform a simple melody into an opportunity for transformation and healing.

As we chant, we learn to monitor and balance our strength of will to fully engage with the practice, with our ability to surrender to its power. We establish within us a vertical axis—the energy that grounds us and connects us to our highest guidance. We establish a horizontal axis—openness of heart that connects us with everyone in our chanting circle and with all the concentric circles of souls engaged in prayer. And we cultivate stereoscopic consciousness, which is the ability to be completely focused simultaneously on our own deepest center point *and* on the energy of the group as we build the *Mishkan* of the chant together.

Entering the Silence

1. Gentle breath into the heart
2. Exploration of inner space
3. Noticing shifts of consciousness
4. Surrendering to God's transforming presence

The last phase of the chant happens in the silence that follows. When the music stops, the power of the chant is really just beginning. This is the point when our finest attention is required. One of the ways to refine your attention is to focus on the breath and imagine you are breathing in the flavor and nurturance of the chant. Imagine that the breath is entering directly into your heart and touching the deepest place inside you. As the heart opens in response to the energy of the chant, it is possible to explore the inner landscape, and as Rabbi Heschel describes, *"we become aware of the riches our own souls contain."* When the chant ends, there is a door that must be opened in the silence. In the practice of chant we learn to find that door and enter through it to discover the depths of our soul's wisdom and the expansive spaciousness of our souls.

&

Intention

*M*any years ago I worked at Disney World. I was a monorail pilot, and it was my job to transport as many people as possible, as safely and as swiftly as possible, from the parking lot to the Magic Kingdom and back. (Some of my students have commented that I am still doing this job, in my own way.) I wore what I referred to as an old-fashioned futuristic costume—blue and green polyester with a pilot's helmet. I studied the safety procedures and, in my spare time, drew flow charts, determined to improve the efficiency of the system. I even set up meetings with my superiors to share my ideas, which were politely ignored.

One night I had a dream. In my dream, we had finally found a way for the trains to run perfectly on time. They stopped at each station for exactly the right amount of time. But the doors didn't open ... and then the train just continued on to the next station. (What had kept the train from running smoothly before were all those unpredictable people—old people who moved too slowly, young children who were distracted, families trying to stay together.) In my dream, I watched the train move gracefully around its circuit, keeping to schedule, keeping its doors neatly closed. What beauty, what efficiency!

I woke up and immediately realized that this was a dream about *prayer.*

The train represented the words of prayer, moving from station to station in our service. Yet they were empty! We needed to stop, open the doors wide, and fill the sacred word with intention.

The great Hasidic master we call the Baal Shem Tov came to this same conclusion on his prayerful way to the Magic Kingdom. In a commentary on the story of Noah, he reminds us that the word for "ark" (*teivah*) also means "word":

> Genesis 6:16 says, "Make a window for the *teivah* (word of prayer) ... so that the light can shine in." And in 6:18: "You and your entire household must enter the *teivah* ... enter into the word with your entire body and energy."
>
> (*Tzava'at Rivash* 8b)

Chant is a way letting the light into the word and of filling each word with my "entire body and energy."

The way that "filling" happens is not through the force of my will, but rather through the force of love. I come into relation with the word; I fall in love with the word; I allow myself to become completely vulnerable to its power; I call on all my knowledge of sound, melody, harmony, rhythm, breath, and tone as I play with wild abandon; and finally I surrender.

The word takes me from the parking lot of normal discursive perception and expression to the Magic Kingdom of unitive consciousness. When I get back to the parking lot, I have been transformed. My heart is open. I am fully alive and inspired.

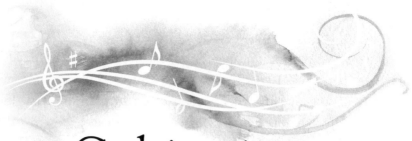

Cultivating Four Pathways of Intention

I remember a conversation with Jonathan Goldman, one of the world's foremost experts on sound healing. He took me aside one day during one of his trainings and whispered conspiratorially, "You know it's really 95 percent about *intention*." Everything we had been learning about pitch, resonance, psychoacoustics, entrainment, toning, harmonics, chakras, and overtones dealt with that small remaining 5 percent. And I wondered, "How might I explore the power of intention?"

I began to understand intention not as a force of my own will or ego (what I want), but rather as a field of potentiality (what God / the Universe / the Great Intelligence wants for me or through me). I approach the practice of chant as a way of connecting with that field. Albert Einstein said that "the field is the sole governing agency of the particle." Scientists of quantum physics are finding that consciousness is central in shaping our world, that we are not separate from our environment; we are a packet of pulsating power, constantly interacting with a vast sea of energy. Chant is a way of bringing awareness and deliberation to that interaction.

When I realized that the power of intention was not sourced merely from the place of my own desire or ego, I began to tune in to the field of intention and perceive a sense of being "intended." In theistic language, I was sensing "the will of God" moving inside of me, calling me toward the realization of my potential. In the words of *Pirkei Avot* 2:4, "Make God's will like your own will, so that God will make your will like God's will." I nullify my small will (my whims and preferences) in order to open up to the greater will.

In the language of the Hasidic masters, I am moving from *mochin d'katnut* (small mind) to *mochin d'gadlut* (big mind).

When I chant, I am activating my potential, which is the God-force within me. I am aligning myself with the greatest possibility. I am stepping up to the challenge of becoming a co-creator of my world, a vehicle through which divine creativity might flow.

The word for intention in Hebrew, *kavanah*, is associated with direction. Energy is flowing through me all the time, but if I direct my heart toward a specific purpose, then the energy flows toward that goal. As I prepare the ground of the chant and establish my intention, I am directing my heart, orienting myself toward a certain potential.

The four pathways of intention that I have been exploring, four different ways of approaching the work of building intention, are *memory*, *imagination*, *presence*, and *attunement*.

Memory

There are two different ways that I understand the role of memory as I do the work of building intention. First, I learn how to call on and activate the power and qualities of the memories that are stored in my body. And second, I use the power of my chant practice to create memories that can be called on when needed.

CHANNELING THE POWER OF MEMORY INTO MY PRACTICE

Let's look at an example of a practice that is activated by the power of memory:

ASHREI

אַשְׁרֵי יוֹשְׁבֵי בֵיתֶךָ עוֹד יְהַלְלוּךָ

Ashrei yosh'vei veitecha od y'hal'lucha.
Happy are those who dwell in Your house; they keep on praising.
(Psalm 84:5)

There is a state of consciousness I call *Ashrei*. It is the kind of unconditional joy that comes from being in the "God-house," which means being in God-consciousness, which means having the experience of *knowing* that we are all connected, all integral to the whole and the holy. Have you ever had a moment of experiencing that great joy? Where were you? On a mountaintop, perhaps? Or in the arms of a lover? Or looking into the eyes of a child? Or witnessing a birth? Or deep in prayer or meditation?

I remember an "*Ashrei*" moment. I was outside connecting with my land through prayer. I felt so very blessed to be living in this beautiful, holy, spacious land. My prayer took the form of a vow to care for and love all the creatures that shared this land with me. I sat beneath the branches of a tree and spoke to the rocks, the trees, the birds, foxes, raccoons, bears ... vowing my attention, honor, and love. As I spoke, a flock of birds quietly landed in the tree. I spoke my promises, felt my love, and watched those birds fill every branch. When I finally stopped speaking, the entire flock flew up into the sky all at once in a rush of wind. And my heart lifted with them in such joy.

I close my eyes and remember that moment—the feeling of wings in my heart, connecting me to the sky—the joy of knowing that I had been heard and that my prayer was fully received. Well, really the "knowing" came afterward. In the moment of "*Ashrei*" there was only surprise, and a timelessness, as if I had entered the infinite space between moments, between the in-breath and the out-breath, the meeting place of love and awe.

That moment is still inside me, and I can call on its power to help return me to that place the liturgy calls "God's house." In that place, critical mind, with all its worry and complaining, falls away, and all that's left is praise. *Od y'hal'lucha!* All I can do is praise.

I let the memory of that "*Ashrei*" moment fuel the chant, and the chant becomes a vehicle of remembrance, connecting me back to that wordless truth that I know but so often forget. I let the memory of that "*Ashrei*" moment become my compass that can guide me back toward its truth and treasures.

I want to stress that chant is an *embodied* practice; we can't stay in our heads, merely thinking *about* or contemplating ideas, no matter how sublime. When I chant, every molecule of my body is vibrating, jarring loose the power of stored memories and making that force available to me as I build the power of intention.

Memories that are painful or terrifying sometimes get trapped in the body and form blockages that obstruct the free flow of energy. I believe that those energy blockages eventually manifest as disease. Chant has the potential to free those obstructions, allowing us not only to release painful, "stuck," calcified memories, but also to utilize their energy in the building of positive intention.

The path of the chanter is a path of healing trauma. When we experience trauma, we no longer fully inhabit our bodies. When difficult memories are stored in the body, that's the last place we want to be. A kind of numbness sets in. Being cut off from our bodies makes us less alive; our breath becomes shallow; we live in our heads, our experiences completely mediated by ideas. Being numb and cut off from the power and wisdom of our bodies is such a great price to pay for the illusion of safety. Chant reconnects us. And with that reconnection, I have access to the power of memory. In chant, I dedicate the energy of all memory (even painful ones) to the building of intention.

Here is an example of using a painful memory in building the power of intention. This practice, which I call "Sowing Our Tears," is inspired by Psalm 126, one of the Songs of Ascent:

SOWING OUR TEARS

הַזֹּרְעִים בְּדִמְעָה בְּרִנָּה יִקְצֹרוּ

Hazor'im b'dimah b'rinah yik'tzoru.
Those who sow in tears will reap in joyous song.
(Psalm 126:5)

Some tears lie fallow. They dissolve into dust or splatter on pavement, and are not planted. These tears leave us bitter and exhausted. Yet, when we know our tears as precious, they can be carefully and tenderly planted. We can do this planting for one another by giving each other the kind of attention that creates fertile ground for tears. By acknowledging the value of grief as tears flow through us, we can plant each tear as a seed of joy. Our grieving can wash us clean, open the ground of our hearts, and clear the way for new life, new song, and surprising joy.

With this practice I reach into the stored memories of grief. I reencounter my own tears, shed and unshed, and know my tears as precious seeds that can grow into greater love and compassion for myself and others. As I chant these sacred words, I let the power of my grief pour through my voice and presence. Memories fuel my intention, the intention to surrender to the power of transformation.

CREATING MEMORIES OF STATES OF CONSCIOUSNESS

The second way that I understand the role of memory in the building of intention is the *creation* of memories that can happen in the silence that follows a chant. Each chant practice, each unique text married to melody, rhythm, intention, and tone, engenders a particular state of consciousness. Our state of consciousness determines the lens through which we perceive Reality; it determines the kind of thoughts that our brains produce; it determines our patterns of moods, as well as the extent of our vulnerabilities to the outside world; and it determines the depth and breadth of our creative abilities.

And here is the rule to remember: *The awareness of a state magnifies its benefit.*

We move through different states of consciousness all the time. It's often very haphazard and accidental, and it's easy to become the victim of our own fluctuating states of consciousness.

It is possible, though, through the practice of chant, to bring awareness to my state. Through awareness, I create a pathway so that I can access that particular state when I need to. In the silence after a chant, I engage in quiet inquiry. I ask, "What is this? What is possible from here? What door has been opened by the chant? How might I enter?" These questions do not just engage my intellect. They activate my curiosity and my appreciation. Sometimes I call this process of awareness "spiritual photography." I am taking a picture of the state that has been generated by the chant. I remember it by breathing it in deeply and imprinting it in my physical body. The benefit of that state is magnified through awareness, because the memory of that state will always be there, enriching my inner life. I can access that state because my cognitive mind has created a pathway of access.

Here is an example:

GRATEFULNESS

אוֹדְךָ בְּעוֹד תִּהְיֶה נִשְׁמַת אֱלוֹהַּ בִּי

Odach b'od t'h'yeh nishmat Eloha bi.
I will thank You as long as the divine breath is in me.
(Solomon ibn Gabirol, eleventh-century Spanish poet and philosopher)

This line from a poem by Solomon ibn Gabirol expresses my intention so well—to feel God's breath in me, and to use that breath in gratitude ... no matter what! When I chant these words I am lifted up into a kind of unconditional gratefulness that comes from the inside and is not dependent on outer circumstance. In the silence after the chant, I breathe in this intoxicating energy. I notice where the chant has brought me—I notice the rhythm of my breath, feelings in my body, my sense of spaciousness, both inner and outer. I imagine breathing the energy of the chant into my heart and "tasting" it.

Through the power of association, I allow images to arise. Sometimes I'll feel the energy as a color, flavor, or texture. All this is happening under the watchful eyes of an attentive inner witness. I am watching, noticing everything about this state as it emerges ... and it is this awareness that makes all the difference. Awareness magnifies the benefit of the chant by creating a pathway that I might return to that state, just by remembering. The words and melody of the chant become a memory key.

Then one day when I'm having trouble finding my way to gratefulness, I can either use the chant or find the memory of the chant in my body and just breathe into that memory.

As I develop my repertoire of chants, each with its own particular energy, it's as if I am adding to my medicine bag. The power of a chant is its "medicine," its unique power to move me or open the door into a distinct state of consciousness.

In the work of transforming states of consciousness, I'm not trying to value one state above another. What matters is fluidity and awareness; what's important is that I don't get stuck and I don't go unconscious.

The memory that I have planted of that state of unconditional gratefulness, or expanded awareness, or the deep essential joy of being itself can save me from my own negative patterns.

Imagination

As a child I gloried in my imagination. I could play all day long without tiring, and my imagination opened up worlds of experience, joy, and adventure. My imagination set me free from the limitations of place, age, culture, expectations, and agreed-upon possibilities. I could be an explorer. I could try out every profession and try on every identity. By playing, by imagining myself as the hero of my own life, I could unearth my buried strengths and shine my hidden radiance.

I remember the first time I overheard an adult talking about me. This grown-up looked over at me and said, "She has such a good imagination." And I knew by his tone of voice and by the way he rolled his eyes that this wasn't a compliment. I felt confused and just a little ashamed. Something that I thought was so wonderful was degraded, devalued, was relegated to "childishness." I gradually lost some of my enthusiasm for play because I wanted to be taken seriously.

As an adult, as I stepped consciously onto the spiritual path, I knew that I had to recover, then cultivate, then refine the imagination that I had as a child.

I had a great thirst for knowledge, but there were limits to where my rational mind could take me. "Imagination is more important than knowledge," Albert Einstein tells us. "Logic will get you from A to B. Imagination will take you everywhere."

My path has been the recovery of imagination and then the refinement of that faculty (partly through intellect and partly through love). I think of that process of refinement as becoming a pure, clear channel for the divine overflow.

I use my imagination to build the power of intention. The more that I use my imagination, the more powerful and clear it becomes. Here is an example of a practice that incorporates the imagination:

SPACIOUSNESS

הַרְחִיבִי מְקוֹם אָהֳלֵךְ

Harchivi m'kom oholeich.
Enlarge the place of your tent.
(Isaiah 54:2)

As I chant, I am visualizing, feeling, imagining my inner spaciousness getting wider and more expansive. I celebrate the spaces between each molecule of my body. I imagine the space inside my heart expanding.

This practice is very useful in dealing with emotional or physical pain. Pain is a pattern of contraction. I become overwhelmed because the pain takes up the entire space of my awareness. I have found that even when I can't "make the pain stop," it is possible to create a sense of spaciousness around the sensation, so that in that very large space of my awareness, the pain can be experienced as just a small part of who I am. When I can become spacious, "enlarging the place of my tent," then the pain becomes manageable and I am not overwhelmed. With this practice of imagining spaciousness, I experience the vastness of my true Being. Instead of contracting around the pain, I expand my awareness into that spaciousness. The expansive harmonies really help. In the silence after the chant, I focus on my breath and imagine my breath as God's breath being breathed into me, opening up the inner spaces. In a hadith (a story about the prophet), God says to Muhammad, "The whole universe cannot contain me, but the human heart *can* contain me." That's how spacious we can become.

In chant we can call in a vision, by entering an altered state and then opening to wisdom. That vision often comes to us through the gateway of imagination. By working with the imagination, I am making myself into a vessel, so that I might receive the overflow of God and then transmit the highest wisdom, sweetest love, and wildest possibilities.

Here is an example of a practice that invites a vision to enter through our imaginative faculties:

INVITING OUR FUTURE SELVES

הוֹדִיעֵנִי יהוה קִצִּי וּמִדַּת יָמַי מַה־הִיא

Hodi'eiani Yah kitzi, umidat yamai mah hi?
O God, show me my end, and what is the measure of my days?
(Psalm 39:5)

I discovered this practice many years ago at a time when I was deeply depressed. My despair just kept me in bed that morning; I didn't have the energy to move. I was startled out of my paralyzed state by a vision. My future self came to me. She was there to comfort me and to show me who I was becoming and to assure me that everything was going to be OK ... and even better than OK!

It was such a powerfully healing vision that it got me to thinking, "If my future self could visit me, why can't I go and visit my past self?" I embarked on a series of imaginative journeys to the sad, shy, lonely little girl I had been. I imagined embracing her, comforting her, letting her know that it would be OK, and even better than OK!

I really believe that I changed the past, and in consequence my present was impacted and my future possibilities were enlarged.

With this chant we can pray for a vision of who we are becoming. At the end of the chant, open up to receive a visit from your future self. Let your imagination lead you to your vision and trust what comes. Receive the gift, wisdom, guidance, or blessing of your future self.

Presence

As I build the power of intention and enter into the practice of chant, I ask myself, "Where is the chant coming *from*? Who's chanting? Who's *not* chanting? (I call toward my inner multiplicity, my inner complexity.) How can I activate the fullness of my presence, so that the chant can come from the very deepest place within me?" Through the practice of chant, it is possible to integrate all of my disparate parts. When I can learn to chant from that deepest place within me, from that inner spark of divinity, then perhaps I can also learn to live from those depths. When I can live from the depths and source that God-spark within me, then I have access to the fullness of my love and wisdom.

In Torah, when God calls, the correct answer is, "*Hineini*! Here I am!" God calls us to presence, because only when we are fully present can we step onto the path of our own destiny.

Presence can be understood as the *prerequisite*, the *path*, and the *goal* of our practice.

Presence is the prerequisite. As Abraham, Isaac, Jacob, Moses, and many of the prophets step up to their holy work, they answer God's call by saying, "*Hineini*! Here I am, ready to hear your voice."

Presence is the practice. As I chant or meditate, my mind wanders off, and I am called back again and again to presence. *Hineini*! I got lost for a little while, but now I'm back.

And presence is the goal. My practice calls me back to God's presence. That Great Mystery has been patiently waiting for me all along. When I stand in the fullness of *my* presence, God's presence is vibrating within me, making itself known.

Sometimes we can get lost in the shallows, tangled up in the irritability of the surface. I remember one day I was having a fight with my beloved husband Rachmiel. It was one of those fights where right in the middle of it, neither of us could remember what we were fighting about. We called a "time-out," and we each retreated to our respective meditation rooms.

I did the following practice, so that I could recover the depths of my presence and with it my calm love and wise perspective. It really worked. With presence came the remembrance of my deepest intention for love.

CALLING FORTH THE HIDDEN POWER

קוּמָה יהוה הוֹשִׁיעֵנִי אֱלֹהַי

Kumah Adonai, hoshi'eini Elohai.
Rise up, YHVH; save me, my God.
(Psalm 3:8)

With this practice, I call forth the hidden power. I sing to the force that is hidden in my depths and in the secret places of this world. I sing with a bold demand and with a humble plea for that force to reveal itself. As I chant, I dedicate myself as a vessel for that power. I pray to be saved from the traps of superficiality. I pray to have access to depths of meaning and purpose rather than be a prisoner to the surface of things.

In building the power of intention, I am continually refining the quality of my presence. The very first question that God asks in Torah is, "*Ayekah?* Where are you?" (Genesis 3:9). That question is still reverberating, and I hear it each time I set my intention, each time I open my mouth to chant.

Attunement

The most powerful way of establishing an intention is *not* by asking for something, but by stepping into that possibility with the fullness of my passion and faith. Attunement is a way of harmonizing my energies with that field of potentiality, the best that is in me. When I practice attunement, it feels as if I am claiming my rightful inheritance and stepping into the larger life that I was meant to live.

I first learned about the process of attunement back in the 1970s when I embarked on a simple experiment that changed my life. I had an annoying problem of having warts on my hands. I went to the doctor, who tried burning them off, freezing them off, cutting them off ... but they kept growing back. They were very ugly and caused me a lot of shame.

I was reading a book by Jane Roberts called *The Nature of Personal Reality*, which was part of a body of channeled material from a spirit called Seth. I decided to apply its principles with an experiment to finally get rid of my warts. After all, what did I have to lose?

There were two components to this experiment:

One: Each morning I lay in bed, and for exactly five minutes I basked in the beauty of my hands. I waxed poetic and spoke out loud in a very musical way, describing the glory and wonder of my smooth, luxurious hands. With great feeling I gracefully lifted my hands in the air and exclaimed, "Oh, what beautiful smooth, magnificent, marvelous hands I have. How wonderful! How soft!"

Just five minutes.

Then the second component: Usually when I noticed my warts, I would react with a feeling of revulsion—nothing big, just a little feeling of "Oy." So, during this experiment, whenever I had that averse reaction, I would notice and cut it short and just release the tension and relax. I'd interrupt my normal response and just gently let it go. I was surprised at how many times a day I had to do this and also how easy it was to do.

In less than a week, all my warts were gone, and they never returned.

I wondered, "Why was this method so successful? How can I apply this to other aspects of my life? How can I use the principles of attunement to build and activate the power of my intentions?"

Attunement is about coming into harmony with the highest possibility. Here is an example of a practice of attunement:

RUTH

עַמֵּךְ עַמִּי וֵאלֹהַיִךְ אֱלֹהָי

Ameich ami veilohayich Elohai.
Your people are my people, and your God is my God.
(Ruth 1:16)

On Shavuot, we read the book of Ruth, which recounts the story of love and loyalty. As we chant Ruth's vow to Naomi, we can each find our own love and loyalty. Though Ruth was a Moabite (Moab was an enemy of Israel), she became the honored ancestor of King David, whose bloodline produces the Messiah. Through her steadfast devotion to Naomi, her people, and her God, Ruth found her own way. So too may we find a sense of belonging and birth *mashiach* (messianic) consciousness into the world.

I chant these words as a practice of belonging. Each repetition allows me to address wider and wider circles of relations, letting that sense of belonging expand. I begin by chanting these words to my family, my students, my close friends. As I chant, I am filled with the joy of connection and kinship. After chanting to all the people I love, I begin to chant these words to everyone else, to people I don't yet know, to people who might seem different than me, to people who I don't even like or I might consider my enemies. "Oh, you are also my people. We come from the same root in God." When I run out of people, I chant these words to all the animals, to the plants, to the rocks. And as I chant, I am glorying in the truth that "we are all related; we all come from the same root in God." I chant these words of power to the stars and know myself as one of them, shining, belonging to the cosmos. I am attuning myself to this truth.

And in this knowing, I am releasing the old patterns of alienation, the pain that comes from feeling like I don't belong.

It turns out that this work of building intention for my practice of chant is exactly the same work as building intention for my life. This is how I want to live:

> With full access to the power of *memory* that is locked away in my body and the ability to create fluid memory pathways to altered states,

> With the free flow of *imagination* that can take me beyond conditioned perceptions of reality and open up worlds of possibility,

> With access to the fullness of *presence*, so that I can be in my power, act from my wisdom, and answer God's call,

> And with *attunement* to the highest, deepest, most expansive possibilities of who I am becoming, so that I might come into harmony with the flow of "milk and honey" and enter the Promised Land.

"That This Song May Be a Witness"

THE POWER OF CHANT

*L*ike many Jews, I am a lover of words. I loved Hebrew, even when I didn't "understand" a word of it. The sounds seemed to open up the place inside me that wanted to pour itself out to God. The sounds turned me inside out in ways that made me feel visible to God. Seen and known and loved. As my love for the sounds and my knowledge of the words grew, I found myself seriously out of step with formal communal prayer.

My thirst to drink deeply from certain phrases in the liturgy that called to me was constantly being frustrated by the pace and sheer volume of traditional prayer. I began to look for what was essential in prayer and to search for the deep structure of the prayer service, which would help me to understand the function and not merely the content of each prayer. My background in music and many forms of meditation prepared me in developing a chanting practice, which treated the sacred phrase as a doorway. Repetition became a way of stilling the mind and opening the heart wide. In that wide space it felt as if the sacred phrases were planting seeds.

In Deuteronomy, God instructs Moses to "write this song for yourselves and teach it to the Israelites; put it in their mouths, that this song may be a witness" (31:19). God goes on to predict that when the people enter the Land, they will "get fat" (31:20), mean-ing they will grow complacent and forgetful, breaking the covenant. When that happens, even though they might ignore every teaching, the song that has been planted within them will not be forgotten, and it will serve as a reminder, a witness, which can help redirect the hearts of the people toward the One God.

The practice of chanting cultivated in me a garden of devotion, yearning, joy, and vision—reminders of my connection to God. Gradually I became familiar with the wide range of mind-states that the chants engendered. I was drawn especially to the ecstatic states, which were both healing and empowering. At some point in my train-ing I became less attached to those ecstatic states and began to notice the silence that followed the chant. I felt myself drawn into that silence. I had known that the chant was a doorway, but before I really understood the invitation of the silence, I had not really entered.

Entering the *Mishkan*

Being drawn into the space within, learning to enter it without dis-turbing its form, is like coming into the *Mishkan*, the Tabernacle in the desert. So much tender care and attention to detail are described in the building of the *Mishkan* in the book of Exodus. Artistry, skill, inventiveness, and sheer generosity were called forth in that building. When I lead chanting, I feel like B'tzalel, the chief artist, directing this building project whose purpose is to create a dwelling place for God in our community, in our hearts.

Learning each particular state of mind that it is possible to attain through a certain chant has been a piece of this work. These are the tools I develop. As I expand the repertoire of tools, I feel called to constantly deepen my connection to tradition, so that I may know the prayer service as a transformational process, trust the power of prayer, and integrate the teachings of Torah into the heart that has been opened by that power.

Another piece of this work is understanding and utilizing the inter-dependent relationship between the "ecstatic" and the "contemplative."

The ecstatic component of chant allows me to move into contemplative space with vitality and with the strength and fullness of my devotion. Framing chant within the context of a contemplative silent practice creates a space in which the power of the chant can deepen and evolve, allowing its power to unfold in the silence. I want to make clear that my intention is not for the chant to continue in the silence, but rather for the chanter to enter through the door of the chant into the depths and vast expanse of the silence.

Developing a Chant

In developing a chant I will first choose a phrase from the text that reaches out to me with its beauty or mystery. I pay close attention not just to the meaning of the words but also to the sounds, both consonant and vowel, and the feelings that those sounds evoke. I've learned that certain sounds are particularly powerful in affecting the mind or heart or body. I've learned that certain rhythms of breathing will produce specific states of mind. I've learned to expand the range of "tones" that will inspire and evoke memory, meaning, and depth. I've learned that the power of the chant can sometimes be increased through adding certain body movements or visualizations. I work with the tools that I know so well—melody, harmony, syncopation. And yet I don't use these tools just to make something that is pleasing or beautiful. The chant is not a song.

The difference between chanting and singing is crucial. Chanting is primarily a meditative process, which requires an inward focus, on the one hand, and a sensitivity to the energy of the group and a willingness to serve the group, on the other. Through the chanting practice, both these foci are cultivated and strengthened. As with any type of meditation, effort is required, and yet at some point you must simply surrender to the power of the chant, the presence of God that has been invited in, and the transformation that is working through you.

I will give an example of a chant and how it might be used. The chant consists of a phrase taken from Psalm 23. It is *Kosi r'vayah*, often translated as "My cup runneth over."

MY CUP

כּוֹסִי רְוָיָה

Kosi r'vayah.
My cup overflows.
(Psalm 23:5)

In introducing the chant I would bring something of its context to life: Though I walk through the valley of the deepest darkness, I will not fear evil, for You, God, are with me. How do you manifest Yourself to me? I have come face-to-face with my own demons across the lavish table that You spread before me. And on that table is a cup that is overflowing.

In building the *kavanah*, the intention for this chant, I would invite the community to begin to become aware of two different dimensions of "cup." One cup is located in the heart. It is the connection to the Source of life and love within us, and no matter what befalls us or what "enemy" faces us from across the table, that inner cup continues to flow and to overflow. The sound of the chant reconnects us to that flow. The other "cup" is the cup that is formed in community. The sound of our voices and the strength of our shared intention create that cup, which both contains the divine flow and serves as a vehicle for our nourishment. As we form the cup of community, we enable each person to access exactly what they need, to drink individually from the flow that we create together.

This chant is composed of three parts, which through different rhythmic patterns evoke the feeling of rivulets flowing mellifluously together and apart. Chanting is done with eyes closed, to promote greater concentration and less self-consciousness. The chant moves through a number of phases as the community gradually surrenders to its flow and as each heart begins to open in response to the gentle beauty of both the inner and the outer flow. Some people may feel a surge of emotion welling up in them. They are instructed to pour that emotional energy into the chant, in service to the group, and to let go of each thought or feeling as it passes. Each repetition is an opportunity to be more present to the fullness of the chant, to bring more attention to listening and receiving the "whole" of the chant and to refining your own intention and generosity.

It is the leader's responsibility to understand the direction, function, and potential of the chant in the context of a service or meditation and to know when to end the chant. Often chant leaders will end too soon, because there is a powerful message that the mind transmits when it is bored. The message to stop the chant arises from normal consciousness when it is threatened, when it can't hold on much longer. The goal is to chant through the boredom and through the momentary anxiety of losing control or losing the fixed boundaries of self. As I keep on chanting, I remind myself, "Beyond boredom is breakthrough." Past the boredom there is a shift in consciousness, a sudden expansion, and a simultaneous cohesion of the group.

The most powerful moment of the chant happens in the silence that follows. The chant inclines the mind toward a certain state of consciousness, which can be accessed in that moment after the chant. The discipline of chanting teaches how to discern the potential of that moment, let its fullness unfold, and walk through the door that is opened by the chant. That "walk" is taken by means of a gentle, deliberate, directed breathing and an expanded awareness of the energy that has emerged. A key element to using that energy is a willingness to serve and to surrender your "personal" experience. Thus the self expands beyond its normal boundaries, and there is a taste of connection. In order to grow beyond just tasting, we must encounter certain obstacles to practice and be careful of certain traps that lie along the way.

Obstacles and Traps

I make a distinction between obstacles and traps. It's important to identify both. Sometimes I look at my practice life as a searching for just the right balance between "surrender" and "will." The will is expressed through our commitment to rigor, regularity, moving through difficult places, expending effort, not giving up.

Each of us faces obstacles to the emergence of will, whether it be laziness, apathy, confusion, loneliness, despair, or cynicism. The trap of the will is in feeling that we are in perfect control and all spiritual attainments are within the grasp of our effort. When we get so caught up in the power of the will that our egos take over, we are in danger of inflation, a serious and destructive malady that eventually excludes the flow of divine grace and separates us from each other.

The main obstacle to surrender is fear. Fear of the unknown, fear of letting go, fear of not being "in control," fear of opening up to an insight that will compel us to change. The trap of surrender comes in not being able to discern inner voices, of following blindly, and of rejecting the responsibility of becoming a partner with God rather than merely God's subject.

All spiritual practice brings us face-to-face with our particular resistance. In the facing we come to know ourselves, and in that knowledge comes the growth of compassion and spiritual power. It's important to remember that resistance isn't what keeps us from the work. It *is* the work. Sometimes what we yearn for the most is also what we are the most afraid of.

The practice of chant is powerfully effective in awakening that yearning and in giving us the energy and courage to face our fears as well. The danger in spiritual practice is that each of us has our "blind spots" in regard to either the nature of resistance or our particular trap. Having either a spiritual friend or a teacher to lend us a mirror for those difficult blind spots is important. Just knowing that those blind spots are there can help keep us humble and careful.

Meditative Practice in Relation to Prayer

My chanting practice evolved out of my search for a form of prayer that would bring me to an experience of the Divine and would continue to deepen and develop with practice. The experience of chant has enhanced and inspired my silent practice. I have what I call a "base" practice that remains the same and has become the foundation for other practices that evolve and change according to whatever feels needed. That base practice is a silent twenty-minute daily sit that I call *d'veikut* (cleaving).

It is a practice of intention. My intention is to be in God's presence and to gently let go of all thoughts that come by, returning to my loving intention to just be in God's presence. One of the purposes of this meditation is to develop an ongoing vital relationship with the Divine. That relationship then becomes the foundation for prayer. The deep silence that can be tasted in *d'veikut* becomes the wellspring from which a chanting practice can flow. I believe that different forms of Jewish meditation can strengthen your prayer life. When I work with a sacred phrase from the liturgy, exploring its meaning with the intuitive senses of the heart, letting that meaning expand and affect my inner life, then that phrase will always have power. The cumulative experience of using many phrases from the siddur in meditation gradually injects new life and depth into prayer.

The power of the chant can help connect a group to one another. This is especially important in the context of a prayer service. It allows for the experience of praying in the voice of community as well as from an individual perspective. It is important to gradually connect your solitary meditative practice with formalized communal prayer, so that the spiritual benefit from one can inform the other.

In leading a chanting service, I study the Torah portion and look for the spiritual challenge that it presents. With that challenge in mind, I will build the *kavanah* for the chants in ways that will inspire a "rising to meet" that challenge. A chanting service is a seamless process. The structure of the traditional prayer service becomes a vehicle for healing, self-expression, visioning, inner journeying, and connection—to oneself, each other, the community, the world, and God.

God told Moses, "Put it in their mouths, that this song may be a witness" (Deuteronomy 31:19). Chanting takes the song that is in our mouths and plants it deep in our hearts. There it can grow and flower and bring forth the fruits of constant remembrance.

The Lineage
of Chant

his precious practice of igniting the fire in one sacred phrase
at a time and using its light to illuminate the landscape of
Torah and the geography of my heart was my way of receiving the
gift of my inheritance. This was what worked for me.

I began leading a Shabbat chanting service in my apartment in
Jerusalem when I was still a rabbinical student. (A chanting service
follows the structure of a traditional prayer service but uses consider-
ably fewer words. It treats the prayer service as a transformational
journey, which includes periods of silence.) Participants came by invitation only ... and I only invited those who were willing to collaborate
and bring an open-hearted humility and bold passion to this prayer
experiment. As the word spread, some people asked to be invited.
Besides American rabbinical students, there were a number of Israeli
Orthodox women who had felt excluded from prayer and were looking for a way to express their devotion.

I remember being accosted by a young man from the Conservative
seminary. "I think what you're doing is disgusting. It's a travesty. You
are desecrating the service. It's revolting and shameful!" He waited
just a moment and in a softer voice asked, "Can I come?" (I gently
said, "No.")

People often ask me, "Well, is it Jewish? Is it kosher? What are
the precedents for what you're doing? What gives you the right to

change something that's been around so long? Isn't this a betrayal of your ancestors?"

I appreciate these questions because they help me clarify my intention and strengthen my resolve. In my book *Torah Journeys: The Inner Path to the Promised Land*, I wrote:

> Judaism is a great storehouse of treasure and blessing. And it is a vital, dynamic, living conversation that spans the globe and the centuries. Every generation inherits the accumulation of text, music, commentary, law, custom, recipes, and secret wisdom. And it is the responsibility of each generation to fully receive, re-interpret, add to the treasure and pass it on in a form that is more relevant and more alive to our present-day challenge.
>
> (p. 4)

For me, becoming a rabbi was my way of stepping up to that responsibility of creating new forms that might carry forward the beauty and wisdom of my inheritance. I was drawn to being a full participant in a "living tradition," which for me meant using every tool I had to revive the words that seemed to have died on the page.

I remember a dream I had when I first started rabbinical school: I found myself riding down a raging river together with my classmates. We suddenly realized that we were riding on a sleeping giant. He looked quite powerful and dangerous, and at first we were glad he was sleeping. But then, I looked downstream and there was an even more dangerously powerful monster that was sure to devour and destroy us all. I knew that our only hope was to wake up the sleeping giant.

Only a "living tradition" can save itself from irrelevancy, devolution, or extinction. The conversation of Judaism will die if we don't hold up our end of it. My part of the conversation is to share what works for me. Chanting works to wake up that sleeping giant. And what a ride it's been!

I began with an assumption that chant in its essence is not new; it is a spiritual technique that is universal. Because I wanted to connect myself to the lineage of this practice of chant, I turned first to Yuval.

Genesis 4:21 tells us of Yuval, the ancestor of all musicians. Thus we are reminded that music is at our very roots as humans.

One of Yuval's descendants who knew the power of music was Serach, Jacob's favorite granddaughter.

Legend tells us that when Joseph's brothers learned that he was still alive, they had to go and tell their father, but they were afraid that he would die of shock upon learning the truth. They were afraid that this news would be too great a blessing and that Jacob's soul would fly out of him when he heard it.

They argued with each other about who would deliver the news. There is a legend that recounts the solution to their problem. Jacob had a favorite granddaughter, Serach, who was the daughter of his son Asher. Serach was a musician with a gentle voice and a powerful spirit. Only she knew how to comfort Jacob during his dark nights of wrestling. When he called for Serach, her song became a healing balm and he was comforted.

It was agreed that only Serach would be able to reveal this great news, because when Jacob's soul, overcome by blessing, flew out, Serach would know and would sing the song that would call his soul back to this world.

The song that Serach sang to Jacob was the most beautiful melody she had ever sung. Everyone who heard it wept with joy because in it Joseph's spirit was revealed. The melody carried Joseph's beauty, pain, longing, love, and devotion. Her words told the story of his journey, and it was woven with his dreams. Serach's song also told the truth about the whole family, a truth that would have been hard to hear if it were not delivered with such purity.

When Jacob heard Serach's song, his soul indeed flew out and left this world ... but it was called back by the beauty of her song. For this gift, Serach was rewarded with a very long life. It is said that she sang through four hundred years of slavery in Egypt. When the people were about to leave Egypt, they were held back by their promise to bring Joseph's bones with them. Fortunately, having lived long enough to both witness Joseph's burial and be present at the time of the Exodus, Serach located exactly where Joseph was buried, and the liberation could begin.

Every day we remember the Exodus from Egypt, our escape from *Mitzrayim* (the narrow places). The moment we cross the sea, Miriam the prophet (sister of Moses and Aaron) leads us in a celebration with music and dancing (Exodus 15:20). The energy that is generated from that song and that dance is what sends us toward our freedom. Without the song, we might wither in the wilderness. Music calls up our strength, inspiration, and sense of purpose. The rhythm of our song propels us through every challenge and opens our hearts to receive the flow of milk and honey that is the Promised Land.

The book of Samuel tells us about the bands of prophets who would roam the Holy Land, calling in the divine spirit of prophecy through their practice of ecstatic song (1 Samuel 10:5–11). When I chant with my friends and students, I feel that we are continuing in their tradition.

David, the archetypal king from whom the Messiah will come, is best remembered by his psalms, which have became so central to our liturgy and practice. It always feels slightly crazy to me to race through and mumble the psalms so tonelessly, when they are filled with exhortations to make music.

> Call out to God, all the inhabitants of the earth; open your mouths in joyous song and play music. Play music to God on a harp, with harp and the sound of chanted praise!
>
> (Psalm 98:4–5)

> *Halleluyah*! Praise God, O my soul! I will praise God with my life. I will sing to God as long as I exist.
>
> (Psalm 146:1–2)

> *Halleluyah*! For it is good to sing to our God, for praise is beautiful and fitting.
>
> (Psalm 147:1)

For David, praise is how we lift ourselves into God's presence. And to praise without music would be unthinkable.

Another central prayer of our liturgy is called the *K'dushah*, which is recited daily and is composed of excerpts from Isaiah and Ezekiel's visions of angels who are chanting to one another. In the Talmud, *Sotah* 49a, the Rabbis emphasize the importance of this prayer when they say, "The world is maintained by the *K'dushah*."

Sometimes when I am chanting in community, I feel that we are imitating those angels who call to one another, giving each other full permission to express their holiness and stand tall in their beauty.

I've learned from a fascinating text called *Perek Shirah* that it's not just the angels who are chanting. This ancient mystical text is composed of a series of quotes from *Tanach* (Torah, Prophets, and Writings), Talmud, and *Zohar*, put in the mouths of all of Creation— the sun, moon, clouds, stars, wind, fig, date, vegetable, apple, grasses, rooster, dove, vulture, crane, fish, frog, camel, horse, elephant, lion, bear, wolf, ant, fox, snake, scorpion, dog ... each has a voice and a message of praise. This is the perfect text for chanters because it understands that the whole of Creation is chanting songs of praise to its Creator.

In studying this text, I ask, "Can I listen well to Creation? Can I join in the cosmic chorus and sing my own song of praise in concert with all the voices of Creation?"

Traditionally *Perek Shirah* is attributed to King David. Modern scholars have traced it back, through *genizah* fragments, dating to around the tenth century, but it may have been connected to earlier *Heichalot* or *Merkavah* mystical literature.

Mystical commentaries refer to the existence of angelic archetypes who mediate between God and Creation. *Perek Shirah* was intended and used as a liturgical text and was included in both *machzorim* and siddurim. In fact, a version of *Perek Shirah* is included in the Reconstructionist Shabbat and holiday siddur (p. 704). In Rabbi Art Green's commentary of *Perek Shirah*, he says, "Prayer is also a universal act, one that binds the whole human community together with all of Nature, calling forth in us an appreciation of life as an ongoing celebration of the gift of being."

Green goes on to say, "We seek a religious language that will deepen our appreciation of divinity within the natural world. Faced with the threat of environmental destruction, we find ourselves led back to this ancient poetic vision of our tradition. Here all of nature is joined together in calling out through song to its single source."

My own immersion in *Perek Shirah* has given me a glimpse into a way of perceiving nature as *praise*. In the moment when I can see in that way, I can also join in and become part of the chorus. My chant practice connects me with all of Creation.

Chant is a lifestyle. In the Talmud (*Sanhedrin* 99a–b) there's a discussion about the importance of learning Torah and reviewing it. Rabbi Akiva's opinion is that we must "sing every day, sing every day." Rashi explains that when you sing Torah, then it follows you even to the next world.

I sing my Torah every day so that rather than having something I merely think about, its wisdom can become a part of me and guide my every step.

The Baal Shem Tov was also a believer in the power of song. I call on his spirit as my lineage as I engage in the practice of chant.

The Baal Shem Tov, "Master of the Divine Name," was a healer and miracle worker in the 1700s in Poland. He is known as the founder of Hasidism, a great movement of the revival of the spirit in Judaism. In my chant practice, I drink from the fountain of his legacy. He lifted the veils of the illusion of separateness, saw the whole universe as a manifestation of God, and taught the practical significance and implication of this truth. The Baal Shem Tov taught his followers to look for the good in everyone and everything and to call forth that goodness through prayer and song and loving awareness.

He lived at a time when the rigorous and detailed study of Talmud and the scrupulous attention to law made the treasures of Judaism nearly inaccessible to the common people. The Baal Shem Tov stressed prayer as a path of love that was open to all. At a time when the rabbis were teaching asceticism, mistrust of pleasure, and hatred of the body, the Baal Shem Tov called the Jewish people to expand their capacity for joy. He showed us a dimension of prayer that is beyond petition or praise, called *d'veikut* (literally, "cleaving").

Contemporary teacher and storyteller Maggid Yitzhak Buxbaum defines *d'veikut* as "God-consciousness imbued with love" (*Jewish Spiritual Practices*, p. 4).

The underlying purpose of my chant practice is to learn how to live every moment of my life in the loving awareness of God's presence.

As I developed this practice of chanting for myself, I began sharing it with others, and there were always people for whom it resonated, who felt that this was the doorway through which they could enter into a Jewish life. And I also met with a great deal of resistance, ridicule, and resentment.

Once while still a rabbinical student, I was invited to a synagogue in Canada to teach and lead services. It was a pretty conservative place, and there were quite a few people upset with what I was doing and saying. On Shabbat afternoon a group of us sat around a table, and I taught them a chant.

A very old man at the end of the table sat there obviously very moved by what was happening. Tears were streaming down his face. After a long moment of silence he said, "I haven't experienced this since I was a little boy, sitting at the Rebbe's table. This is just what he used to do ... sing one phrase over and over till we were all transported. I am so happy to have lived long enough to have this experience again."

I was so grateful to know that my practice was connected to an amazing lineage and that through chant, I could become a channel for the flow of blessing through the ages.

Chant as a Core Spiritual Practice

*C*hanting is the melodic and rhythmic repetition of a Hebrew phrase drawn from our sacred text. It is a practice that allows for the exploration of the deeper levels of meaning and experience that lie beneath the surface of our religious lives. For many, chanting has become an important method of opening the heart, connecting with the community, quieting the mind, and viscerally embodying our liturgy and scripture.

Why We Value This Practice as a Core of Contemporary Jewish Spirituality

It's important to bring our sustained and loving attention into building and refining the strength of our inner lives. Chant is a practice that connects the outer dimensions of sound and group dynamics with the inner dimensions of awareness. As we grow and nurture our inner lives, it is important to have ways to express and share with community the gifts we receive in the solitude of our practice. Chant is the bridge between the inner life and the outer expression, between the solitary practice and the shared beauty of fellowship. When we chant, we are using the whole body as the instrument with which to feel the meaning of the sacred phrase. We study the meaning of the words and the context from which they are drawn. We explore the range of our feelings so that they can be dedicated to the purpose of the chant. And we use the power of the practice to enter into the silence and stillness at our core. Thus the practice of chant integrates our spiritual, intellectual, emotional, and physical energies.

The Relationship between Chanting and Other Spiritual Practices

MINDFULNESS MEDITATION

For many, the practice of silence can be daunting. Our minds are so filled with clutter, and our thoughts move in habitual circles. The practice of chant can provide an entranceway to the silence, by focusing our intention and gathering up our attention into a form that is both compelling and beautiful. In the silence after a chant, many people experience an inner spaciousness for the first time. Because the chant is often energizing, they are able to sustain that spacious silence for much longer than ever before. The silence after the chant invites them then to rest and be renewed in the sanctuary that the chant has built.

PRAYER

The practice of chant takes the words of prayer and uses them as doorways into deeper meanings and into the spaces of our own hearts. It does this through the clarifying and refining of our intention. Sometimes the sheer volume of prayers that we have collected over the centuries becomes an obstacle to diving deeply into their meaning or using their power for transformation. The practice of chant allows us to explore one phrase at a time, igniting the fire of our enthusiasm and pouring our passion into those particular words. Once we've had a personal and passionate experience with those words, our prayer life will never be the same. Chanting wakes up our liturgy and brings it to life within us.

TEXT STUDY

The practice of chant gets us "out of our heads" so we can begin to approach the text from an expanded understanding—from our hearts, bodies, and experience as well as from what we know intel-lectually. In addition to preparing us for text study by expanding our perception of the words in front of us, we can also use chant in the comprehension of a text. We do this by taking a phrase from the text that has some power or mystery for us and experiencing it with melody and rhythm and repetition until it unlocks its secrets for us.

SPIRITUAL DIRECTION

Often during the ongoing practice of chant, the complexities of our inner life are brought to the surface. For this reason it is recom-mended that we who engage in chant also have access to a spiritual director, who can acknowledge the mysteries and challenges that are called up by the chant and help us appreciate the complexities of the inner life as they are revealed by the practice. Both spiritual direction and chant rely on the ever-deepening of our capacity to listen and then express the truth of our inner knowing.

YOGA

Like yoga, chanting is an embodied practice. As chanters, we are encouraged to feel the sound resonating in every part of the body and to use that sound to open up places of tension or resistance. Chanting supports the practice of yoga by energizing the body, opening the heart, and clearing the mind. Chanting has often been used in con-junction with yoga to put our efforts into the context of a devotional practice.

MIDOT

We are dedicated to supporting the work of cultivating *midot*—quali-ties such as the conscious awareness of God's presence, compassion, wisdom, love, open-heartedness, justice, spiritual community, and humility. Chanting can be an effective and powerful tool in this work. In the practice of chant, we choose a phrase that expresses or embodies the quality that we wish to cultivate. As we chant, we can step inside that quality, feel its beauty, and also explore the obstacles that arise in response to its presence. For instance, in exploring the *midah* of patience, we might chant from the Psalm 37:7, "*Dom l'Yah v'hitcholeil lo*" ("Be still and wait for God"). As we repeat and embody that phrase, we experience both the feeling of patient waiting *and* our rising impatience. In the practice of chant, we can strengthen and appreciate the stillness of waiting as well as explore the roots of our impatience. This exploration can be done with compassion and understanding as we direct the beauty of the chant to soften hard places in the heart and melt our defenses.

SPIRITUAL COMMUNITY

When we chant together with a community, we are creating something so much more beautiful than what any one of us could make alone. We begin to appreciate the shared project of a chant and see that it is a microcosm of our lives. We can shape our differences to create fascinating harmonies. We can time our varying rhythms to create counterpoint. Each of us learns to bring the fullness of our presence to the group in ways that will enhance the overall feeling and tone of the chant. Even people who feel that they cannot sing can learn to chant and contribute their unique tone and feeling to the whole of the shared creation. As we enter the silence after the chant, each of us lays down our differences and experiences a collective silence that is framed by the highest intentions of everyone in the group.

Meditation as the Foundation for Chant Practice

When I entered rabbinical school I had a real problem with the prayer book. Somewhere along the way, the traditional liturgy had died for me, and I knew that a large part of my training would be to bring those words to life inside my heart and to renew my relationship to prayer. My meditation practice was born out of a desire to turn my life itself into a prayer. Prayer for me is the flow of connection between the finite and the infinite. My work in meditation is aimed at keeping that channel of connection open by cultivating a constant awareness of God's presence. That awareness then becomes the foundation of my prayer life, the place from which I can connect with and interpenetrate the Divine.

The object of my practice is to live every moment in the awareness of God's presence. This is my foundational practice, and part of the way I refine it is through teaching it. I call this constant awareness a devotional practice because it is fueled by my love and longing and intuition of wholeness. It is a practice of intention, the pure and simple intention of just being, which means being in God's presence. Though it begins as the simplest of practices, I find that so much is required of me and so much is revealed as my spiritual work is given to me layer by layer.

The deepest layer I call *d'veikut,* "cleaving." Here in the absence of content, essence is revealed. Boundaries of self dissolve; the mind becomes spacious, and the heart expands. Over time a foundation of God's presence is laid beneath my life. This foundation of God's presence is what makes prayer work. When that foundation is established, then every word of prayer breaks through to the infinite, and every word I speak becomes God's own words to me.

The Functions of Consciousness

In order to know the purity of just being, I have found that four distinct functions of consciousness must be cultivated:

1. The ability to focus attention
2. *Korban*—the art of letting go of content
3. *T'shuvah*—the art of returning (to the intention to be in God's presence)
4. *M'sirat nefesh*—surrendering of the small self to that transforming presence

And so my practice becomes the building of these functions. The first function, the ability to focus attention, I have found to be a prerequisite or complement to letting go. Though the practice of simply sitting in God's presence itself is not a "focus" meditation, if I have not learned to focus, then I also cannot let go of focus and "just be." This ability or "muscle of the mind" must be methodically conditioned and strengthened. Most meditation techniques work with this function, and perhaps in building a practice life, this is where we must begin.

When I examine the second function, the art of letting go of content, I find that certain qualities are needed to let go in a way that will bring me to the level of *d'veikut,* cleaving. I call it an "art" because it matters *how* I let go of a thought. If I push that thought away with annoyance, if I indulge it too long, identify with it, or disdain it, that thought will be given the power to keep me from my depths. In the art of letting go, I see that I must cultivate a certain gentleness, self-compassion, and an awakened relaxed alertness to the workings of my mind. These, then, are the *midot* (attributes) that I must have access to in order to be an artist of letting go. I find that I can access these attributes through working with sacred phrases, using the words of our liturgy to unlock the particular quality, taste it, strengthen it, and face the obstacles that block my way.

The third function, *t'shuvah*, the art of return, serves to strengthen my intention. After the moment of letting go of a thought, there is a gesture of return ... return to the intention of "just being in God's presence." How that return happens and what fuels it matter. As I examine and build this function within me, I find that the qualities of wholeheartedness, persistence, patience, and rigor are required. As I explore each of those qualities, I begin to identify my obstacles and challenges. If I am to have access to those qualities when I sit with the intention of just being in God's presence, then each of those obstacles must be attended to, understood, and dissolved in the light of my awareness and love. When I can understand the source of those difficulties and complexities, I can direct my prayer with compassion toward their resolution.

When I sit with the intention to just be in God's presence, each thought that I sacrifice sends me deeper into presence, and when I wander, each return strengthens my intention, which fuels the fires of sacrifice.

The first function, the ability to focus, prepares me to enter the holy space. The second and third, *korban* and *t'shuvah*, describe the moment-to-moment process of dealing with thoughts in a way that opens the door to God's presence.

The fourth function, *m'sirat nefesh*, describes the overall process of surrender. It is an awareness of the effects of these practices and the extent to which they constitute consent to God's presence. It is this consent to God's presence that transforms our hearts.

The third layer of practice, the cultivation of *midot*, can be described as ecstatic practice. It employs heart-opening techniques of breath work, melody, rhythm, movement, inner journeying, imagery, and the building and refining of energy. This ecstatic energy is then used in the cultivation of the four functions of consciousness, and those functions are accessed as we simply enter the silence to "just be." My prayer life has become the field of practice in this third layer, for every word of praise for God awakens that quality in me. Every *halleluyah* waters the seed of God within me.

I find that each moment of silent meditation is a microcosm of my life. I must deal with physical pain, mental distraction, conflicting voices. And as the stillness in me rises, as my heart opens to the pervading presence of God, I both experience the fullness of my incarnation and receive glimpses through to the vastness beyond. Moment by moment, I am given the opportunities to enter into that spaciousness. The qualities that I must cultivate in order to step through that doorway in meditation are the same qualities I need to live a life in which the fullness of my love is realized. As I practice each day, I am growing that love. And from that watered garden each fragrant breath calls out an invitation. "Blow upon my garden that its perfume may waft out. Let my Beloved come into his garden, and eat its precious fruits" (Song of Songs 4:16).

Rhythm

*A*t some point on my Jewish journey, I fell in love with Torah and prayer. Not just the meanings that unfold endlessly, but the sound of the sacred phrase. When I find a Hebrew phrase that is compelling, I say it out loud, and one of the first things I notice is that these words have a rhythm. I feel this rhythm in my body. It moves me. The rhythm calls forth a melodic story, and then that story suggests harmonies and tonal subtleties. As I continue to repeat the phrase, I notice its effects on my consciousness. I notice the rhythm of breath that it engenders. I notice feelings in my body, images that appear in my mind. I acknowledge the transformative power of the phrase, and I look for ways of magnifying that power. When I first began chanting, I picked up a *dumbek* and developed my own style of one-handed drumming. The drum felt like an extension of my body. Holding a drum reminded me to stay anchored in my body. I soon found that the wisdom of my body could best be expressed through the sound of the drum. With my drum I could signal subtle dynamics of the chant: loud, soft, dreamy, bold, sweet, daring. It wasn't so much a matter of drumming technique as it was feeling in my hand a certain truth and expressing it through how I touched the drum. When I chant with other drummers, it's very important to me that they get a feel for the intention of the chant and then put that intention into their bodies and transmit that intention through the drum. This is what my husband Rachmiel calls kavanistic drumming. The *kavanah* (intention) is embodied and expressed.

My own simple style of drumming taught me the importance of hearing and feeling the downbeat of a chant. If the downbeat is weak or missing, then there is a good chance that we'll all get lost. When there's no one holding that downbeat, all the fancy drumming, intricate technique, and wild expression will only distract us from the true power of Torah. When the downbeat is solid, it becomes our dance floor. With a strong foundation we can ascend to ecstatic heights of meaning and pleasure.

When I lead chant and someone else is drumming, I need to create a psychic mind-meld with the drummers, so that they will be attuned to the nuance, story, dynamics, and transformative process of the chant. Throughout the course of the chant, I am aiming somewhere—toward a particular state of consciousness. Before the chant begins, I remember that state and feel it in my body so that I can then lead people there, through the power of chant. Ideally, the drummers will also know in their bodies where we are going and be able to communicate that knowing with sensitivity in the holy place where hand touches drum.

One very important place where the sound of the drum is crucial to the effect of the practice or prayer is in how the chant comes to its conclusion. A good chant is one that leads us into the silence, and if the chant has done its job, that silence will be filled with potential. The last couple of repetitions of the sacred phrase must communicate not only that the chant is ending soon but also that a door will be opening into the silence and we will be invited to enter and receive God's presence. It is this subtle change of rhythm that prepares us to open to the potential for transformation in the silence.

Drummers, you hold a great power in your hands. When you unconsciously speed up, you accelerate our heartbeats, and this can bring anxiety to emotions and body. When you unconsciously lag, you can cause us to lose energy or fall into sentimentality. And when you bring steadiness, generous vitality, and mindful purpose to your drumming, then we are all lifted up into the heavens and grounded in love.

THE SECRETS OF
CHANT

The Inner
Dimensions of Chant

*W*hen you have learned the words and the melody of the chant, you have only mastered its surface. And you have only engaged your own surface. As you practice the chant in the spirit of adventure and exploration, and with the humility to know that you really don't yet know what it *means*, you are clearing away preconceptions and opening to new possibilities. You are discovering the vast dimensions of your own soul.

Even if I have chanted these words hundreds of times, I have not yet experienced them in the context of this moment, this place, this situation, this combination of circumstances. I know that fresh meanings may very well emerge out of this new synergy. Psalm 149 says, "Sing to God a new song!" Every song is new when you approach it as a bold adventure with the surprising combination of humility and curiosity.

When I open my mouth to chant, I come with a sense of expectancy (something amazing is sure to unfold) but without expectations (I really don't know exactly what will happen or who I will be at the end of the chant).

We live in a world that is continually calling us to the surface. Appearances seem to be everything. The sheer pace of life seems to require superficiality. The quick wit is rewarded. It feels like we are always trying to keep up with the momentum of our lives and with the speed of this spinning world. Yet when I slow down, I am rewarded with the richness and depth of each moment's gifts. When I slow down, I marvel at how much I've been missing in my rush to keep up.

I'm sorry to say that the prayer service that I inherited, with its style and obligation to say so many words, so very quickly, became for me an obstacle to prayer. My solution was to take one phrase at a time and explore its depths. That exploration required that I would also be exploring my own depths. "From where is this chant coming?" became as important a question as "What does it mean?"

In my goal to become wholehearted in my chanting, I became aware of many facets of self, many inner voices that each clamored for my attention and recognition, and some aspects of self that remained hidden in the shadows. One of my teachers, Paul Ray, called this "the parliament of personality." One of the goals or purposes of chant is to integrate all of these separate parts and become wholehearted before God. As I'm chanting, I turn within and ask, "Who's *not* chanting?" I call in and welcome the fullness of who I am and who I'm becoming.

The following practice, from Psalm 130, is a sacred phrase that has usually been interpreted negatively. Rabbi Samson Raphael Hirsch, in his commentary on the psalms, calls these depths "the deepest misery of all, misfortune coupled with the burden of guilt" (*The Hirsch Psalms*, p. 395). When I chant these words, they become the fulfillment of my innermost longings—to live from my depths and thus to know the fullness of life. My "call" to God is the life that I live, the expression of my unique essence.

FROM THE DEPTHS

מִמַּעֲמַקִּים קְרָאתִיךָ יהוה

Mima'amakim k'raticha Yah!
From the depths I call to You, O God. Hear my voice!
(Psalm 130:1)

Calling out to God is a practice of dropping down into those infinite depths and allowing my deepest and truest expression to emerge.

With the power of my chant, I open the door at the center of my heart, so that I can be filled with inspiration and become the vehicle for God's presence. It is the "innerness" of the practice that makes it transformative.

In the book of Exodus, which tells the story of our journey to freedom, Moses realizes that the only way to accomplish this journey and reach the Land of Promise is for God's presence to be within, between and among us as we go. Even after all the trouble of the Golden Calf, the murmurings and rebellions, Moses knows that it is only this "innerness" that makes our holy journey worth all the bother.

With the following chant, I address myself to You, God, the Great Mystery, with the knowledge that "I can't and don't want to do this without You!" In the silence after the chant, I make a place inside me for that Divine Presence to dwell.

יֵלֶךְ־נָא אֲדֹנָי בְּקִרְבֵּנוּ

Yeilech na Adonai b'kirbeinu.
Please, God, go within us.
(Exodus 34:9)

Eight Functions of Consciousness in a Spiritual Group

I used to shy away from groups, and I perceived myself as the proverbial "outsider"—someone who would never fit in. Being the outsider, my habit was to judge. I would be secretly critical, look for what was not working, and then become disappointed and alienated. As I began to become aware of my own heart, I realized that this habit was self-destructive. It separated me from the possibility of connection and collaboration and perpetuated my role as an outsider. I realized that my habit of judging was painful and destructive to my own heart.

In stepping into leadership and truly opening to the spirit of service, I began to see that the quality of presence I embodied in any relationship or group actually had an effect. The question was whether I might bring that quality of presence deliberately in response to what was needed ... or just accidentally in response to my changing moods. The realization of the power of my own presence was coupled with a growing curiosity about "group energy." I spent about a year assisting Paul Ray, a great teacher of energy work, in his meditation groups. We would meet after each group and talk about the quality of energy that had been raised, noting the moments of shift and transformation. Paul taught me to tune into the energy of the group (not just the individual members) and ask the questions, "What is this?" "What is the potential here?" and "What is needed in this moment that I might bring with the quality of my own presence?" Asking these questions changed my relationship to the group. Instead of standing outside and criticizing, I could dedicate all my energy to bringing my presence in a way that might help. It felt subversive (because I could do it without anyone knowing), and at the same time, this new stance unlocked a flowing generosity that I didn't know was possible.

In my first years of rabbinical school, I had the honor of studying Bible with a great scholar, Tikva Frymer-Kensky (may her memory be a blessing). After participating in a service that I led, Tikva said, "Shefa, you have great gifts as a leader, but it's not something that can be taught." Well, whenever someone says that something *can't* be done, I receive it as a challenge. Perhaps I *could* teach this. I took it on as an experiment. My "gift" was in perceiving what was true in this moment, sensing the potential of a group, and being willing to respond to the energy before me. I always had a plan, but I was also willing to change the plan at any moment if it wasn't working. The weakness that I observed in many leaders was that they didn't seem to notice when the plan they had made wasn't working and they just plowed ahead.

I also began noticing what components were present when the group energy felt complete, when the energy soared and was transformative. I became very curious about why something "worked," what qualities were present, and how those qualities fit together to create a sum that was greater than its parts.

In order to teach about these qualities of presence and their effect on the group, I needed to develop a vocabulary that might begin to describe what I was perceiving. I identified eight functions of consciousness, eight distinct ways of bringing the gifts of presence to a spiritual group. These include:

The Empowerer
The Guide

      The Observer
      The Container
      The Exalter
      The Foundation
      The Secret Heart
      The Bridge

When all eight functions are manifested at once, something wonderful emerges from the whole, which is so much greater than the sum of its parts, and all the members of the group benefit.

Working with these eight functions inspired a collaborative model of leadership. The person who is the perceived leader of a group needs the full attentive and responsive participation of each member. So, when it "works," that leader can't take full credit. The credit belongs to the workings of the whole. As we each learn the power of our own presence, we can learn how to bring those qualities responsibly, collaboratively, and generously in response to our perceptions about what is needed.

In my leadership training course, Kol Zimra, I teach how to become aware of and work with all eight functions. These functions become the energy-worker's repertoire that we can draw on in responding wisely to the challenges of the group engaged in prayer or spiritual practice.

Eight Functions of Consciousness in a Spiritual Group

The following are explanations of the eight functions and how they work in the context of a spiritual group.

1. THE EMPOWERER

Dedicated to the group energy; channels energy through themselves to the center of the group so that everyone can be nurtured and empowered.

TASK: Building up group energy.

The first function of consciousness is one that I call the Empowerer. Before I begin a chant, I know something about its potential, its medicine. As I enter into the practice, the group will need to generate enough energy to activate that medicine. The role of the Empowerer is to build up the group energy to the level of activation.

As Empowerer, I channel energy through myself to the center of the group so that everyone can be nurtured and empowered.

When you're chanting, power is different than volume. The sound carries energy but is not equal to it. When I do the function of Empowerer, I open up a channel behind my heart (or in the soles of my feet and the top of my head) and imagine channeling energy from the God-source into the center of the circle. At that center point, I imagine a fountain of energy that is being charged up, which can then send nurturing and empowering energy to everyone in the circle. I resist the temptation of sending energy to particular people or points in the circle that seem weak, because if I try to do that, those people will resist and those points of weakness will suck out all the energy of the group, and I will get exhausted from the effort. Instead, I focus my attention on the point of potential between us. I call forth that flow from the center with persistence, faith, gratefulness, and ease. I become a channel for energy to pour into the center. (It feels like priming the pump.) And then I become receptive to that energy as it showers the circle from the Infinite Source between us.

2. THE GUIDE
Sees and holds to higher purpose of the group, builds structure and plan; sees and nurtures the potential of the whole and the capabilities of each part.

TASK: Perceiving guidance and steering the ship.

The second function, the Guide, is usually fulfilled by the apparent leader of the group. As the Guide, I tune into both the higher purpose of the group and the group's potential. When I am the Guide, I rely on the other seven functions so that I can dedicate the energy toward the fulfillment of that higher purpose. I actually check into each of those other functions to make sure they are happening, and if needed, I support those functions and unify their energy in service to the higher purpose. I open myself to the spirit of guidance so that I can respond moment to moment to the possibilities as they emerge. I open my crown chakra (energy center at the top of my head) and connect that center with my heart. My heart begins to feel like a bowl, filling up and overflowing.

When I teach these eight functions, the Guide is the last one I will teach. It is necessary to master the other seven first, so that I can see, nurture, and call forth the potential of each of the parts while staying connected to the flow of guidance.

As the Guide, you might begin to notice that certain people have natural abilities that fulfill one of the eight functions.

For example, Anna is just naturally a Secret Heart. When she comes into the room, the energy just feels "deeper" because of Anna's presence. She probably doesn't know that she has that effect on the group; she is just being herself. When, as the Guide, you can communicate how precious she is to the group energy, Anna can begin to use her gifts more deliberately and refine that Secret Heart function.

Each person has the power to affect the energy of the group just through the particular quality of their presence. The role of the Guide is to notice, acknowledge, and appreciate those natural abilities, so that the power of presence can be cultivated and refined and dedicated in service to the group energy.

3. THE OBSERVER

Conscious attention on behalf of the group; maintains awareness of group's energies while still being a part of it; discriminates shifts without being judgmental.

TASK: Perceiving the energy of the whole.

The third function is called the Observer. As Observer, I expand the field of perception to take in the *whole* group, rather than be caught by the details of its individual components. When I am involved in this function, it feels as if I am sending a periscope up from the top of my head so that I can get a wider perspective on the whole. And then I begin to notice shifts of energy. This might feel like the energy of the whole group getting lighter or deeper or sharper or sweeter. It might feel like a color or a flavor or a texture. I "watch" these shiftings of energy with curious, loving attention. It is the quality of my attention itself that has an effect on the group. As Observer, I am carefully discerning yet never judgmental. I am fully participating and adding my own contribution, yet I maintain an awareness of the "big picture." My stance of careful, loving attention becomes a powerful force in itself. I don't have to fix anything. I may want to check in with the group at some point about what I have been noticing, but I know that just my presence (as Observer) has an effect on the group; it makes everyone more aware and carries an electric vitality and refinement that are contagious.

4. THE CONTAINER
Guardian of the group; creates safe/sacred space by containing the energy, using three methods—imaginal arms, heart, and voice; guards against outside intrusion.

TASK: Protecting and embracing the energy of the whole.

The fourth function, the Container, is so fundamental to group energy that if I can teach only one function, this is the one that I teach. When we feel "held," we relax and thrive and can reach levels of strength, clarity, and inspiration that would otherwise be impossible to attain. When someone is "holding" the energy, it feels as if I can lean back against a wide embrace of unconditional love. All the energy that might go into measures of defense can be redeployed, channeled into creative endeavors. The sense of safety that the Container inspires allows us to take risks. Spiritual growth often requires a "leap of faith," but unless we feel embraced by unconditional love, we won't risk making mistakes. And I am beginning to realize that it is only through mistakes that we learn.

At a very practical level, the Container sees to it that the time and place of a spiritual group is conducive to practice. As the Container,

I guard against interruptions, work to keep the integrity of the circle, and bring a fierce mothering love that embraces the group energy and allows those within the circle to become vulnerable. In spiritual work, this vulnerability is our power. When we lower our defenses, the divine flow pours in, filling the space between us. That flow also pours into the heart, expanding inner space to its vast soul dimensions.

A rule to remember in our work: *Energy follows intention.*

There are many ways to do the work of the Container, all of them involving the practice of clear, powerful, focused intention. I'll describe three of these "holding" techniques:

- Imagine your own arms stretching out, embracing the whole group. This wide embrace of strong loving protection has in it the intention of allowing and support, so that each person in the circle can do the inner work he or she needs to do.

- Let your own heart become the microcosm of the group. One at a time, invite the pure soul of each member of the circle into the space of your heart. Allow your heart to expand as you receive each one. Offer your own heart as the Container on behalf of the group. Surround the image of the whole group inside your heart, with blessing.

- Imagine your voice (or breath) weaving together with the voices or breath of everyone in the group. Using your imagination and intention, you can actually be the weaver, uniting the disparate strands of energy into one beautiful tapestry.

5. THE EXALTER
Raises up the spark of the Divine by seeing and celebrating it; lifts the group through joyful presence.

TASK: Loving whatever is Divine "in this"—exalting it and bringing it out still further.

The fifth function is the Exalter. "Getting high," raising the vibration of the group, is an essential function that requires both careful attention and playfulness. As Exalter, I look for what is beautiful "in this." I search for the spark of the Divine, and when I find it, I raise it up, celebrate it, and appreciate it. Through my attention, that spark bursts into flame and is made available to the group. As Exalter, I must continually let go of judgment and rivet my attention on that spark of beauty or goodness. My entire presence becomes a radiant smile, a burst of applause in appreciation for the potential that is manifesting. As Exalter, I am "grateful in advance" for what is emerging. And my optimism is contagious.

There are certain people who are natural Exalters. When they enter a room, the energy gets lighter, higher, and more "sparkly." Exalters breathe in the hidden beauty and magic and then breathe out the joy of that secret.

6. THE FOUNDATION
Creates solidity; brings grounding; lays one's consciousness beneath what is happening as a dance floor that supports the group's energies.

TASK: Establishing the foundation for the group energy.

We can't get "high" unless there is a firm, strong foundation holding us up. Our dance can become ecstatic when we feel a solid yet springy dance floor beneath our feet. The Foundation grounds us, gives us a feeling of balance, connection, and safety. The Foundation connects us to our own heartbeat and to the heartbeat of the planet.

As the Foundation, I learn to lay my consciousness underneath the energy of the group with the intention of providing a steady, stable base. The function of Foundation is also about the practical matters like remembering to bring the key to the building or send out the e-mail reminders. When we know that the Foundation is there, we all get to surrender, relax, and enjoy, knowing that we are supported. If the Foundation function is weak or missing, our ascent will be wobbly and dangerous.

7. THE SECRET HEART

Is completely effaced in God/Devotion; the deepest part of the group, the least known part to outsiders and to the superficial; God in the silence.

TASK: Surrendering to the depths on behalf of the group, thus connecting the group with those depths.

This seventh function, which I call the Secret Heart, brings depth and profundity to our spiritual work. As the Secret Heart, I am continually surrendering to God in the depths of my being. As energy moves through me, I am giving it over, offering it up to the Great Mystery, to God in the darkness, to the unknown. This devotional function, which might usually feel very solitary, is paradoxically done *on behalf* of the group. As Secret Heart, I dedicate this work for the benefit of the spiritual group; thus, my presence connects everyone to the mysterious depths of God and to the possibilities of surrender.

In ecstatic work, raw spiritual energy must be refined and distilled if it is to be useful in healing. The Secret Heart does this work of refinement and distillation through a willingness to surrender power, ambition, pleasure ... and dissolve the hard edges of self in the infinite Sea of Self/Consciousness. When I am doing the function of the Secret Heart, it feels as if I am bowing in devotion to the Mystery, breathing out everything that I think I know, and breathing in the vast unknown. I dedicate this unknowing to the depth of the group.

8. THE BRIDGE

Makes connections through interdisciplinary awareness; enlarges the meaning and the context for the group; bridges different states of consciousness and levels of meaning.

TASK: Holding paradox, cultivating stereoscopic mode.

The function of the Bridge channels a wild and passionate energy into the texture of the group. As the Bridge, I am allowing my mind to be "blown" on behalf of the group. I enter into the consciousness of "Wow!" of radical wonder. In chanting, I can get to that place by focusing on the expanding meaning of the words of the chant. I use the power of mind to go beyond the mind. I ride the energy of the chant and let it take me to an expanded state of consciousness where I can hold more than one perspective.

Here is an example. We are chanting the following words from liturgy: *Baruch she'amar v'hayah ha'olam* (Blessed is the One who spoke and the world came into being). As the Bridge, I chant these words and let them take me to a perception of the Holy One in the act of creating this reality. At the same time I become aware of the reality of these holy words emerging from my heart and mouth, and I know that I, created in God's image, am also creating worlds. Suddenly the word *olam* (which I know to mean both "universe" and "hidden") begins opening a new perspective for me. I feel the hidden universes inside my own heart begin to be revealed. There is an infinite flow of diverse realities pouring forth from my heart, which I realize is also the heart of God. As the Bridge, I am exploring the implications of my experience. I am blown away, wondering, "How can I live in the light of this moment?" Whether or not I share my experience or insights with the group, they have benefited from the quality of presence that I manifest as the Bridge. They feel my enthusiasm as it fuels the group energy.

I do the work of the Bridge by cultivating stereoscopic consciousness, which is the ability to hold two perspectives at once. I am aware of the larger perspective of the group while at the same time completely connected to my own depths.

How This Works

The quality of presence that we bring to a group always affects the energy. Why not learn to bring that quality consciously and deliberately, expressing our loving, generous impulse toward service?

By learning and practicing these eight functions, I can expand my own capacity for service, refine my perceptions of energy, and explore and cultivate new capabilities. I can expand my energetic spectrum and learn about parts of myself that would otherwise remain hidden or dormant.

In working with these eight functions, I begin to see how they rely upon each other. The Exalter receives the benefit of the Foundation's efforts, dancing higher because of that support. The Bridge is sent to a vision by the presence of the Observer, who is strengthened by the Empowerer, who is held by the Container. The Guide is inspired and opened to guidance by the devotion of the Secret Heart.

We create this energy together.

And we connect with spiritual circles across the planet—all doing this work of transformation, each in our own sacred way.

Power and the Open Heart

One of the main benefits to my chant practice is to help me keep my heart open, no matter what changing circumstances life throws in my path. When my heart is open, I can embrace those changing circumstances and look for the opportunity in every challenge. The benefit of an open heart in relationship with others is that when my heart is open, compassion flows. I can connect with others and break free of the prison of my illusion of separateness. The benefit of an open heart in relationship to God and to my self is that when my heart is open, I have access to the flow of God—wisdom, love, and vitality—that is within me. When my heart is open, all those divine resources are available and accessible. My commitment to keeping my heart open requires that I do the practices that support an open heart *and* that I bring a careful awareness to the patterns of just how and why my heart closes.

In Leviticus, Deuteronomy, and the writings of the prophets, we are commanded to "circumcise our hearts," which means we must cut through or dissolve the layers and layers of defense that we construct to protect our fragile and vulnerable hearts. The trouble is that that very same defense we thought would protect us cuts us off from the divine flow of life, love, and goodness.

With my chant practice, I am focusing in on those layers that cover my heart and keep me insulated from those divine flows. At the end of a chant, I focus on my breath and imagine the power of the chant riding the breath into my heart. I direct the energy of the chant so that it penetrates my defenses and leaves my heart wide open.

Once I was leading a weeklong meditation retreat, and by the end of the week we were all feeling wonderful, in love with each other and with life itself, overflowing with generosity.

One of those open-hearted students came up to me, and I could see the terror rising in her eyes. She pointed to her heart and said, "You have to shut this down! If I go out in the world like this ... I'll be devastated, demolished, destroyed!"

Well, I could see her point, but instead of closing down the heart, I thought that another strategy might be more beneficial. I realized that practices that open the heart must be balanced with practices that build and sustain the integrity of our personal power, presence, or energy field.

The way to protect myself without being cut off from the divine flow is to develop and refine the power of my presence. Within the field of that powerful presence, I can keep my heart open. Here is a practice from Psalm 7 that describes the work:

MY PROTECTION

מָגִנִּי עַל־אֱלֹהִים מוֹשִׁיעַ יִשְׁרֵי־לֵב

Magini al Elohim, moshia yishrei leiv.
My protection is all about the God-field;
that's what saves the upright heart.
(Psalm 7:11)

When the source for my own energy field is the *Shechinah*, that indwelling Divine Presence, then I am protected, shielded, and ultimately safe. That sense of ultimate safety allows my heart to risk being open and expansive no matter what the circumstance. My heart stands up within me and takes the lead.

My energy field is like a *Mishkan*, into which I can invite the Divine Presence to dwell. The strength and integrity of that *Mishkan* will determine my ability to receive the divine flow of blessing and miracle. "Strengthening the vessel" becomes, then, one of the main goals of spiritual practice.

I learned this lesson the hard way.

When I was first coming into leadership and I was determined to live my life with an open heart, no matter the circumstances, I felt incredibly vulnerable. It seemed that the more visible I was as a leader, the more I attracted negative projections and attack. I felt defenseless, repeatedly devastated, and wondered if I could possibly continue on the path of leadership to which I felt called.

That's when my friend Shaya taught me a simple shielding practice that he had learned from a body of spiritual work called Arica. It became just the first phase of a practice that I have developed over the years, called EFR (energy field recharge). This first phase consists of setting up an energy pattern, visualizing an egg of light completely surrounding me, and filling that egg with light from the center of my heart. When I began doing this practice, it quite literally changed my life. Every day my field and the power of my presence grew stronger and lighter. It seemed that when someone sent negative energy my way, the quality of my presence just transmuted that negativity. I began to feel safer and more confident. It seemed that the practice was cumulative; each day I added to the strength of my energy field and maintained its integrity.

I added the second phase of the practice, which included a concentration of the breath, because I realized that whenever I focused my attention on the breath, whatever I did was magnified by that concentration. EFR became an important part of my daily practice. After a couple of years, I progressed to the third phase.

One day I was leafing through the *Encyclopaedia Judaica* (just for fun) and I came across a picture of an ancient shield of an Israelite warrior. On it was inscribed the words of Psalm 67. This was very exciting, so I ran to get my book of Psalms and began immersing myself in the words of that psalm. As a chanter, I was looking for the line that might hold the power or medicine of the psalm. When I found it, I began chanting that line until its power was revealed. Then I connected the chant with the energy pattern. I found that the chant magnified the energy pattern and infused it with beauty and power.

For the next few years I did the third phase of EFR, which incorporates the chant, the energy pattern, and the visualization.

Finally, when the chant was so much a part of me that I could hear it inside without chanting it aloud, I could move to the fourth phase of EFR, which reincorporates the concentration on the breath, while I am chanting silently, setting up the energy pattern, and visualizing the egg of light.

Here is a full description of the practice:

EFR—ENERGY FIELD RECHARGE

This practice can be used for protection, for clearing, and for strengthening the energy field.

אֱלֹהִים יְחָנֵּנוּ וִיבָרְכֵנוּ יָאֵר פָּנָיו אִתָּנוּ סֶלָה

Elohim y'choneinu vivarcheinu ya'eir panav itanu selah.
God, grace us, bless us; may its light shine among us, selah.
(Psalm 67:2)

First Phase: Visualization and Energy Patterning

1. Find a point of light deep in your belly and bring it up through the body, out the top of your head until it's about a foot above your head.

2. Weave an egg of light clockwise from the point above your head down the body until you reach a point at the bottom of the egg about a foot below your feet.

3. Pull that point of light up through your perineum back to the beginning point in your belly.
4. Connect the point in your belly to a point within your heart.
5. Radiate out from the heart, filling the entire egg with a white/golden light.
6. End by rooting your attention back in the belly.

Second Phase: Visualization, Energy Patterning, and Breath Concentration

1. *On the inhalation*: Find a point of light deep in your belly and bring it up through the body, out the top of your head until it's about a foot above your head.
2. *On the exhalation*: Weave an egg of light clockwise from the point above your head down the body until you reach a point at the bottom of the egg about a foot below your feet.
3. *On a partial inhalation*: Pull that point of light up through your perineum back to the beginning point in your belly.
4. *Continue the inhalation*: Connect the point in your belly to a point within your heart.
5. *Breathing in and out from the heart*: Radiate out from the heart, filling the entire egg with a white/golden light. End by directing the breath into the belly.

Third Phase: Chant, Visualization, and Energy Patterning

1. *Elohim*: Find a point of light deep in your belly and bring it up through the body, out the top of your head until it's about a foot above your head.
2. *Y'choneinu*: Weave an egg of light clockwise from the point above your head down the body until you reach a point at the bottom of the egg about a foot below your feet.
3. *Vivarchei*: Pull that point of light up through your perineum back to the beginning point in your belly.

4. *Nu*: Connect the point in your belly to a point within your heart.

5. *Ya'eir panav itanu selah*: Radiate out from the heart, filling the entire egg with a white/golden light. End by rooting your attention back in the belly on the word *selah*.

Fourth Phase: Silent Chant

Chant silently with breath concentration.

What is wonderful about this practice of EFR is that it promotes a sense of safety and protection without insulating you. Your "shield" is completely permeable, but the quality of that energy field allows you to become so radiant that negativity is neutralized. Furthermore, the practice of EFR trains you to access the divine source within you and fill your field with its light.

It's important to note that an imbalance of these two aspects of spiritual practice result in some peril. To cultivate an open heart without also building the power of presence might leave you so vulnerable that you become the walking wounded, fearful of criticism and attack. To cultivate the power of presence without also doing the work of opening your heart is also dangerous because it can lead to corruption, ego inflation, and addiction to power.

I am continually rebalancing these two aspects of practice.

Longing

FUEL FOR SPIRITUAL PRACTICE

*W*hen I sit down to chant or meditate, I address myself to God, the Beloved, the Great Mystery who wears the disguise of this strange and amazing life ... And I say, "I just want to *be* with You." In that moment of focused intention, my heart is stirred and awakened. Inwardly I turn away from the surface of things and I turn toward that which is essential. I open up the treasures of my depths; I unlock the power of longing.

That power sustains me in my practice, fuels the passion of my prayer life, and sends me to a state of attentive, vital, open, loving expectancy. That power is so very essential to my spiritual practice. Without access to this deep and abiding force that is hidden away inside my heart of hearts, I could not sustain my practice, and my prayer life would be a dry and pointless habit.

Years ago, when I was first stepping into the blessing of being a teacher, Reb Zalman Schachter-Shalomi gave me this one assignment: "Go to your people and awaken the power of yearning," he said.

The Song of Songs, the sacred text of yearning and consummation, says, "I was asleep, but my heart stayed awake. There it is—the sound of my Lover knocking" (5:2).

All of us are asleep to some extent, lulled by the constant din of media and commerce. We are constricted by past disappointments, habituated to a narrow version of reality, blind to the unexpected.

And yet ... each of our hearts is imprinted with a memory of Home, a knowledge of the infinite, and a great love. Inside each of our hearts is a spark of holy desire, waiting to be ignited into flame.

Our hearts lie awake, waiting to be roused by God, our true love, who is knocking, who calls us to become ourselves and to be connected in sacred union with all of Creation and with the Source of All. God is knocking with the reality of each moment. The truth of this moment is distorted when anxiety compels me to reach out for what's next and thus miss what is right in front of me, or when I am so preoccupied with the past or my ideas about what should be that I miss what is. My awakened heart vibrates like a bell so that the whole of me might wake up and stay present to the truth that is before me, to the miracle of my ongoing rebirth. I engage in practices that cultivate longing, directing my attention toward that bell of the heart so that its ringing will awaken, enliven, encourage, and motivate me to wholeness and to the holiness that is my destiny.

A good healer will awaken and nurture the power of healing that is built into our bodies. A good healer helps us heal ourselves. So, too, a spiritual teacher awakens the power of longing, the divine homing device planted in us that will propel and guide each of us to our divine potential.

I take two approaches to this work of awakening the force of longing. I believe that both are necessary. And then, once that force is unlocked, care must be taken to direct its power in service to the evolution of our soul-path.

One approach is in really knowing, experiencing, and expressing the pain of separation from God, from the Oneness. The pain of separation becomes the motivating force that finally turns us toward our Source and sends us on the journey of awakening and liberation. When the Israelites went down into Egypt, it took them four hundred years to realize that they were enslaved and to cry out to God. It was that powerful cry that set in motion the process of liberation. And when Moses began to act, life only got harder and more oppressive. So, too, when we awaken to the pain of separation, all of our well-built defenses begin to crumble; places in our hearts that had been shut down by disappointment or despair are suddenly feeling again. Our former numbness is replaced with the excruciating anguish of isolation and alienation from the Wholeness of Being. We become strangers in the land of our own lives. The pain shows us just how far we have strayed from our own truth. Through the agonies of separation and the buildup of our defenses against feeling pain, we have gone unconscious and hurt those that we love the most. These realizations have the power to strip away our excuses and defenses, to turn us toward God, to send us on a new path. In our brokenness, we find the force of longing that can move us to wholeness.

And every tragedy that I suffer in my life opens the possibility of soul growth as I choose the option that affirms life and deepens compassion, rather than the one that leads me to bitterness.

This approach to the cultivation of longing would not be very popular or sustainable if there weren't also another approach to this most essential spiritual work. The other way, which is equally rigorous but sometimes more attractive, is through ecstatic practice.

Through the practices of chant, dance, drumming, breath, visualization, or focused intention, it is possible to receive a glimpse of the "Promised Land." That glimpse is the momentary identification with a state of consciousness that is abundantly flowing with "milk and honey," with the realization that God is right here, embracing us, pouring the Great Love through the vessels of our life. In that glimpse we see and know our oneness with Creation and with the Source of All. We are nurtured by milk that flows directly from the breast of God, and we taste the honeyed sweetness of existence itself.

It may be just a moment. And that moment may be terrifying, as the boundaries of Self and Reality dissolve to reveal the wide expanse. However terrifying or delicious that glimpse may be, we can take the memory of that state back into the wilderness of our lives. That memory can be used to awaken the power of longing, the force that will sustain us on this journey. The memory of expansiveness sets up a painful dissonance with the narrow constructs we have built. As old and limiting beliefs shatter, we are propelled onto our path—sent by the impossibility of going back into slavery, drawn by the beauty of our vision of the Promised Land, and inspired by the taste of freedom. That memory becomes the compass that can guide us, as we learn to love and be loved, as we choose life again and again at the crossroads of each and every moment.

Focus, through Pleasure, All the Way to Basking

A chant practice requires me to learn how to focus my attention. I use the breath, various aspects of the sound, the ever-deepening meaning of the words, the rhythm, the pathways of intention, the vertical and horizontal axis, and stereoscopic consciousness to help me return to the sacred phrase every time my mind wanders, every time I space out.

Most of the hard work of meditation is learning how to focus our attention. This work is simple but certainly not easy. The mind tends to wander, free-associate, and be easily distracted. Often, meditation teachers give the instruction of focusing on the breath because it is relatively unproblematic and readily available. In meditation, we train the mind by bringing the attention back to the breath every time it wanders.

Once, as I sat at a weeklong meditation retreat with Thich Nhat Hanh, a renown Buddhist meditation teacher from Vietnam, I had a revelation that turned my practice upside down and sent me deeper into the treasures of chant.

After sitting for many hours, working so very hard at my practice, I suddenly heard Thich Nhat Hanh's instruction, both his words and the tone of his voice. He said, "Enjoy your breathing!" And he said it in a tone that was tremendously loving, sensuous, and luxurious. I suddenly felt wide awake and completely relaxed. The next breath filled me with delight. I savored its fragrance and felt nourished by its life force. I felt the power of the breath filtering through my entire body. Each breath was an opportunity to savor *this* very moment of blessing. I stepped inside the present moment to completely inhabit it ... to show up fully in order to receive the gift that God was giving me just now.

By "enjoying the breath," I was able to achieve exquisite focus of attention, but I also experienced something even more compelling. What had been simply unproblematic (the breath) was transformed through my delighted attention into a beneficent miracle.

Rabbi Abraham Joshua Heschel said, "Just to be is holy."

Focusing my attention was just the beginning, just the doorway. I could enter through the doorway of focused attention and discover the immense pleasure of being.

Here is a chant practice that describes that pleasure:

IN HIS SHADE

בְּצִלּוֹ חִמַּדְתִּי וְיָשַׁבְתִּי וּפִרְיוֹ מָתוֹק לְחִכִּי

B'tzilo chimadti v'yashavti, ufiryo matok l'chiki.
In His shade I delight to sit, tasting His sweet fruit.
(Song of Songs 2:3)

When I chant these words from the Song of Songs, it feels like I am putting down all my struggle. I am leaning back against the Tree of Life, resting into this moment. In the silence after the chant, I taste the sweet fruit of God's presence through my breath. And then I can bask in the light of pure being.

In chapter 8 of the book of Proverbs, Wisdom herself calls to us and exclaims:

My fruit is better than gold, better than fine gold,
And my produce is better than fine silver,
I walk on the way of righteousness, on the paths of justice,
I bequeath those who love me existence itself,
I will fill them with treasures.

(Proverbs 8:19–21)

If I can learn to "enjoy my breathing," then how much more so can I learn to enjoy the chant, which is beautiful, evocative, and alluring.

The beauty of a chant lures me in and opens the door to my heart. The pleasure of a chant keeps me attentive and present and willing to keep surrendering. With a chant, I am focusing my attention and then opening to the immense pleasure of this moment. Then I get to bask in "existence itself" and receive the treasures that God is giving.

I really learned about the pleasure of "existence itself" from my practice of Shabbat (the Sabbath). All week long I try to get things done. Through my effort, creativity, intelligence, and passion, I work at transforming my world into a *Mishkan*, a dwelling place for the Divine. I am busy fixing, beautifying, preparing, arranging, resolving, figuring it all out, and learning from my mistakes. The work of my life is intense and beautiful. When the time comes to enter Shabbat, I let all that busy intensity and all that intricate beauty send me through the doorway of delight into a state of spaciousness. I let go of my usual busyness, worry, and ambition. I let go of my focus on all that doing, and I enter into the realm of pure being, where my senses are heightened and I become receptive to the subtleties of pleasure that I might have missed in my busyness.

The Sanctification of Pleasure

Shabbat is the sanctification of pleasure; it is dedicated delight. All week long I try to focus my attention on the task at hand. I need to focus on accomplishing, acquiring, creating, and achieving (not to mention keeping up with my e-mails). On Shabbat, I stop (turn off my computer) and open to receive the fruit of my effort and God's grace. I let go of the illusion of control, and I surrender to "what is." I let the delight of Shabbat send me there. I receive the simple splendors of light, color, breath, connection, taste, fragrance, touch, or sound ... and I let that beauty send me from *doing* to *being*. Even one moment of basking in the light of Pure Being can be so nourishing, inspiring, and encouraging that it can sustain me through great challenges when I return to my work, to my doing. Through Shabbat, I am given a wider perspective on my life and an inner calm that can center me when life gets turbulent. It really works.

Well, the practice of chant is a microcosm of that Shabbat miracle.

I begin the chant with intensive focus and a deepening sense of purpose. The beauty of the chant transforms the sacred phrase into a doorway. I am drawn through that doorway into a sparkling spaciousness where I can then bask in the light of God's presence.

I absorb that light and become radiant. This is the light that illuminates my way.

THE USES OF
CHANT

Chanting as a Healing Modality

hanting, the repetition of a sacred phrase, is a way of transforming the words of liturgy into doorways. They become entrances into expanded states of consciousness. From those expanded states, we can have access to the fullness of our power to bless and to heal, both ourselves and others. The sacred words become the lanterns by which our inner treasures, the unique medicine that we each carry, may be revealed. We kindle a light in the words through careful and loving attention to breath, intention, meaning, sound, melody, harmony, tone, and rhythm and through the will to repeat a phrase long enough that a shift in consciousness can occur. Energy that is generated in the chant can then be focused and refined for healing.

The art of chanting in community requires a double focus—on the ever-deepening center of one's being, and on the group energy that is emerging. With each repetition of the phrase, the chanter has an opportunity to strengthen and refine both these points of focus. By opening the heart, the chanter finds within herself more to give the group. And by becoming a servant to the group, the chanter is given access to the deeper realms of her own heart.

When the sound of a chant has ended, the most subtle, transformative, and powerful part of the practice can begin. By entering into the silence after a chant, we can receive both the divine influx and the gifts that bubble up from the soul. The silence after a chant is a completely different, yet complementary practice to the chant itself. At the end of a chant, the silence allows us to focus attention on the breath moving gently in and out of the heart. We surrender to the power that the chant has generated, letting it do its work within. In the silence, the chanter notices everything possible, knowing that a heightened attention is necessary in order to enter through whatever doors have been opened by the power of the chant. Awareness of a state magnifies its benefit.

The healing power of a chant depends on the ability to create a vehicle for energy. That vehicle can be understood to be like the *Mishkan*, the movable sanctuary that housed the Holy Ark that was built during our wandering in the wilderness. Into that *Mishkan* we invite the presence of the Divine to dwell. It becomes the nexus point between the infinite and the finite realms. The stronger, more spacious, and clearer the *Mishkan* is, the more energy it can receive and transmit.

When we chant, we are building a *Mishkan* at four distinct, yet interconnecting levels. The *Mishkan* exists at the level of the group, in relationship, in the body, and in the heart. During a chant for the purpose of healing, we call on the fullness of our passion and generosity to build and strengthen the *Mishkan* at all four levels.

In Kabbalah there are four worlds, which correspond to the following realms:

1. The physical world of action
2. The emotional world of expression, feeling, and creativity
3. The world of knowing
4. The spiritual world of being and interconnection

The chant becomes a healing force when all four worlds within the chanter are engaged. The chant vibrates through the body, opening up and enlivening the physical world. The emotions are engaged through the building of intention. The world of knowing is engaged through learning about the content and context of the sacred phrase. And the spiritual world is activated in us as our sense of separateness dissolves and we open up to the One through expanded states of consciousness. Through the practice of chant, we can activate all our disparate parts at once and become the vehicle for God's healing power.

Chant in Ritual

*R*itual is a way of responding to the spiritual need of the moment, by stepping outside of the flow of time and accessing the eternal now of mythic truth that includes and yet transcends our ordinary daily rhythms.

As we step into ritual space, we achieve the priceless advantage of perspective. We can perceive our own stuck places of blame, fear, worry, attachment, or despair, and we can rise up in ritual to move that energy, break old patterns, open up the channels of flow within and between us, and thus open up to greater aliveness and deeper love.

Chant is the perfect modality for this movement of energy and for addressing the spiritual challenge and opportunity of the moment. As I develop and practice a chant and "make it my own," I am continually inquiring into the nature of its "medicine," its transformative or healing power. When that becomes clear, I put that chant into my medicine bag. Then, as I feel the need for ritual, I can call on those chants as vehicles of transformation.

Here is an example: This is a ritual for Mother's Day. Mother's Day was originally conceived as a day to harness the power of motherhood to inspire us toward the making of peace in our world. It often devolves into something less ... obligations, Hallmark cards, cut flowers. Perhaps there is nothing wrong with this, but I sense in this holiday an (often lost) opportunity for healing and empowerment.

In examining the phenomenon of motherhood, I discern four distinct functions: nurturing, protecting, empowering, and initiating. (I learned about these functions of mothering from Phillip Moffitt, *Vipassana* meditation teacher.)

In rising to the challenge of Mother's Day, I see that it's possible to spend a lifetime blaming our mothers for not doing a good job of this or blaming ourselves for not mothering well enough. All of the din of our complaining and blaming might drown out the voice of God, the Great Mother, whispering to us in the depths of our own hearts, "I am here. Turn to me. It's never too late to be mothered well."

In ritual space, we set an intention of turning to God to fulfill these functions of mothering. We share with each other moments when those functions were glimpsed and remember the healing that brought us. And then we use a chant to turn toward God, the Great Mother. The chant opens us to a flow of blessing that has always been flowing. The chant magnifies or focuses that flow and lets us receive it.

RETURNING TO THE GREAT MOTHER

Mother's Day Ritual/Celebration

NURTURING

On Mother's Day, the Great Mother comes to you as Nurturer and opens her arms in an inviting embrace. There is no shame too great, no ugliness in her eyes, no sin you could commit that would bar you from Her love. She sees the place in you of insatiable hunger, the emptiness you vainly try to fill with entertainment, unhealthy food, drugs, or your busyness. All the prayers we say are meant to open us to Her abounding love, and remember that it is *that* love that we have been seeking all along. It is only *that* love that can nurture us and quench our awful thirst. We can open to that God-love in the everyday details of our lives and in our relationships with family, friends, and strangers.

Sharing moments of feeling nurtured and comforted:

נַחֲמוּ נַחֲמוּ עַמִּי

Nachamu, nachamu ami!
Comfort, comfort My people!
(Isaiah 40:1)

וְנָהָר יֹצֵא מֵעֵדֶן לְהַשְׁקוֹת אֶת־הַגָּן

V'nahar yotzei mei'Eden, l'hashkot et hagan.
A river comes forth from Eden to water the garden.
(Genesis 2:10)

PROTECTING

On Mother's Day, the Great Mother comes to you as Protector. She comes to remind you that whatever happens to you in this unpredictable life, you are ultimately safe. Though our lives seem filled with dangerous adventures, the Great Mother whispers to you that She was, is, and will always be there for you, and the knowledge of Her presence will protect you from despair even through your greatest suffering. "Even death is safe," She whispers. What seems a tragic ending is, in the greater reality, a joyful homecoming.

Sharing moments of feeling well-protected:

וַאֲנִי מָצָאתִי מְנוּחָה   מִתַּחַת כַּנְפֵי הַשְּׁכִינָה

Va'ani matzati m'nuchah mitachat kanfei HaShechinah.
Under the wings of *Shechinah* I have found my rest.

כִּי־עַזָּה כַמָּוֶת אַהֲבָה

Ki azah kamavet ahavah.
For love is as strong as death.
(Song of Songs 8:6)

EMPOWERING

On Mother's Day, the Great Mother comes to you as Empowerer. She reminds you that you always have allies and that Her strength is within you. She challenges you to act righteously, to be good stewards for Her creation, to repair the broken places of Her world. She reminds you how powerful you are in that each word, each action, each thought, every intention really matters. She also reminds you of the power of your beauty.

Sharing moments of feeling empowered:

קוּמָה יהוה הוֹשִׁיעֵנִי אֱלֹהָי

Kumah Adonai, hoshi'eini Elohai.

Rise up, YHVH; save me, my God.

(Psalm 3:8)

הִנָּךְ יָפָה רַעְיָתִי הִנָּךְ יָפָה

Hinach yafah rayati, hinach yafah!

How beautiful You are, my Friend, how beautiful!

(Song of Songs 1:15)

INITIATING

On Mother's Day, the Great Mother comes to initiate us into Her mysteries. With this initiation, She sends us onto our life's path with an awareness that each of us has a mission to fulfill. Each of us must grow into the unique being that we truly are. Each of us must accept the gifts and the challenges that are given through this initiation. The Great Mother asks us to hear Her voice, a voice that cries for our pain, yet sends us to our wholeness. This initiation connects us with our ancestors and makes us loyal servants to the ones who will follow behind us in the days to come.

Sharing moments of initiation:

מַה־נּוֹרָא הַמָּקוֹם הַזֶּה

Mah nora hamakom hazeh!

How awesome is this place!

(Genesis 28:17)

So if you've ever felt a lack of nurturance in your life; if you've ever felt deathly afraid; if you've ever felt disempowered; if you've ever suffered a lack of meaning for your life ... then your hunger, disappointment, sadness, anger, or hopelessness can lead you back to the Great Mother, who awaits your turning with an eager embrace.

Here is another example of using chant in ritual: Gaia is another name for earth. We personify the presence of our planet in order to be in loving relationship with her. We come into loving relationship with our planet so that we can be empowered to cherish and protect her and receive blessing, beauty, and wholeness in the process.

Sometimes we fall into despair, and that despair robs us of our energy, motivation, and commitment. And then we need a ritual to restore our faith and inspire us to do the work of healing our planet.

The following Gaia Healing Ritual begins with the prayer from our morning liturgy that refers to the miraculous self-healing power of the body. With this prayer, we are calling that amazing intelligence of the body to heal itself—God. In this Gaia Healing Ritual, we are addressing that great divine intelligence in the body of the earth, affirming our faith in its self-healing mechanism. Perhaps we are part of that self-healing mechanism of our planet.

As the ritual continues, we chant to call on each of the elements of earth, water, fire, and air as our allies in this work. A good ritual engages all of the senses, so in addition to the chant, we are seeing touching, smelling, and tasting the symbols of these powerful elements as a way of knowing their power within us.

The ritual concludes with a blessing and then a chant to move us through the gates of this moment into the fullness of our love and empowerment.

GAIA HEALING RITUAL

רוֹפֵא כָל בָּשָׂר וּמַפְלִיא לַעֲשׂוֹת

Rofei chol basar umafli la'asot!
O wondrous Healer of all flesh!
(from the morning liturgy)

אַדְמַת־קֹדֶשׁ הוּא

Admat kodesh hu!
It is holy ground!
(Exodus 3:5)

כּוֹסִי רְוָיָה

Kosi r'vayah.
My cup overflows.
(Psalm 23:5)

נֵר יהוה נִשְׁמַת אָדָם חֹפֵשׂ כָּל חַדְרֵי בָטֶן

Neir Adonai nishmat adam chofeis kol chadrei vaten.
My soul is the flame of God that searches the inner chambers.
(Proverbs 20:27)

כֹּל הַנְּשָׁמָה תְּהַלֵּל יָהּ הַלְלוּיָהּ

Kol han'shamah t'haleil Yah.
Every soul praises Yah with every breath,
From the moment of birth until death! *Halleluyah!*
(Psalm 150:6)

Bless us, O Yah, through the moon above,
through the earth below,
Through flowing waters, through bright fire,
swirling wind and gentle breath.
May Your blessing pour through us ... to all living creatures.
May our hearts open in startling wonder and empowered love.

עִבְרוּ עִבְרוּ בַּשְּׁעָרִים פַּנּוּ דֶּרֶךְ הָעָם

Ivru, ivru bash'arim, panu derech ha'am!
Go through, go through the gates, clear the way of the people!
(Isaiah 62:10)

Chanting During *Taharah*

*A*fter someone dies and before the body is buried, a *chevra kadisha*, a group of "holy friends," is given the honor of *sh'mirah* (watching over the body) and *taharah* (preparing it for burial). There is a special liturgy that is said, and I believe that this ceremony can be enhanced and made even more beautiful through the practice of chant.

The ritual of *taharah* requires us to step into "the between," that sacred space between life and death, in order to escort the soul on her journey. Performing *taharah* is like being a midwife to that soul. We do this soul-midwifery by coming into a state of heightened awareness and reverence.

The practice of chant can help us cultivate that state in which our reverence for the life that has been lived merges with our awareness of the great expanse that is opening beyond death. Chant can clear away any fear or reactivity, so that we can be fully present to both honor the body and celebrate the awesome journey of the soul. The chant helps us transcend our individual stories and personalities, in order to connect the *chevra kadisha*, the "holy friends," to each other in shared intention and purpose.

With a chant, we can use a kernel of the liturgy to focus that shared intention so that the words of the liturgy lift us up into sacred space. We use the words to go beyond the place of words. The sacred sounds of Hebrew, the melodies, harmonies, rhythms, and our concentrated attention help expand our awareness of the import of this awesome moment. Chant works to clear the mind of distraction, open our hearts, deepen our love, and focus our attention on the task at hand.

Chanting has the power to open the inner dimensions of our being and connect us to the reality and radiance of our own soul. If we are identified only with our bodies, then we'll only see and relate to the body before us. If we are identified with the great expanse of our own souls, then we can be in communication and communion with the soul before us, who is embarking on an amazing journey.

PREPARATIONS

Ideally, the *chevra kadisha* would practice and know these chants well. (They can also assign a subset of the group to be chanting for everyone.) Then we will have the tools that will help us rise to each of the challenges of the *taharah* ritual. The first challenge is to prepare ourselves by coming into the presence of a great mystery.

כִּי אַתָּה מְחַיֶּה הַמֵּתִים וּמֵמִית חַיִּים

Ki atah m'chayeih hameitim, umeimit chayim.
For You revive the dead and bring death to the living.
(from the *Taharah* liturgy)

WASHING

During the washing, we chant words of comfort and confidence to the soul, who is now expanding beyond the confines of her incarnation and stepping into its more expansive dimensions. Knowing and affirming the presence of God is a way of sanctifying this time of transition.

We also bring the words of the Song of Songs to this sacred act of washing. These words of love create an atmosphere of reverence for our embodiment, while luring the soul into the place of pure love. Rabbi Akiva said that while all the writings of Torah are holy, the Song of Songs is the "Holy of Holies." We wash the body and, through our chant, call in the remembrance of the High Priest. It is only the High Priest (the *Kohein Gadol*) who enters the Holy of Holies and encounters the Divine Presence. The Song of Songs reminds the soul of the gift of love that life has given ... the only gift that matters as we leave everything else behind.

כִּי־תַעֲבֹר בַּמַּיִם אִתְּךָ־אָנִי וּבַנְּהָרוֹת לֹא יִשְׁטְפוּךְ

Ki ta'avor bamayim it'cha ani, uvan'harot lo yisht'fucha.

When you pass through the waters,
I am with you, yes, I am with you.
I won't let the rivers overwhelm you,
I will be with you.

(Isaiah 43:2)

זֶה דוֹדִי וְזֶה רֵעִי

Zeh Dodi v'zeh Rei'i.

This is my Beloved; this is my Friend.

(Song of Songs 5:16)

הִנָּךְ יָפָה רַעְיָתִי הִנָּךְ יָפָה

Hinach yafah rayati, hinach yafah!

How beautiful You are, my Friend, how beautiful!

(Song of Songs 1:15)

כִּי־עַזָּה כַמָּוֶת אַהֲבָה

Ki azah kamavet ahavah.

For love is as strong as death.

(Song of Songs 8:6)

THE *TAHARAH*

During the ritual pouring, this chant affirms the essential purity of the soul while assigning the water the power to break up rigid life patterns and clear the way for the soul to move forward on her path.

כָּל־מִשְׁבָּרֶיךָ וְגַלֶּיךָ עָלַי עָבָרוּ
טָהוֹר הוּא, טְהוֹרָה הִיא

Kol mishbarecha v'galecha alai avaru.

Tahor hu, t'horah hi.

All of Your breakers and Your waves have swept over me.

He is pure; she is pure.

(Psalm 42:8)

DRESSING

As we dress the body in the clothes of the High Priest, we rejoice in the imminent journey. As we dress the body, we are preparing the soul for her passage into the beyond ... and into the realization of salvation.

שׂוֹשׂ אָשִׂישׂ בַּיהוה תָּגֵל נַפְשִׁי בֵּאלֹהַי
כִּי הִלְבִּישַׁנִי בִּגְדֵי־יֶשַׁע

Sos asis badonai tageil nafshi beilohai,

ki hilbishani bigdei yesha.

I will rejoice in God, who has dressed me in the garments of salvation.

(Isaiah 61:10)

FINAL BLESSINGS

We acknowledge the completion and fulfillment of a life lived to its conclusion, and we send the soul to her journey with the Priestly Blessing.

כִּי מָלְאָה צְבָאָה

Ki malah tz'va'ah.

Her time of service is fulfilled.

(Isaiah 40:2)

יְבָרֶכְךָ יהוה וְיִשְׁמְרֶךָ

יָאֵר יהוה פָּנָיו אֵלֶיךָ וִיחֻנֶּךָּ

יִשָּׂא יהוה פָּנָיו אֵלֶיךָ וְיָשֵׂם לְךָ שָׁלוֹם

Y'varech'cha Adonai v'yishm'recha.

Ya'eir Adonai panav eilecha vichuneka.

Yisa Adonai panav eilecha v'yaseim l'cha shalom.

May God bless you and guard you.

May God shine His face upon you and grace you.

May God lift up Her face to you and give you peace.

(Numbers 6:24–26)

Chant

TRANSFORMATION, PURIFICATION, HEALING, AND RENEWAL

*W*hen someone comes to me for guidance, coaching, comfort, inspiration, encouragement, support, or spiritual friendship, I listen with a heart that has been informed by my own powerful chanting practice.

Hebrew chanting is the melodic and rhythmic repetition of a phrase drawn from our sacred text. It is a practice that allows for the exploration of the deeper levels of meaning and experience that lie beneath the surface of our religious lives. For many, chanting has become an important method of opening the heart, connecting with community, quieting the mind, and viscerally embodying our liturgy and scripture. In the context of *hashpa'ah* (spiritual direction), the practice of chant can be used as a method of inquiry and as a vehicle for expanding our capacities to receive and integrate the vast mystery and wisdom of our souls.

It's important to bring our sustained and loving attention into building and refining our inner lives. Chant is a practice that connects the outer dimensions of sound with the inner dimensions of awareness. As we grow and nurture our inner lives, it is important to have ways to express and share with our community the gifts we have received in the solitude of our personal practice. Chant is the bridge between the inner life and the outer expression; between the solitary practice and the shared beauty of fellowship. When we chant, we are using the whole body as the instrument with which to feel the meaning of the sacred phrase. We study the meaning of the words and the context from which they are drawn. We explore the range of our feelings so that they can be dedicated to the purpose of the chant. And we use the power of the practice to enter into the silence and stillness at our core. Thus the practice of chant integrates our spiritual, intellectual, emotional, and physical energies.

The practice of chant takes the words of prayer and uses them as doorways into deeper meanings and into the spaces of our own hearts. It does this through the clarifying and refining of our intention. Sometimes the sheer volume of prayers, collected over the centuries, itself becomes an obstacle to delving more deeply into their meaning or using their power for transformation. The practice of chant allows us the luxury of exploring one phrase at a time, igniting the fire of our enthusiasm and pouring our passion into those particular words. Our prayer life will start to reflect the personal and passionate experience we have had with those words. Chanting wakes up our liturgy and brings it to life within us.

The practice of chant allows us to begin to approach the text from an expanded understanding—from our hearts, bodies, and experience as well as from what we know intellectually. In addition to preparing us for text study by expanding our perception of the words in front of us, chant may also be used in the comprehension of a text. We take a phrase from the text that holds some power or mystery for us, and we experience it with melody and rhythm and repetition until it unlocks its secrets for us.

Often during the ongoing practice of chant, the complexities of our inner lives are brought to the surface. In the context of a counseling relationship, the seeker can acknowledge the mysteries and challenges that are called up by the chant and begin to appreciate the complexities of the inner life as they are revealed by the practice.

One facet of *hashpa'ah* is support for the work of cultivating *midot* (qualities) such as the conscious awareness of God's presence, compassion, wisdom, love, open-heartedness, justice, spiritual community, or humility. Chanting can be an effective and powerful tool in this work. In the practice of chant, we choose a phrase that expresses or embodies a quality that we wish to cultivate. As we chant, we can step inside that quality, feel its beauty, and also explore the obstacles that arise in response to its presence.

Richard asks me to help him learn about patience. We chant from Psalm 37:7, *"Dom l'Yah v'hitcholeil lo."*

WAITING ...

דּוֹם לַיהוה וְהִתְחוֹלֵל לוֹ

Dom l'Yah v'hitcholeil lo.
Be still and wait for God.
(Psalm 37:7)

As we repeat and embody that phrase, he experiences both the feeling of patient waiting *and* his rising impatience. Through the practice of chant, Richard works on strengthening and appreciating the stillness of waiting, and he has the opportunity to explore the roots of his impatience. This exploration can be done with compassion and understanding as he directs the beauty of the chant to soften hard places in the heart and melt his defenses.

Laura comes to me filled with anxiety about getting old. We explore her fears and see that she has ignored some of the gifts of aging. I sense that these gifts might be important in strengthening her sense of wholeness as she faces the challenges of getting old and frail. Together we study the words from Psalm 92:

AGING AND SAGING

עוֹד יְנוּבוּן בְּשֵׂיבָה דְּשֵׁנִים וְרַעֲנַנִּים יִהְיוּ

Od y'nuvun b'seivah
D'sheinim v'ra'ananim yih'yu.
They will be fruitful, even in old age; they will be juicy and luxuriant.
(Psalm 92:15)

The intention that I bring to this chant is to get in touch with the kind of fruitfulness, luxuriance, and juiciness that emerges from my depths after many years of experience. This is a fruitfulness of wisdom and subtlety, and it's not always obvious if you're attuned only to the surface of things. Even as our outer skin dries and wrinkles, there is an inner softness that can be cultivated from years of rubbing up against the Mystery. Even as outer sight dims and hearing falters, there are inner senses that can become fine-tuned as we age.

As we practice together, I ask her to use this chant to bless the elders who have been models of aging and saging as they continue to blossom, burgeon, and flourish in full-hearted glory.

I send Laura home with this practice, with instructions to chant these words daily and use them to open up to a new vision.

Paul has been through a devastating divorce. He is just beginning to see glimmers of hopefulness again, but he feels weighed down by the past. He would like to examine and eventually heal the wounds that he has suffered through this painful time, but he feels overwhelmed by anger, shame, and remorse.

Together we study the words of Isaiah:

THE MIRACLE

וַיָּשֶׂם מִדְבָּרָהּ כְּעֵדֶן וְעַרְבָתָהּ כְּגַן־יהוה

Vayasem midbarah k'eiden, v'arvatah k'gan Adonai.
He transforms her wilderness into delight,
her wasteland into a divine garden.
(Isaiah 51:3)

I ask Paul to remember another time in his life when he came through a period of devastation and found himself again filled with hope and beauty. I ask him to remember the feeling of miraculous rebirth. We use the chant to call up the possibility of transformation and of miracle. In the silence after the chant, I instruct Paul to breathe this possibility into his broken heart.

Susan comes to me because she's feeling overwhelmed and afraid. She is starting a new job, entering into an intimate relationship, beginning to know her own strength and calling ... but she is plagued by self-doubt. Together we look at Psalm 112:

SUPPORTED

סָמוּךְ לִבּוֹ לֹא יִירָא

Samuch libo lo yira.

סָמוּךְ לִבָּה לֹא תִּירָא

Samuch liba lo tira.
Heart supported, fearless.
(Psalm 112:8)

Samuch libo lo yira. We sing this in the feminine as *Samuch liba lo tira,* and I translate it for her as "Heart supported, fearless." This practice opens up a new way of approaching the cultivation of courage. "What if we became fearless," I ask, "by allowing our heart to feel completely supported? Can you imagine what that would feel like?"

With Susan's permission, I place my right hand gently over her heart and put my other hand at the back of her heart. I ask her to close her eyes, dance gracefully, and notice what it feels like to have her heart supported as I chant to her. She moves tentatively at first, but then as Susan's body relaxes into the sensation of being held as I follow her movements, with my hands gently supporting her heart, her dance becomes more deliberate and beautiful. When the dance is completed, I remove my hands but ask Susan to remember what it felt like to receive support and to breathe into that feeling until it is anchored in her bodily memory. The chant itself becomes a tool of remembrance. I suggest that every time the old fears come up, she bring this chant to mind as a reminder to open her heart to the sensation of receiving support.

As I study a text, I read with a sensitivity to subtle shifts in my own energy. A certain phrase will intrigue me or disturb me or make me curious. And so I'll begin to explore that phrase through melody, rhythm, or gesture. My exploration also takes me to the dictionary and concordance so that I can learn the nuance and meaning of these powerful words. I experiment with tempo, tonal quality, movement, or visualization. At some point in my exploration, the sacred phrase begins to emerge as a distinct "medicine." I discern and experience its particular power and transformative quality by noticing its effect on me.

This ability to notice is key to the art of chant. After every chant I stop to notice so that I can learn its particular power and understand its potential as "medicine." At the end of a chant, my work of noticing begins with staying very still and bringing my attention to the breath. I gently breathe the energy that has been built by the chant into my heart center. My heart becomes an organ of discernment. I carefully notice feelings in my body. I observe the texture of my thoughts, and I watch for memories or insights that may arise. I allow the energy of the chant to nurture the power of loving awareness. The more that I practice this kind of noticing, the more the observer in me grows in wisdom, clarity, and compassion.

Sometimes the medicine of a chant shows me a "disease" that I didn't even know I had.

Here is an example. One Friday afternoon as I was getting ready for Shabbat, I came across the following line from Isaiah: *Ki malah tz'va'ah* (Isaiah 40:2).

DIVINE CONGRATULATIONS

כִּי מָלְאָה צְבָאָהּ

Ki malah tz'va'ah.

Her time of service is fulfilled.

(Isaiah 40:2)

Her time of service is fulfilled. In exploring the power of this phrase, I allowed myself to receive its message as a practice of receiving divine congratulations. God was chanting to me and saying, Shefa, in this very moment, you are complete; you have done enough and you *are enough*. Tears began to roll down my cheeks, and something in me relaxed that I hadn't known was tense. The chant was delivering to me a contradiction to a very deeply ingrained belief—a belief that was so a part of me that I just experienced it as "normal." The belief or way of being in the world said that "you're never done … you'll never finish … your to-do list keeps getting longer and you'll never keep up with it." Underneath that voice lay a dreadful accusation that whispered, "You'll never be enough (smart enough, beautiful enough, good enough)." As I chanted the words of Divine Congratulations, I suddenly became aware of a low-level anxiety about ever getting things done that had been with me for as long as I could remember. That anxiety had become the fuel for my accomplishments. As I let the power of the chant in and that newly revealed anxiety dissolved, I experienced a vision of a completely new way of being. In this vision, each moment was completed in joy, and I could rest in that joy. The work of the next moment was given to me, and the fuel that helped me rise to the new challenge was not my anxiety about getting something done, but rather my joy for the work.

At the end of the chant, I brought all of the power of the observer to this new way of being, to this clear vision of switching fuel tanks from anxiety to joy. That moment has become the compass point that guides me in my work now.

Before I ever teach or prescribe a practice to someone, I have worked with it first in my own practice in order to make its "medicine" my own. As a healer/shaman/rabbi, I am continually practicing my art and adding to my "medicine" bag so that I will be able to tune in to the need or challenge of the one who sits before me and find just the right treasure from the vast store of my inheritance that might bring beauty and power to the holy process of transformation, purification, healing, and renewal.

Inquiry and Shadow Work

The practice of chant relaxes and invigorates the body, calms the mind, opens the heart, and allows the deep wisdom of the soul to rise up and be revealed. I use chant to engage in the process of inquiry. And then, when I discover some hidden dimension of the self that might otherwise be projected on the "other," I can reintegrate that part in order to become whole and holy. This process of awareness and integration is called shadow work.

First comes the inquiry.

Often, we know something deep in our *kishkes* (at our core), but that something is buried under layers and layers of worry, anxiety, conditioning, disappointment, or expectation. Sometimes that deep knowing bubbles up from the subconscious through dreams.

Dreams can illuminate an insistent message of the truth that we've been ignoring or point us toward a situation that needs our attention. I've learned that if I can formulate a question or articulate a dilemma just before I fall asleep, and I ask for a dream, I am often rewarded with vivid, insightful, and surprising visions that can help show me the way forward. The language of dream consists of image, metaphor, and word-play, so I must be creative, clever, and receptive if I am to receive and integrate the messages of my dream life.

Well, chant is a way of stimulating a *waking* dream. The power of chant can shine a light on the inner landscape, showing us what's true beneath the cluttered surface of our lives.

As I am building the ground of the chant, formulating the intention that will fuel these sacred words, I often "lay a question on the altar of the chant." Then I work at building the energy, vitality, and force of the chant by mining its riches—bringing awareness to breath, melodic story, harmony, rhythm, and ever-deepening levels of meaning. In the silence afterward, I return to the question that I had so carefully placed on the altar of the chant. But now my mind has been cleared, my heart has been opened, and I have come into a receptive state of consciousness. In response to my question and in that rarified silence engendered by the chant, sparkling new insights and revelations emerge from the depths of my soul-wisdom. In that moment it feels as if I am remembering something that I have always known. The veil between awareness and truth dissolves, and I am given the gift of understanding.

Here is an example of using chant for the process of inquiry and self-knowledge: This chant comes out of an extraordinary and dramatic moment in the book of Genesis. Our ancestor Rebecca is suffering a difficult pregnancy. It feels as if there is a war being waged within her, and in her torment she cries out to God:

אִם־כֵּן לָמָּה זֶּה אָנֹכִי

Im kein, lamah zeh anochi?
If this is the way it is, why am I?
(Genesis 25:22)

Crying out to God is essential to the unfolding of our truth and freedom. It is the crying out of the people enslaved in Egypt / *Mitzrayim* / the narrow places that sets the process of liberation in motion.

When we cry out from our own narrow place, God hears, remembers, sees, and knows us (see Exodus 2:23–25).

After Rebecca cries out to God, she engages in deep inquiry and is answered with the truth that she holds a contradiction within her. Esau and Jacob wrestle in Rebecca's womb. God reminds her, "You are birthing duality. Within you are two nations, two peoples" (Genesis 25:23).

My own process of inquiry begins with this hypothesis: Every narrow place *is* a birth canal.

I begin with an awareness of my own narrow place, my own dilemma.

The Hasidic masters distinguish between *mochin d'katnut* (small mind) and *mochin d'gadlut* (big mind). I realize that this situation is something I won't be able to "figure out" with my small mind. Chant is the vehicle that carries me from small mind to big mind.

Into the chant I pour my passionate inquiry. In the silence, I open to the larger perspective. In my suffering, I cry out. In the silence, I ask, "What am I birthing just now?" I build the intensity of the chant with my yearning, with my determination to find meaning. Then, in the silence, I gently articulate the question in my heart ... and I open, and wait, and pay attention to what emerges ... perhaps a feeling, an image, or a word. When I honor that feeling, image, or word with my full, loving, and expectant attention, I am rewarded with an expansion of *meaning*. Through that expansion of meaning I can manage a difficult situation by seeing it in the context of the larger picture of my life. Through suffering, I can birth compassion; through painful contradictions, I can imagine new and creative pathways of possibility.

The chant helps me move through a difficult time and open to hidden blessings and lessons that I might learn.

Sometimes when I am doing this work of inquiry—when I am searching my heart—I find a place of shadow within me that needs attention and clearing.

Here is an example of using chant to do that shadow work: Each day I look into my heart. I simply close my eyes, concentrate on my heart center, and imagine breathing into the center of my heart. When I encounter a feeling of obstruction, tension, or unease, I investigate. One morning when I did this heart searching, I found a heaviness within me. I realized that it was connected to a situation in which I had been blamed for something that truly wasn't my fault. There wasn't anything I could do to convince the one who was blaming me that I was innocent. I felt besmirched. My usual pattern would be to go to the place of righteous indignation. But I wanted to try something different.

So I held the question of what to do with this awful feeling, and I opened the book of Psalms and pointed my finger at the first line I saw. (I call this practice of oracle "I-Ching-Psalms.")

This is the line that I pointed to, and it became my practice of clearing the shadow that had fallen over my heart:

HEART WALK

אֶתְהַלֵּךְ בְּתָם־לְבָבִי בְּקֶרֶב בֵּיתִי
Et'haleich b'tom l'vavi, b'kerev beiti.
I will walk within my house in the integrity of my heart.
(Psalm 101:2)

That day I did a walking meditation around my house, using this chant to reclaim my personal space, which had been violated by someone's unfair accusation. Instead of reacting, getting self-righteous or defensive, or trying to change the person's mind, I could simply take care of my own heart.

The verb *Et'haleich* is reflexive. When I chant it, I am taking myself for a walk, without needing to "get" somewhere. When I chant *b'tom l'vavi*, I am affirming the integrity, wholeness, innocence, and purity of my heart. And when I chant *b'kerev beiti*, I am reclaiming the safety, security, and boundaries of my own personal space.

This chant was just the right medicine for my clouded aching heart. I realized that the situation I was responding to was similar to other hurts of the past, other burdens of shame, guilt, and despair that I carried. Those old hurts were also being healed by this practice, which I named "Heart Walk."

The practice of chant opens up a new path of healing old wounds and letting go of old baggage from past hurts. In the book of

Leviticus, the priests are commanded to clear the ashes on the altar of sacrifice each and every day. Only then can their fires burn clean and bright. Now, we are the priests, and the altar is our heart. When we clear the ashes of past hurts, the fires of our passion and inspiration can burn clear and bright, shining a light for everyone.

This work of inquiry, shadow work, and clearing is essential if we are to become channels for the divine flow that is pouring into this world.

Ecstatic Practice and the Establishment of Basic Trust

hanting is both a contemplative and an ecstatic practice. It is contemplative because it is a form of meditation that opens the door to deep, reflective, and silent communion with Reality/God. And chant is an ecstatic practice because it facilitates a kind of rapture that allows the soul to expand beyond the confines of ordinary discursive consciousness.

Ecstasy is so often misunderstood. In a state of ecstasy, I become unself-conscious. Rabbi Abraham Joshua Heschel calls ecstasy "the withdrawal of consciousness from circumference to center" (*The Prophets*, p. 104). When we judge ecstasy from the outside, from the circumference, we miss what is happening at the center. We just can't understand what is going on for a person by observing the outer expression of someone who is experiencing ecstasy. In fact, it might look weird or scary or out of control.

What is happening "at the center" is another story entirely.

As I explore ecstatic states through my practice of chant, I am aware that my ancestors (along with mystics and prophets from every spiritual tradition) have used music, dance, and meditative techniques to achieve these altered states of consciousness for millennia.

In the Bible, we hear how the prophet Samuel anoints Saul and tells him that as part of his preparation for kingship, he will meet a band of roving prophets who prophesy through music (lyre, drum, flute, and harp). When Saul meets them, he begins to prophesy as well (1 Samuel 10).

The word for "prophesy" here is *yitnabei*—a reflexive verb that means "to go into an ecstatic state."

That verb, *yitnabei*, "to go into a prophetic/ecstatic state," is also found in the book of Numbers:

> And God came down in a cloud and spoke to him [Moses] and took the spirit that was upon him and put it on the seventy elders. When the spirit descended on them, they prophesied [went into ecstasy]. At that same moment, Eldad and Medad, who had stayed in the camp, also began to prophesy [become ecstatic], and someone ran to report this to Moses.... "Are you being jealous for my sake?" Moses said. "Would that all of God's people were prophets, that God would put his spirit upon them!"
>
> (Numbers 11:25–29)

Even Moses agrees that being in this state of ecstasy is a very good thing and just might be a sign of our deep connection with divinity.

I am on the path toward ecstasy when, after each repetition of a chant, I have the presence to ask, "What more do I have to give?" Again and again I reach for and open to more energy, presence, beauty, heart, meaning, or fullness.

Philosopher and mystic Simone Weil said, "The highest ecstasy is the attention at its fullest."

This is what happens when I chant: I heighten my attention as I use the music, breath, power, and beauty of the chant to relax the tensions of body, heart, and mind ... and thus get out of the way, so that the Spirit can descend. After a while, it feels as if God is chanting through me.

This is how it feels: I begin chanting, giving it "everything that I've got." I'm chanting ... I'm chanting ... I'm chanting ... I'm chanting ... I'm chanting ... then ... oh my God, who's chanting?! Suddenly it feels as if I am being chanted. It feels like a great relief to no longer be "in control." I surrender to the Greater Flow of Being in which I live. I know myself as part of that flow. In religious language, I surrender to God's will. My surrender feels like an expansion of identity. I am dissolving into the larger Self of the cosmos.

This dissolving of boundaries can be both blissful and terrifying.

Ecstatic practice is not just about "getting high." I've been exploring the long-term benefits of ecstasy for many years, but it was only after reading a chapter about basic trust from a book by spiritual teacher A. H. Almaas, that I really began to understand the value and purpose of my practice.

Almaas defines basic trust as "a non-conceptual confidence in the goodness of the universe." He goes on to explain, "This innate and unformulated trust in life and reality manifests as a willingness to take that plunge into the abyss" (*The Facets of Unity*, pp. 22–23).

As a spiritual guide for my students, I had noticed that as they walked the path of realization, they often would come up against a wall and be blocked in their progress. That wall was made of fear of the unknown and an unwillingness to let go into the mystery. Almaas describes the prerequisite for spiritual growth as "the capacity to accept the most problematic phase of spiritual transformation—the dissolution of familiar structures and identities." He explains that this capacity arises from an "innate sense of safety and security" (ibid., pp. 23–24).

> The more that basic trust is present, the more the process of realization and transformation can proceed smoothly. If we lack basic trust, it becomes important for us to develop it. Development here does not mean building up some new experience of self. It means experiencing the factors which brought about the original profound disconnection from reality and, in particular, experiencing repeatedly the fundamental truth of non-separateness to the point where the soul can again rest in the knowledge of that truth. Each new experience of essential truth deepens the soul's contact with her own basic trust.
>
> (ibid., p. 27)

Ecstatic practice, when engaged in responsibly, purposefully, methodically, and with heightened awareness, can give us glimpses of the fundamental truth of unity consciousness. The experience of that truth can strengthen our basic trust, our sense of security and ultimate safety. And that sense of safety allows us to take the necessary "leap of faith."

The midrash tells us that it is only after Nachshon stepped into the Red Sea up to his nose that the sea parted and we were able to cross to our freedom and journey to the Promised Land.

Like Nachshon, we stand at the threshold of the unknown. When we have established the quality of basic trust, then we can act boldly, courageously, and creatively as we face the new challenge that life is giving us. Without that basic trust, we are paralyzed by fear and may very well regress into old patterns of reactivity or habit.

Here is an example of an ecstatic practice that helps establish basic trust and thus plants the seeds of possibility in the ground of my life:

SHINING

קוּמִי אוֹרִי כִּי־בָא אוֹרֵךְ וּכְבוֹד יהוה עָלַיִךְ זָרָח

Kumi ori ki va oreich uch'vod Adonai alayich zarach.
Arise and shine for your light has come,
and the Glory of God is shining upon you.
(Isaiah 60:1)

This is a practice of connecting with the radiance within me and knowing it as God's light. At the end of the chant, I breathe into the center of my heart and find the image of a flame. With each breath, I let that fire grow brighter, until it begins to shine out into the world with more and more brilliance.

What makes my ecstatic practice different than "getting high" is that through awareness, the impact of my practice is integrated into the fabric of my life. My practice is infused with this question: How do I live in the light of this truth that I have glimpsed?

Soulful,
Wholehearted,
Embodied Text Study

These are things the fruits of which a man enjoys in this world,
while the principle remains for him in the world-to-come:
Honoring father and mother,
acts of kindness,
and bringing peace between a man and his fellow.
But the study of Torah is equal to them all.

(Talmud, *Peah* 1:1)

Three who dine at a table and exchange words of Torah are
considered as having eaten at God's table.

(*Pirkei Avot* 3:4)

God's Torah is perfect, restoring the soul.

(Psalm 19:8)

orah study is a cornerstone of Jewish practice. In many communities it is valued above all because it is understood to encompass all. Jewish study includes the expectation that the lessons of Torah will be applied to life. My experience is that "it ain't necessarily so." I've engaged in some kinds of Torah study that bring out the worst kind of competitive, quarrelsome, and arrogant spirit in people who are determined to master a text. I spent a year studying at a yeshiva in Jerusalem. When I got home, my husband commented, "You know, Shefa, you're much more argumentative since you started studying Talmud." Well, that kind of stopped me in my tracks, and I had to pause and wonder, "Who am I becoming through the study of Torah?" Am I "eating at God's table," or am I eating at the table of my ambition, at the table of my need to be right?

I wondered how I might raise up the study of Torah so that it might truly restore the soul and become a Tree of Life, bridging heaven and earth, connecting me to the Living God and to Creation. I began to see that it really mattered what questions I was bringing to a text, what assumptions I was making, and the purpose that was driving my inquiry.

When I decided that I really didn't need to get any smarter—or prove how smart I was to anyone else—I began to walk into the sacred text as if it were a doorway. I found that in order to walk through that doorway, I had to let go of all my preconceptions.

This is how it works: I come upon a piece of text that intrigues me. I may be drawn in by its beauty, its apparent contradictions, its rhythm, its poetry, or its depth.

I study that text, read various translations of it, look at commentaries, and talk about it with my friends.

Then, I hone in on one phrase from that text that seems like the key to its power. I explore each word of that phrase to understand both meaning and nuance. I use both a dictionary and a concordance. The dictionary helps me understand meaning and grammar, while the concordance shows me every other place where that word appears in scripture. Like a detective, I follow the clues, until I can taste the word, feel its texture, and hear its tone.

For example, in Psalm 6:3 there is a fascinating word, *umlal*, that is usually translated as "feeble," "faint," or "weak." I roll this word around in my mouth, and it feels so mournful. I learn that the prophets Isaiah and Joel (Isaiah 16:8, 24:4, 24:7, 33:9; Joel 1:10, 1:12) used this word to refer to the vines that withered after being cut by the enemy and to the land that cries out in suffering after the devastation of war.

I recall a line from a poem by D. H. Lawrence that describes the feeling of *umlal.*

> *This is what is the matter with us: we are bleeding at the*
> > *roots*
> *because we are cut off from the earth and sun and stars.*
> *And love is a grinning mockery because, poor blossom,*
> *we plucked it from its stem on the Tree of Life and*
> *expected it to keep on blooming in our civilized vase on*
> > *the table.*

In order to do the soulful, wholehearted, embodied text study that might "restore my soul," I first look at why I *need* this text. In what way might I be cut off from my roots, disconnected from my Source?

When I find that place of disconnection, of withering thirst, I begin chanting these words, asking for grace, opening to the possibility of reconnection. I experiment with tone and pitch and rhythm, looking for the melody that will reach across the chasm between devastation and hope. I might add a harmony that brings mystery, passion, or deeper dimension. As the chant/practice develops, I'll notice where it brings me, what its "medicine" is, what treasured potential it opens. I'll live with the chant and invite it to live inside me. I'll let it vibrate through my body, and I'll move to its rhythm.

PREPARATION FOR RECONNECTING

חָנֵּנִי יהוה כִּי אֻמְלַל אָנִי

Choneini Yah ki umlal ani.
Grace me, Yah, for I am withered [disconnected].
(Psalm 6:3)

After chanting this for a while and harvesting its riches of intimacy and immediacy, I realize that I couldn't possibly have known what these words meant or have understood their power until I had taken them into my practice as chant. I realize that no matter how smart I am and how hard I study, the true meaning of a sacred phrase might elude me unless I am willing to risk embodying that mystery and letting it live inside me.

I remember encountering the following line from Psalm 24, and having no idea what it could mean.

שְׂאוּ שְׁעָרִים רָאשֵׁיכֶם וּשְׂאוּ פִּתְחֵי עוֹלָם

S'u sh'arim rasheichem, us'u pitchei olam!
Lift up your head, O you gates; lift them up, you everlasting doors!
(Psalm 24:9)

What? Do gates have heads? How do you lift them up? What is an everlasting door?

So in the spirit of soulful, wholehearted, embodied text study, I began to chant.

When I chant for a long while, something wonderful happens. Suddenly it feels as if I'm not the one who is chanting; it feels like God is chanting to me or through me, and then the meaning of the chant transforms. God is chanting to me, saying, "Lift up your head—raise your consciousness, Shefa, for you are the gate through which I might come into the world."

It is significant that this is the psalm designated for the very first day of the week. When I leave the garden of Shabbat and step up to the work I have been given, this chant can inspire me to know that when I raise my consciousness I can become the doorway for God's presence to enter and permeate the world.

Sometimes the meaning of a text can become obscured by centuries of interpretations. There is a beautiful passage in Jeremiah (31:30–33) in which God describes a new covenant that is not like the old one that was violated. This one will be different. Here's how:

A NEW COVENANT

נָתַתִּי אֶת־תּוֹרָתִי בְּקִרְבָּם וְעַל־לִבָּם אֶכְתְּבֶנָּה

Natati et Torati b'kirbam, v'al libam echtavenah.
I will put my Torah into their inmost being and
inscribe it upon their hearts.
(Jeremiah 31:33)

I am well aware that the Christian community has used these words as their proof text for the coming of Jesus as Messiah. I have seen countless churches that proclaim the name "New Covenant" on their billboards. And yet, I have a sneaking suspicion that these words conceal a mystery and a treasure for me that I must work to uncover.

As I chant these words that describe the nature of this "new covenant," I realize just how "new" it is. Is it possible that every moment holds an opportunity to renew my agreement with the underlying Mystery of Being? A covenant is always a two-way agreement. When I show up fully for this encounter with that mystery we call God, then God will whisper to me through the promptings of my heart. Showing up for this moment of encounter means putting aside everything that I think I know, stripping myself bare of defenses, and surrendering to "what is."

When I have the calm determination to become fully present for the life I have been given—both its blessings and its challenges—then God will also be present as the truth of my inmost being and in what is written on my heart.

That's the deal.

By chanting this prophecy of Jeremiah, I am stepping up to sign the contract. With the power of my voice and intention, I am making a commitment to fulfill my end of this "new covenant" and to renew it each day or as often as possible.

Through the practice of chant, I engage in the kind of soulful, wholehearted, embodied text study that fulfills the expectation that the lessons of Torah will be applied to life. Through chant, I am studying with all my heart, with all the strength and grace of my body ... as well as with my intellect. Then the perfection of God's Torah can truly restore me to wholeness.

Gratefulness as the Foundation of Practice

*W*hen I made a commitment to dive deep into the liturgy instead of skimming along the surface, I decided to enter through one phrase at a time. I opened the siddur (prayer book) to the very first words, words that are meant to be prayed even before getting out of bed in the morning:

מוֹדֶה אֲנִי לְפָנֶיךָ

Modeh ani l'fanecha.

Modeh ani: "I gratefully acknowledge."

L'fanecha: "You," or literally, "to Your face," and the word "face" in Hebrew is plural, so even more literally, "Your faces."

This is the formula for awakening. The very first thought as I emerge from sleep: "When I open my eyes, I will see Your many faces, God. You wear the mask of this world. I am so grateful to be able to recognize You. Today I promise not to be fooled by your elaborate and imaginative disguise. I will see and acknowledge You everywhere and in everyone."

In Hebrew, the word for "Jew," *Y'hudi*, comes from the same root as *modah*. The Jewish people might be called the Grateful Ones. Judaism might be called the Path of Gratefulness. By waking up in gratefulness, we set the tone for the day; we step into a particular groove; we open our eyes in search of both the obvious and the hidden blessings that God has set before us.

Many years ago I was in a state of terrible despair. I was suffering in overwhelming physical and emotional pain. I couldn't stop crying. My teacher, Paul, looked at me dispassionately and instructed me simply to "say, thank You." I looked at him with astonishment and incredulity, wondering if I had heard him correctly. I was furious. Because I trusted Paul, I didn't follow my first impulse, which was to hit him in the face and stomp away in rage.

Instead I went home and began saying, "Thank You." At first my "thank You" was shaped by the sharp angry edge of sarcasm. "Thanks a lot! Thanks a f***ing lot!" But as I kept thanking, the edge in my voice began to soften. The tone of my "thank You" kept changing. It took me a few hours, but I finally found my way to gratefulness. And in the miracle of gratefulness, I experienced a glimmer of hope and the seeds of a new life.

I learned that gratefulness is not a feeling; it's a practice.

Gratefulness opens me up to receive the flow of blessing *and* connects me with the Source of that flow. Gratefulness opens up the possibility of profound and transforming relationship with the gift of Creation and incarnation.

I once participated in a morning prayer experiment with Rabbi Jill Hammer at a rabbinical conference at a rural hotel in upstate New York. She sent us out to pray with the trees and grasses. I found my tree, and soon I was praying to God, inspired by the beauty that surrounded me. It was nice, easy, sweet, comfortable. After a little while, I noticed the tree, really noticed it. I reached out and caressed its rough bark. I addressed the tree directly and just said, "Thank you."

Quite abruptly everything shifted in the most dramatic and surprising way. The tree responded as if it had been waiting all of its life for this moment of recognition. It gratefully revealed its own beauty, grandeur, and wisdom to me. Where my hand had been touching the bark, I suddenly felt as if the tree were touching me. In that moment of mutuality and holiness, I felt intimately known.

By addressing the tree directly, I was encountering a face of God. My prayer to an abstract idea of God paled in comparison to this holy encounter. This face of God, in all its majesty, was addressing me, responding in perfect reciprocity. Or was God addressing me through this magnificent face?

Philosopher and mystic Meister Eckhart said, "If the only prayer you ever say is, 'Thank You,' that would be enough."

That one small thank you, addressed to a tree, opened the door to an encounter that changed my life by showing me what prayer can accomplish. I will never again settle for nice, easy, sweet, comfortable words that decorate an abstraction, when I know that real meeting is possible.

Looking back on this encounter, I realize that it was those nice, easy, sweet, comfortable words of prayer that awakened me so that I could open to the present moment and meet the face of God. The lesson I take is to let the words of prayer send me and then to let all those words go. (Imagine a multistage rocket launching into outer space, leaving behind its launchpad, dropping each of its now empty burned-out boosters, continuing on to meet the unknown with a lighter precious payload into the mysterious darkness of space.)

Spiritual teacher Brother David Steindl-Rast (*Gratefulness: The Heart of Prayer*, p. 12) equates the growth process of gratefulness with the process of awakening.

My chant practice opens the door to gratefulness and leads me toward greater aliveness. The state of full, abundant, overflowing aliveness is radiant with mystery and paradox. The first prayer of the morning is about gratefulness because, if I find that quality, I will have access to the energy that I need to step onto the path of spiritual practice. Gratefulness is the foundation of my practice because it wakes me up and gives me the strength and clarity to face my challenges, resistances, and obstacles. Gratefulness is the foundation of my practice because it gives me access to the gifts I'll need to meet those challenges.

When I am working to cultivate a quality, I do that work in two ways. First, I tune in to that attribute so that I can know it, taste it, feel it, understand its complexities, and appreciate how it functions in my life. Then I begin to explore the obstacles that keep me from embodying that quality. When I understand the obstacle, I can develop a practice that might help me rise to the challenge before me in order to fully embrace the quality that I have tasted.

Steindl-Rast describes the extraordinary state of gratefulness as a condition that binds together apparent opposites. Gratefulness is:

> *Calm ... and yet energized,*
> *fulfilled ... and yet receptive/empty,*
> *uplifted ... and yet humbled,*
> *connected/acknowledged ... and yet self-forgetful*

It is an extraordinary state. My gratefulness opens me to the flow of abundance and connects me with the Source of that flow. My gratefulness flows back to that Source, and I become part of a circle of flow.

Until something stops that flow.

I asked my students to tell me what gets in the way of being grateful. Here's the list they came up with: overwhelm, worry, anxiety about getting things done, being distracted, the challenges of aging, being on automatic, being too busy, feeling weighed down with responsibilities, jadedness/cynicism, fatigue, chronic pain, fear of not having/being enough, fear of engaging with life, entitlement, being too full of myself, being attached to my preferences, beliefs about what is supposed to be, comparing mind, caught up in too many details, not receiving, not trusting, focusing on what's wrong or on what/who is missing or lacking, feeling wounded, resentment, bitterness, anger, sadness, depression and/or numbness, feeling sorry for myself, disappointment, lack of generosity, need to always be in control, negative small-minded programmed thoughts, lack of perspective about what really matters.

When I recognize in myself one of these obstacles to the flow of gratefulness, I look for the practice that might meet this particular obstacle. If I am overwhelmed, distracted, or worried, I look for a practice that heightens my sense of presence and focuses my attention on the miracle happening right before my eyes.

This is a practice that always helps shift my attention to the miracle of this present moment:

SHEHECHEYANU: A MEDITATION ON THIS MOMENT

שֶׁהֶחֱיָנוּ וְקִיְּמָנוּ וְהִגִּיעָנוּ לַזְּמַן הַזֶּה

Shehecheyanu, v'kiy'manu, v'higianu laz'man hazeh.
O Mystery, Grace unfolding, O Miracle, it's You alone,
O Mystery, Grace unfolding, O Miracle, who brings us Home.

If my obstacle to gratefulness is cynicism, fear, a sense of entitlement, attachment to preferences, or preoccupation with details, I might look for practices that send me to wonder and rapture and open me to the Great Mystery.

This is a practice that lifts me above my pettiness into the state from which praise flows:

אַשְׁרֵי יוֹשְׁבֵי בֵיתֶךָ עוֹד יְהַלְלוּךָ

Ashrei yosh'vei veitecha od y'hal'lucha.
Happy are those who dwell in Your house; they keep on praising.
(Psalm 84:5)

If my obstacle to gratefulness is bitterness, anger, sadness, a lack of trust, or self-pity, I might look for practices of heart healing that will help me address old patterns and wounds, to clear the harmful and poisonous residue from the past.

When I have identified those old patterns of hurt, I can embrace them with compassion and begin the work of releasing them with this beautiful practice. Each time I chant the word *lach* (Yours) I reach into my heart and give over to God the burden of shame, pride, or grudge that has clogged the streams of grace.

דּוֹדִי צָפַנְתִּי לָךְ

Dodi tzafanti lach.
My hidden (treasure) is Yours, my Beloved.
(Song of Songs 7:14)

As I begin clearing the obstacles to gratefulness, the flow is restored.

The flow of gratefulness begins with a sense of surprise. You might be stopped in your tracks by a rainbow or a sunrise or the most ordinary sight of a child playing or your partner deep in thought. Unexpectedly, the beauty, poignancy, sweetness, and depth of a moment touches you and you are suddenly *alive*; the world around you takes on a shimmer and a mystery.

Gratefulness, beginning in surprise, gradually expands into a sense of wonder. When you are in a state of wonder, you remember what a miracle this life is. You are able to actually enjoy the absurdities; you let yourself be astounded by the enormity of Creation; your mind is blown by synchronicities, coincidences, and a glimpse of the infinite. Then your heart opens. From a state of wonder it's impossible to judge another or commit a crime against this amazing Creation.

Gratefulness, beginning in surprise, expanding into wonder, gradually grows into generosity as we look for ways to respond to this gift of life that we are given. Our eyes are opened to the suffering around us, and we realize that "we" are not separate from "them"; we are all a part of this gorgeous tapestry ... and as even one thread unravels, the whole pattern is diminished. We stop judging one another and start serving each other. We look for ways to give, in response to how much we have received. And each one's gifts are acknowledged as precious and unique.

Healing the Spirit, Transforming the Mind, Deepening Love

HEALING THE SPIRIT

*I*t's so easy to become discouraged. Every day in the news we are bombarded by images of senseless violence. The gap between rich and poor keeps widening. We watch helplessly as our precious resources are being depleted. Everywhere it seems that the greed that creates short-term gain is destroying the possibilities of our long-term well-being. We are surrounded by a kind of cynicism that covers up a deepening despair. Beneath the crushing weight of that despair, our spirit withers.

I understand spirit as the part of us that is connected up with the Eternal and with the holiness at our core. It is that connection that sustains us through challenging times. It is that connection that allows us to find our courage and take the next step on the path of righteousness. Disconnection from Source leads us to the dangerous condition of being paralyzed by fear or drained by despair.

Through my practice of chant, I connect my spirit with the Great Spirit—that force of life that breathes through all Creation. Through my practice of chant, I am reminded that "love is as strong as death" (Song of Songs 8:6).

Through my practice of chant, I also connect with others. When our voices rise in harmony, when the sound that we make together is so much fuller, richer, brighter, stronger than anything I could imagine creating alone ... I am encouraged. I am reminded that I do not face these challenges alone and that together we can awaken the spirit of justice, equality, love, and peace in ourselves and in the world. The chant can help me find the energy to do what needs to be done.

One of my students is a rabbi in a community that had been traumatized by a series of senseless, horrifying murders. I composed the following chant, first to calm my own heart, which felt so shaky and vulnerable when I heard the news of the latest tragedy, and then to offer it as a practice for my student and her community as they stepped onto the path of healing.

THE VALLEY OF DEATH

גַּם כִּי־אֵלֵךְ בְּגֵיא צַלְמָוֶת לֹא־אִירָא רָע

Gam ki eileich b'gei tzalmavet, lo ira ra.
Though I walk through the Valley of Death,
I will not fear,
Though I walk through the Valley of Death,
my God is near.
(Psalm 23:4)

Since that terrible time, I use this practice whenever I need to make a commitment to courage, whenever I need to feel God's presence with me as I face a difficult challenge, whenever I need to walk through that Valley of Death.

Transforming the Mind

The condition of the mind—whether it is cluttered or spacious, calm or turbulent, dull or vibrant—will determine our perception, the quality of our experience, our access to inner resources ... even our ability to be happy. When the mind is churning with negative thoughts and judgments, we'll open our eyes and only see what's wrong with the world. When the mind is calm and expansive, filled with thoughts of love and gratitude, we'll open our eyes and see wonders and miracles abounding.

I like Reb Zalman Schachter-Shalomi's image. He says we're all like pickles. The conditions of mind, the kind of thoughts that we soak ourselves in, constitute the brine. What kind of pickle do you want to be? If your attention habitually is drawn to what's wrong; if your mind fills up with bitter, unkind, or critical judgments ... well, that's what kind of pickle you'll become. The longer you soak yourself in those negative thoughts, the more your mind becomes accustomed to bitterness. Those thoughts just seem like "the Truth."

In developing a chant practice, I learn to notice the quality of my thoughts (my pickle juice). Meditation doesn't stop the mind from thinking. That's just what the mind does. What my spiritual practice gives me is a discerning awareness of the quality of my thoughts, the realization that a particular lens that a mind-state can engender might distort my perception of reality. My practice also gives me a glimpse into the mind-state that produces certain kinds of thinking.

Some days I wake up, look out, and everything just seems broken or wrong. The weather's bad; my breakfast doesn't taste good; nobody cares ... wait ... suddenly I realize that there is a factory in my brain just manufacturing negative thoughts. With this realization comes the glimmer of compassion for myself because I'm in this "state." And then, before I do too much damage, I can turn to my practice. Really, I am turning to God and saying, "Help."

Because, through my chant practice, I have planted hundreds of sacred phrases and they are just "in" me, one will rise up at that moment and ask to be chanted.

It might be this one:

ASCENDING

וְעַל בָּמוֹתַי יַדְרִכֵנִי

V'al bamotai yadricheini.
He prepares a path for me upon the high places.
(Habakkuk 3:19)

This is a practice that helps me see every circumstance of my life as an opportunity for awakening. It lifts me up into a wide perspective and reminds me of the "perfection" of all of it. As I chant this, I surrender to the power of these magic words. When I remember that I am guided and supported and loved, the tumult of my mind subsides. In the moment of stillness, I drop into my heart.

Deepening Love

As I step onto my Jewish path, I am stepping onto a path of love. I understand the following to be the core teachings of my inheritance:

> You shall love *YHVH* your God with all your heart and with all your soul and with all your might.
>
> (Deuteronomy 6:5)

> Love your neighbor as yourself.
>
> (Leviticus 19:18)

> You shall love the stranger, for you were strangers in Egypt.
>
> (repeated thirty-six times in Torah)

I open to the power of these words and I ask, "Well, how do I fulfill these commandments to love?" I dedicate my entire practice to this possibility of love. This means I am also dedicating myself to moving through each obstacle, each resistance, every defense with both tender compassion and fierce resolve.

Through the practice of chant, I explore the geography of the heart. When I talk about the heart, I'm referring to the energetic center where I can find the source of the powers of love and healing. At the center of my heart I discover the nexus between finite and infinite, between the known world and the unknown mystery. I call this place the Holy of Holies. This is where I converse with God. This is where I hear the "still, small voice." This is where I find my love.

How do I love God? I must love God through *this* world, for that is how God, the Beloved, shows Herself to me. Each moment of my life is God-incarnate. The mysterious unpronounceable four-letter name of God (*YodHeiVavHei*) is the verb "to *be*" ... beyond tense. It is *being* itself that I am commanded to love. To love being is to embrace each moment ... and practice radical acceptance of "what is."

When I was applying to rabbinical school, one of my interviewers asked, "How do we know that after you complete this training you won't go out and start your own religion?" Outwardly I responded with proper indignation, but inwardly I was thinking, "Hmmmm ... I wonder what religion I should create?"

I decided that it would be called the Religion of *Zeh* (This!). I wanted to learn how to embrace each moment as God and, through this practice, deepen my capacity for love.

Now, some things I like and some things I really don't like. But love is bigger than all my preferences and predilections. It encompasses all my attractions and aversions. It is the widest embrace of reality and the complete surrender into the divine embrace.

So often I find myself in contention with reality. And it's an argument that I always lose! Here is a practice of befriending this very moment and of opening to the presence of God in "this":

LOVING "THIS"

זֶה דוֹדִי וְזֶה רֵעִי

Zeh Dodi v'zeh Rei'i.
This is my Beloved; this is my Friend.
(Song of Songs 5:16)

As I nurture and grow my relationship to God, the Beloved, who is manifesting as the circumstances of my life, I connect with the Source of love within me. When I am connected with that Source, I feel loved. When I feel loved, then generosity just naturally flows out toward others, neighbors and strangers alike.

Chanting—Alone
and Together

After you have read all of these musings about chant, I bet you just can't wait to start chanting. There are two different yet complementary kinds of chant practice: chanting alone (with God) and chanting with a group.

When I chant alone, I am exploring a sacred phrase, learning its power, activating its medicine. I study each word of that phrase. I look up each of the words in a dictionary or concordance. The dictionary explains meanings and usages. The concordance shows me every other place in scripture where that word appears, because sometimes you can only understand a word through its various contexts. I look at the particular context from which this sacred phrase is drawn from liturgy or Torah, and I try to discern its function in that context. What comes after? For what might this be preparing me? What comes before? What qualities are meant to be raised up in me as I approach this phrase?

After studying the definitions, associations, and functions of my sacred phrase and learning everything I can about it, I humbly admit that I really don't know what it means until I've chanted it for quite a while, until that phrase lives inside my body, until I have surrendered to its power.

Then I begin to play. I experiment with tempo (fast or slow), volume (soft or loud), tone (sweet, bold, stark, dramatic, righteous, reverent, sad, triumphant, royal, deep ...). I might stop at one particular word and repeat it, until that word opens its secrets to me or sends me into the silence. When I chant alone, I call up the intention to *be* with God, the Great Mystery, and allow every word of the chant to be my love song to that Mystery and to allow every word of the chant to be God's love song to me.

When I am exploring the power of a sacred phrase, it becomes the soundtrack for my life. I chant it in the shower, or as I walk, or while I'm driving; it is chanting itself silently to me as I sit on the airplane or stand on line at the supermarket. I let that sacred phrase penetrate my defenses, layer by layer.

I believe that every good leader of group chant also has an alone practice that allows for exploration and play. The gifts that I receive in my alone practice of chant become the offerings that I bring to the group.

The energy and inspirations that I receive when I chant in a group send me back to my solitary practice with renewed vitality. I need both kinds of chant practice.

Chanting in a group is such amazing opportunity. There are few activities more intimate, more healing, or more connecting than chanting with a group of people who step forward deliberately, fueled by the shared power of their intention, with all their vulnerability and curiosity, and with an openness to being surprised by the magic of chant.

Chanting in a group is as much about listening as it is about singing. When we're chanting together, we're not just listening to the sound of voices; we're also listening for the energy that is being carried by the sound; we're listening for the love.

Chant is a practice of generosity. As we sit in a circle, we are there to serve each other. And we are creating something together, each of us bringing our unique love and presence to this collaboration. The whole that we create together is so much more than the sum of its parts. Each opportunity to chant with a group opens up a precious, new, never-before alchemical mixture of these particular soul energies.

I don't want to miss this opportunity, so I need to pay special close attention; looking into the energy between us, I ask, "What is this? Who are we together?"

In ancient times, a certain person of a specific family held the secrets of the preparation of the incense for the Temple sacrifices. Of the many ingredients, there was one that, if burned alone, would give a very bitter smell, but when mixed with all the other elements, it added a richness, depth, and holiness to the fragrance of the incense offering.

Sometimes when I am leading a group in chant, I feel like that compounder of incense for our offering. Each ingredient is precious and unique. And only together can we blend precisely to form the fragrance that will open all of our hearts and be our offering to this very moment. "Who are we together?" I ask.

With every group it is as if a new being is born. It's the job of the leader to discern the unique possibilities *here* and to midwife this new potential.

For many years I traveled around leading groups in chant. Sometimes there would be one person in the group who simply fell madly in love with the practice and said, "I don't want to live without this." And he would start a chanting group in his community. Chanting began to feel like a path to me, a path that opened up my inner being, a path toward the mysteries of God, a path of connection to community. Over and over again, people were healed during the experience of chant. The healings were sometimes physical, sometimes emotional, and oftentimes spiritual. I wondered, "What are we doing right?"

I discovered that when a group learned to chant together, their potential could be deepened over time. With practice, a group learned how to blend their various "fragrances," build and raise energy, and then dedicate that energy to healing, connection, and integration. I learned that safe space equals sacred space. To create safe space, I needed to make a strong, loving commitment to each member of the circle.

So I invited all those daring souls who were drawn to this practice to join me in the first cohort of Kol Zimra, a two-year training for chant leaders. Because Phyllis Berman was already such a master at creating safe space, I asked her to assist me. My husband, Rachmiel, also added his healing wisdom to the mix. When that very first group of Kol Zimra gathered at Elat Chayyim in the summer of 2004, it felt as if we had all come home to each other. We developed a shared language to talk about energy. We prayed for each other and established a soul connection among us.

As each Kol Zimra cohort forms, I remember that we don't have to "like" each other. When we all fall in love with God together through chant, we are bound together in that love. And when we are connected at the level of soul, it's much easier to unravel the tangles that inevitably arise as our personalities rub up against each other.

Chant has facilitated lifelong spiritual friendships.

I know these friendships as the gifts of chant.

THE
PRACTICES

Liturgy

מוֹדֶה אֲנִי לְפָנֶיךָ

Modeh ani l'fanecha.
I gratefully acknowledge Your face.
(from the morning liturgy)

Each day I wake up with an intention that when I open my eyes I will see and recognize God's face in the details of the day I am about to encounter. I have many different melodies for the chant. I make up a new one almost every day that expresses my particular mood, inspiration, anticipation, attitude, or flavor of my gratefulness.

This was the very first chant that I developed into a practice. The melody line repeats the phrase three times. The first time, I bow to my left and gratefully acknowledge the face of God in my past, knowing that everything that has happened has been a gift and a lesson. The second time, I bow to the right, opening up to the future, thanking God in advance for all that will be given to me. The third time, I bow deeply to the center, acknowledging in gratefulness the presence of God in this very moment (which, after all, is all there is).

BETROTHAL: THE SEVEN CHANNELS
OF COMMITMENT

וְאֵרַשְׂתִּיךְ לִי לְעוֹלָם
וְאֵרַשְׂתִּיךְ לִי בְּצֶדֶק
וּבְמִשְׁפָּט
וּבְחֶסֶד
וּבְרַחֲמִים
וְאֵרַשְׂתִּיךְ לִי בֶּאֱמוּנָה
וְיָדַעַתְּ אֶת־יהוה

*V'eirastich li l'olam, v'eirastich li b'tzedek, uv'mishpat, uv'chesed,
uv'rachamim. V'eirastich li be'emunah, v'yada'at et Yah.*
I will betroth you to Me forever, I will betroth you to Me with
justice, and with impeccability, and with love, and with compassion.
I will betroth you to Me in faith. And then you will know
[be intimate with] God.
(Hosea 2:21–22)

This is the prayer that is said while putting tefillin on in the morning.
It is a ritual of betrothal—receiving God's commitment to us, while
finding our own commitment through the qualities of eternity, justice, impeccability, love, compassion, faith, and intimacy.

The chant itself holds the binding power of tefillin. As I chant, I
am connecting myself to the whole of life, to the Source of All, and
to God as Beloved.

I can get so caught up in the details of my life that I am in danger of losing my wide perspective, forgetting my connection to the
entirety of the cosmos. This binding of vows that I give and receive
is meant to set me on a path of remembrance. My commitment has
within it the requirement to stay open to the flow of blessing so that
it flows through me into the world. That flow happens through seven

distinct channels. As I chant, I am checking to see if each of those channels is open. With each line of the chant, I am calling up that quality through the tone in my voice and through the quality of my presence. It is a diagnostic practice that will allow me to know where the spiritual work of the day might be focused. If I find a channel that is blocked or a channel of flow that is weak, then I might focus my loving attention on that aspect of my life and see how I might repair the channel. As I sing the words of betrothal, I am checking in to each of these seven channels and connecting up to the Great Source of Blessing. I begin the practice by chanting slowly and pausing between each quality to take a deep gentle breath of discernment.

"I will betroth you to Me forever (*v'eirastich li l'olam*)": This refers to my sense of the infinite both in time and in space. Is my perspective wide enough to see myself as a tiny yet integral speck in the universe? Am I connected to a hopefulness about the continuation of life through me? Can I feel myself as a link in the chain of tradition and inheritance?

"I will betroth you to Me with justice (*v'eirastich li b'tzedek*)": Do I feel empowered to express my sense of justice in the world? Are there actions that I must take this day in order to be true to the values that I hold? Can I open to the strength of my commitment to *tikkun olam*?

"And with impeccability (*uv'mishpat*)": I understand this as diagnosing the state of my impeccability. How careful am I? How deliberate? How sloppy? How can I wake up my consciousness so that I can pay closer attention to the details? How can I clear the lens through which I perceive my life? How can I slow myself down enough to minimize the mistakes that happen because I am rushing?

"And with love (*uv'chesed*)": How open am I to the flow of God's love? Am I receiving beauty and nourishment through the events and relationships of my life? Can I open my heart to be filled with divine grace? Can I remember how completely lovable I am?

"And with compassion (*uv'rachamim*)": How strong is my compassion? Is my heart open to the suffering in the world? Or am I overwhelmed by it? Can I pour out this compassion to the people whom I come into contact with today? Am I holding a grudge against anyone?

How can I let go of my anger? Are there particular actions I can take this day to express my compassion? Is there someone I must forgive? Is there someone I might reach out to and comfort or encourage?

"I will betroth you to Me in faith (v'eirastich li be'emunah)": This is the channel that connects me with my sense of basic trust—the knowledge that ultimately existence is essentially good and no matter what happens, I will be safe. (Even Death is safe.) I check in to this channel to feel the firm foundation of goodness beneath my life that will allow me to take risks.

"And then you will know God (v'yada'at et Yah)": This is the channel that represents my loving awareness of God's presence in every moment of my life. When this channel is open I remember to look and feel and listen for that mystery as often as possible. This channel represents intimacy with the Beloved. As I sing these words, I lean into the Mystery and open to the interpenetration of the divine essence with my own.

GRATEFULNESS

אוֹדְךָ בְּעוֹד תִּהְיֶה נִשְׁמַת אֱלוֹהַּ בִּי

Odach b'od t'h'yeh nishmat Eloha bi.
I will thank You as long as the divine breath is in me.
(Solomon ibn Gabirol, eleventh-century Spanish poet and philosopher)

This line from a poem by Solomon ibn Gabirol expresses my intention so well—to feel God's breath in me, and to use that breath in gratitude ... no matter what! When I chant these words I am lifted up into a kind of unconditional gratefulness that comes from the inside and is not dependent on outer circumstance. In the silence after the chant, I breathe in this intoxicating energy. I notice where the chant has brought me—I notice the rhythm of my breath, feelings in my body, my sense of spaciousness, both inner and outer. I imagine breathing the energy of the chant into my heart and "tasting" it.

Through the power of association, I allow images to arise. Sometimes I'll feel the energy as a color, flavor, or texture. All this is happening under the watchful eyes of an attentive inner witness. I am watching, noticing everything about this state as it emerges ... and it is this awareness that makes all the difference. Awareness magnifies the benefit of the chant by creating a pathway that I might return to that state, just by remembering. The words and melody of the chant become a memory key.

Then one day when I'm having trouble finding my way to gratefulness, I can either use the chant or find the memory of the chant in my body and just breathe into that memory.

CLEARING THE WAY

אָנָּא, בְּכֹחַ גְּדֻלַּת יְמִינְךָ, תַּתִּיר צְרוּרָה

Ana b'choach g'dulat y'min'cha tatir tz'rurah.
Please, with the strength of your right hand, untie our tangles.

This is the first line of a magical prayer ascribed to first-century sage Rabbi Nechuniah ben Hakanah. The whole prayer contains forty-two words, the initials of which compose the secret unpronounceable forty-two-letter name of God.

With this practice we call on that aspect of God that moves through obstacles, dissolves resistance, and opens the way forward for us.

Begin by asking, "What is the obstacle [inner or outer] that is getting in my way?" Lay that obstacle lovingly on the altar of the chant. As you chant, allow the power of God's right hand to move through you, forcefully opening the way ahead and delicately untying the tangles within you.

I composed this melody while a dear friend was undergoing quadruple bypass heart surgery, praying that the tangles in his heart would be cleared.

O WONDROUS HEALER

רוֹפֵא כָל בָּשָׂר וּמַפְלִיא לַעֲשׂוֹת

Rofei chol basar umafli la'asot!
O wondrous Healer of all flesh!
(from the morning liturgy)

As part of our morning blessings we acknowledge the miracle of healing. It is the divine spark within me that gives my body the intelligence to heal itself. That amazing intelligence is at work at this very moment. With this practice, I recognize my body's capacity for self-healing, and I activate that divine healing power that is latent within each and every cell.

O PURE SOUL

אֱלֹהַי, נְשָׁמָה שֶׁנָּתַתָּ בִּי טְהוֹרָה הִיא

Elohai n'shamah shenatata bi t'horah hi!
O pure soul, in you I see endless possibility!
(liturgy)

A rabbi friend who is a hospital chaplain asked me to write a chant that she could sing to the tiny babies who were born prematurely and were struggling to come fully into their embodied life. When I imagined singing these words to them, I realized that there is a tiny, fragile baby inside of me who also needs encouragement in order to be fully realized. When I sing to her each morning, I am calling forth her potential and gently welcoming her into form.

MORNING BLESSINGS

O God, who sets the captive free,
who opens the eyes of the blind to see,
who heals the lame and loves the just.
I will praise Yah with my life!
(Psalm 146:7–8, 146:2)

אֲהַלְלָה יהוה בְּחַיָּי

Ahal'lah Yah b'chayai!
I will praise Yah with my life!
(Psalm 146:2)

יהוה מַתִּיר אֲסוּרִים
יהוה פֹּקֵחַ עִוְרִים
יהוה זֹקֵף כְּפוּפִים
יהוה אֹהֵב צַדִּיקִים

Adonai matir asurim, Adonai pokei'ach ivrim,
Adonai zokeif k'fufim, Adonai oheiv tzadikim.

As my morning blessings, I acknowledge the Force that sets me free from the bondage of habit and conditioning. I thank the One who opens my eyes to what were once invisible realms. I feel myself lifted up and healed by that Power, as the best in me is seen, known, and loved.

Then I make a commitment to praise Yah with my life as I become a channel for that force of liberation, enlightenment, healing, and love.

HOLY SPEECH

בָּרוּךְ שֶׁאָמַר וְהָיָה הָעוֹלָם

Baruch she'amar v'hayah ha'olam.

Blessed is the One who speaks the world into being.

This prayer opens the part of the prayer service called *P'sukei D'zimrah*, the Songs of Praise. It is meant to lift us up into the wonder of our divine inheritance. We are each created in the image of God, which means that we can receive, embody, and transmit the same creative force that made the world and continues to shape reality.

With this practice, we claim the power of holy speech. What kind of world will you create? One that is filled with beauty, justice, and love? Well, then, pour those qualities into your voice as you chant.

ASHREI

אַשְׁרֵי יוֹשְׁבֵי בֵיתֶךָ עוֹד יְהַלְלוּךָ

Ashrei yosh'vei veitecha od y'hal'lucha.

Happy are those who dwell in Your house; they keep on praising.
(Psalm 84:5)

There is a state of consciousness I call *Ashrei*. It is the kind of unconditional joy that comes from being in the "God-house," which means being in God-consciousness, which means having the experience of *knowing* that we are all connected, all integral to the whole and the holy. Have you ever had a moment of experiencing that great joy? Where were you? On a mountaintop, perhaps? Or in the arms of a lover? Or looking into the eyes of a child? Or witnessing a birth? Or deep in prayer or meditation?

MANIFESTING TORAH

לִלְמֹד וּלְלַמֵּד, לִשְׁמֹר וְלַעֲשׂוֹת וּלְקַיֵּם

Lilmod ul'lameid lishmor v'la'asot ul'kayeim.
To learn and to teach, to uphold and to practice and to manifest.

As we approach the *Sh'ma*, we increase the power of our receptivity and presence by making a commitment to Torah/wisdom. Our commitment is not just to learn, but to teach ... not just to teach, but to uphold ... not just to uphold, but to practice ... and not just to practice, but to manifest Torah in our lives and in our world.

GOODNESS

הוֹדוּ לַיהוה כִּי־טוֹב כִּי לְעוֹלָם חַסְדּוֹ

Hodu ladonai ki tov, ki l'olam chasdo.
Give thanks to God for essential goodness;
His kindness endures forever.
(Psalm 136:1)

By giving thanks, we open our hearts to receive and acknowledge the essential goodness of reality itself. As we open to the flow of divine kindness, everyone and everything becomes our ally. By giving thanks, we enter the perspective that sees the whole world as conspiring to shower us with blessings.

EYES, HEARTS, AND HANDS

וְהָאֵר עֵינֵינוּ בְּתוֹרָתֶךָ, וְדַבֵּק לִבֵּנוּ בְּמִצְוֹתֶיךָ

V'ha'eir eineinu b'Toratecha, v'dabeik libeinu b'mitzvotecha.
Enlighten our eyes with Your Torah,
and connect our hearts to Your *mitzvot*.

When my eyes are really opened, I see your Torah everywhere! And from the deepest place within, I can connect with and embody that heart wisdom. The next step is to allow that deep heart wisdom to flow out across my shoulders, down my arms, and into my hands. These are the hands that will do Your *mitzvot* with heartful compassion and kindness, instructed always by the Torah that this world reveals to me.

SHEHECHEYANU: A MEDITATION ON THIS MOMENT

שֶׁהֶחֱיָנוּ וְקִיְּמָנוּ וְהִגִּיעָנוּ לַזְּמַן הַזֶּה

Shehecheyanu, v'kiy'manu, v'higianu laz'man hazeh.
O Mystery, Grace unfolding, O Miracle, it's You alone,
O Mystery, Grace unfolding, O Miracle, who brings us Home.

There is a blessing that is said whenever we realize the miracle of this present moment. We bless God who gave us life, sustained us, and brought us to this very moment. We say this blessing when we do something for the first time, to honor and express the wonder of having arrived. In meditation, I experience each moment as a momentous arrival. My whole existence has led me to this very moment—the culmination of my life thus far, where I am privileged to experience the fullness of this *now*. God who is that miraculous force of Grace unfolding has brought me Home. In encountering and honoring that force of Homecoming, I turn and receive the gift of my life.

UNIFYING THE HEART

וְיַחֵד לְבָבֵנוּ לְאַהֲבָה וּלְיִרְאָה אֶת שְׁמֶךָ

V'yacheid l'vaveinu l'ahavah ul'yirah et sh'mecha.
Unify our hearts to love and to be in awe of Your name/essence.

These words are part of the prayer that comes in the paragraph just before the *Sh'ma*. The *Sh'ma* opens in us the perception of unity, but before we go there, we must do the work of unification inside our own hearts. This practice guides me to identify with both the love and the awe for the essence that is hidden behind all form. When I chant *"v'yacheid l'vaveinu,"* I journey into my heart. When I chant *"l'ahavah,"* I find my love. When I chant *"ul'yirah,"* I find my awe. And when I chant *"et sh'mecha,"* I call on the wholeness of my heart to perceive/receive the essence of That-Which-Is.

Psalm 86:11 says:

יַחֵד לְבָבִי לְיִרְאָה שְׁמֶךָ

Yacheid l'vavi l'yirah sh'mecha.
Unify my heart to be in awe of Your name.

The liturgist obviously knew this psalm and decided that love was also needed.

INCANTATION FOR HOPEFULNESS

לִישׁוּעָתְךָ קִוִּיתִי יהוה; קִוִּיתִי יהוה לִישׁוּעָתְךָ; יהוה לִישׁוּעָתְךָ קִוִּיתִי

Lishuatcha kiviti Yah; kiviti Yah lishuatcha;
Yah lishuatcha kiviti.
I wait/hope for Your salvation.
(Genesis 49:18; bedtime liturgy)

As Jacob lies on his deathbed, blessing each of his sons, he suddenly stops and cries out this line, then returns to his task of blessing. The bedtime liturgy takes his exclamation and turns it into a magic incantation of power and protection.

UNDER THE WINGS

וַאֲנִי מָצָאתִי מְנוּחָה   מִתַּחַת כַּנְפֵי הַשְּׁכִינָה

Va'ani matzati m'nuchah mitachat kanfei HaShechinah.
Under the wings of *Shechinah* I have found my rest.

I wrote this chant in honor of Sukkot. I imagine sitting in my sukkah under a delicate roof of branches that gives me a glimpse of the vast deep blue sky. The Divine Presence also protects me, yet allows me to see through Her wings and connect with the beyond.

FREEDOM AND HOMECOMING: A CHANT FOR ROSH HASHANAH

תְּקַע בְּשׁוֹפָר גָּדוֹל לְחֵרוּתֵנוּ, וְשָׂא נֵס לְקַבֵּץ גָּלֻיּוֹתֵינוּ

T'ka b'shofar gadol l'cheiruteinu,
V'sa neis l'kabeitz galuyoteinu.
Sound the great shofar for our freedom,
and raise the banner as we all come home.

These words are part of the daily *Amidah*, but they can be chanted especially for Rosh Hashanah as we gather the tribe in celebration of the New Year and all its possibilities. For me, this prayer is an affirmation that while we each are sent far and wide to our freedom—to fulfill the destiny we are given—we can also return in celebration and be welcomed home.

PILGRIMAGE

לִירוּשָׁלַיִם עִירְךָ בְּרַחֲמִים תָּשׁוּב

Li'Y'rushalayim ircha, b'rachamim tashuv.
To Jerusalem Your city, with compassion you will return.
(from the daily *Amidah*)

I composed this chant in preparation for a trip to Israel. I use this sacred phrase to open me to the call of pilgrimage.

Twentieth-century Christian theological ethicist Richard Niebuhr (quoted in *The Art of Pilgrimage* by Phil Cousineau, p. 14) says, "Pilgrims are persons in motion, passing through territories not their own, seeking something we might call completion, or perhaps the word clarity will do as well, a goal to which only the spirit's compass points the way."

Every pilgrimage is a journey inward, even if we travel clear across the world. We can use this chant, which is a "double round," to prepare ourselves for pilgrimage, for journeying inward toward the center of awareness.

GATHERING IN

וַהֲבִיאֵנוּ לְשָׁלוֹם מֵאַרְבַּע כַּנְפוֹת הָאָרֶץ

V'havi'einu l'shalom mei'arba kanfot ha'aretz.
(Bring us in peace from the four corners of the earth.)
Uriel! Micha'el! Rafa'el! Gavri'el!

This phrase comes from the paragraph before the *Sh'ma*, and I use it to prepare myself for that moment of focused attention that the *Sh'ma* is meant to be. I gather in all the disparate energies so that I can stand in oneness and receive the mystery of unity. For me, the archangels personify the energies of each of the directions, the four winds that blow into my life and make me whole. When I face east and call in Uriel, I am opening to the new and allowing myself to be renewed. When I face the south and call in Micha'el, I am calling in warmth, comfort, love, and constancy and allowing myself to be held in that love. When I face the west and call in Rafa'el, I am opening to a vision of where I am called and allowing the healing power of my path to transform me. When I face the north and call in Gavri'el, I am opening to the power of my ancestors and receiving the challenges of my life with grace and courage.

ALL IS ONE

אַתָּה אֶחָד וְשִׁמְךָ אֶחָד

Atah Echad v'shimcha Echad.

You are One and Your name/essence is One.

מְנוּחַת אַהֲבָה וּנְדָבָה

M'nuchat ahavah un'davah.

Rest of love and generosity.

מְנוּחַת אֱמֶת וֶאֱמוּנָה

M'nuchat emet ve'emunah.

Rest of truth and faith.

מְנוּחַת שָׁלוֹם וְשַׁלְוָה

M'nuchat shalom v'shalvah.

Rest of peace and serenity.

מְנוּחָה שְׁלֵמָה שֶׁאַתָּה רוֹצֶה בָּה

M'nuchat sh'leimah she'atah rotzeh bah.

A perfect rest in which You find favor.

These amazing words are from the Shabbat *Minchah* (afternoon) *Amidah* prayer. They illuminate seven gifts of our rest: love, generosity, truth, faith, peace, serenity, and perfection. As we chant each quality, we can open that particular gift and integrate it into our practice of rest.

ROLLING

גּוֹלֵל אוֹר מִפְּנֵי חֹשֶׁךְ, וְחֹשֶׁךְ מִפְּנֵי אוֹר

Goleil or mipnei choshech, v'choshech mipnei or.
Rolling away light before darkness, darkness before light.
(from the evening liturgy)

As evening falls, we say a prayer to bless the coming darkness. This practice opens us to the miracle of light and dark as they mix and then roll away from each other in cycles of day and night. These same cycles roll inside us through the rhythms of mood, through the ebb and flow of our daily drama. Through this practice, we raise ourselves up as holy witness to these cycles, so that we may gratefully receive the gifts of darkness in absolute trust. We surrender to the evening, knowing this darkness will lead us back to the light again.

USHPIZIN

תִּיבוּ תִּיבוּ אוּשְׁפִּיזִין עִלָּאִין, תִּיבוּ תִּיבוּ אוּשְׁפִּיזִין קַדִּישִׁין

Tivu tivu ushpizin ila'in, tivu tivu ushpizin kadishin.
Sit down, sit down, exalted guests; sit down, sit down, holy guests!

At the beginning of the High Holy Days, the Days of Awe and *T'shuvah*, I always ask myself, "Who *don't* you want in your sukkah?" Who have you thrown out of your heart? Who would you rather avoid? For whom do you hold a grudge?... Then I know what my work will be for those days of forgiving. By the time Sukkot comes, I want to be able to invite the whole world into my sukkah and into my heart.

It is the custom on Sukkot that besides inviting our neighbors and friends, we invite our ancestors, and the archetypes they represent, into our sukkah and into our hearts. With this chant I extend that invitation and open to the energies of my ancestors, who come to sit beside "all my relations," who have been reunited by our loving and persistent spiritual work.

LIFE AND DEATH

כִּי אַתָּה מְחַיֶּה הַמֵּתִים וּמֵמִית חַיִּים

Ki atah m'chayeih hameitim, umeimit chayim.
For You revive the dead and bring death to the living.
(from the *Taharah* liturgy)

Standing in the presence of the mystery of life and death, I am both lifted up and humbled. I address myself to that mystery, open my heart and stand between life and death. I honor the journey beyond this known world into the world-to-come, the beyond that awaits us all.

THE MEDICINE FOR OVERWHELM: *TACHANUN*

Tachanun is a petition for grace that is part of the daily morning and afternoon service. It is omitted on Shabbat, festivals, during the month of Nisan, or at a house of mourning. When I'm feeling overwhelmed, I don't function very well; I forget my practice; I forget to open to God's help; I don't have access to the vast treasure of spiritual resources that are in me. I use this prayer as an antidote to overwhelm. If I can remember at the moment of feeling overwhelmed to take refuge in God, in the ultimate Compassion of the Universe, then I will not fall victim to the curse of overwhelm.

TACHANUN

וְהוּא רַחוּם

V'hu rachum.

It is compassionate.

נִבְהֲלָה נַפְשֵׁנוּ מֵרֹב עִצְבוֹנֵנוּ,

Nivhalah nafsheinu meirov itzvoneinu (2x)

אַל תִּשְׁכָּחֵנוּ נֶצַח

Al tishkacheinu netzach (2x)

קוּמָה וְהוֹשִׁיעֵנוּ, כִּי חָסִינוּ בָךְ

Kumah v'hoshi'einu ki chasinu vach! (2x)

Our soul trembles, overwhelmed by sadness,

Do not forget us,

Arise and save us,

For we take shelter in You!

THE SAVING POWER OF
GOD-CONSCIOUSNESS

שִׁירוּ לַיהוה כָּל־הָאָרֶץ
בַּשְּׂרוּ מִיּוֹם־אֶל־יוֹם יְשׁוּעָתוֹ

Shiru l'Adonai kol ha'aretz, bas'ru miyom el yom y'shuato!
Shiru la'Shechinah kol ha'aretz, bas'ru miyom el yom y'shuata!
Hallelu, Hallelu, Hallelu, Hallelu, Hallelu, HalleluYah!

Sing to the Lord, everyone on earth,

announce His salvation daily!

Sing to the indwelling Divine Presence,

announce Her salvation daily!

Praise Yah!

(1 Chronicles 16:23; Psalm 96:2)

I chant these words to both the masculine and the feminine aspects of God as I call forth an awareness of the Divine Presence that shines forth from the daily miracles of my life.

I am saved by the light of this awareness.

BALANCING WILL AND SURRENDER

עָזִּי וְזִמְרָת יָה וַיְהִי־לִי לִישׁוּעָה

Ozi v'zimrat Yah vay'hi li lishuah.
My strength (balanced) with the song of God will be my salvation.
(Psalm 118:14; Exodus 15:2)

In this practice I find and express my strength, my will, my effort, and my desire when I chant "*ozi*." When I chant "*v'zimrat Yah*," I open and surrender to the God-song and let it be sung through me. Then in the last phrase, "*vay'hi li lishuah*," I balance those two aspects of my practice.

SUKKAT SHALOM

הַשְׁכִּיבֵנוּ יהוה אֱלֹהֵינוּ לְשָׁלוֹם,
וְהַעֲמִידֵנוּ מַלְכֵּנוּ לְחַיִּים טוֹבִים וּלְשָׁלוֹם,
וּפְרוֹשׂ עָלֵינוּ סֻכַּת שְׁלוֹמֶךָ

Hashkiveinu Adonai Eloheinu l'shalom
V'ha'amideinu Malkeinu
L'chayim tovim ul'shalom
Uf'ros Aleinu sukkat sh'lomecha.
O Lord, our God, let us lie down in peace.
Our Sovereign, raise us up again to good life and peace.
Spread over us a shelter of peace.
(liturgy)

This prayer, *Hashkiveinu*, is considered to be an extension of the *G'ulah*, our prayer for redemption. We cannot be free as a people unless we do the work of liberation each night as we face our fears of the dark, of the unknown, of the enemy within and without.

We do this work by attuning ourselves to the shelter of peace that is spread over the whole of life, regardless of passing circumstance.

We have no control over the forms of our life that are always passing away, always changing. That constant flux can be frightening. And when we live from fear, we don't have access to the depths of our wisdom and the breadth of our love.

And so the practice of *Hashkiveinu* reminds us of that abiding presence of wholeness and peace that holds all of us within its loving embrace, no matter how the forms of life come and go.

SIM SHALOM

שִׂים שָׁלוֹם טוֹבָה וּבְרָכָה, חֵן וָחֶסֶד וְרַחֲמִים

Sim shalom tovah uv'rachah chein vachesed v'rachamim!

Grant us peace, goodness, grace, love, and compassion!

This prayer was the ancient response of the congregation to the Priestly Blessing during the time of the Second Temple when the *Kohanim* did not pause between each of the three parts, as in synagogue worship.

At the end of the *Amidah* (the standing silent prayer), we receive the blessing of our prayerful state, take those blessings in deeply, and begin to send them out to the world, sharing the bounty with all who are in need. We thus become channels for peace, goodness, grace, love, and compassion.

THE MAJESTY OF NURTURE

לְתַקֵּן עוֹלָם בְּמַלְכוּת שַׁדַּי

L'takein olam b'malchut Shaddai.
Healing the world through the Majesty of Nurture.
(liturgy)

These words are found in the prayer called *Aleinu*. It comes near the end of the prayer service and is meant to energize us for our holy work. This translation was given to me by Rabbi Arthur Waskow, whose dedication to the holy work of healing the world is an inspiration for me. The divine name *Shaddai* is related to the word for breast. It is an ancient name of God that invokes the Source of all nurturance. As we chant these words, we align ourselves with the Majesty of Nurture by expressing the awesome healing power of compassion for all life.

BLESSING OF MY SOUL

בָּרְכִי נַפְשִׁי אֶת יהוה, הַלְלוּיָהּ

Bar'chi nafshi et Adonai, halleluyah!
Bless the place of Sovereignty, O my soul!

I call on the force of my soul to bless the God-spark within me, to call it forth, to let it shine though all the layers of self, so that that part of me can be re-enthroned.

STANDING BEFORE THE MYSTERY

דַּע לִפְנֵי מִי אַתָּה עוֹמֵד

Da lifnei mi atah omeid!
Know before whom you stand!
(adapted from Talmud, *B'rachot* 28b)

These words are inscribed on many synagogue walls and are meant to remind the congregants of the seriousness of prayer. In the past I've dismissed this phrase as being too stern, too much like "Big Brother" watching and judging. Yet now, when I chant this phrase, an entirely new meaning emerges. The verb *yada*, "to know," also means to "be intimate with" (to know someone in the biblical sense). As I chant, I am called into intimacy with the Great Mystery, who stands before me. That Mystery is disguised as this world, as my life. As I stand before that Mystery, I am called into my power, in order to fully engage. The veil between me and the world-as-God drops away, and I can experience the intimate knowing that I am not a separate observer, but rather an integral part of the Mystery of existence.

BEINI UVEIN

בֵּינִי וּבֵין בְּנֵי יִשְׂרָאֵל אוֹת הִוא לְעֹלָם
כִּי־שֵׁשֶׁת יָמִים עָשָׂה יהוה אֶת־הַשָּׁמַיִם
וְאֶת־הָאָרֶץ וּבַיּוֹם הַשְּׁבִיעִי שָׁבַת וַיִּנָּפַשׁ

Beini uvein Yisrael ot hi l'olam ki sheishet yamim asah Adonai et hashamayim v'et ha'aretz uvayom hash'vi'i shavat vayinafash!
Let it be a sign between us forever,
for in six days I made everything
And on the seventh day I made Shabbat, I made Shabbat for my Soul!
(Exodus 31:17)

These words from Exodus are used as the prelude to the *Kiddush* at Shabbat lunch or during the liturgy to affirm the covenant that we celebrate through the practice of Shabbat.

CHANUKAH CHANT

Let the flame be kindled within me, let Your love burn bright,
I hunger for Your light, I hunger for Your light.

When I light the menorah, I chant these words into the flames and then visualize the fire being kindled in my inner Temple. There I do the work of clearing and cleaning and acknowledging whatever desecration has occurred within my energy-body, my Temple. I visualize the flame growing bright inside my Temple to rededicate my energy toward holiness.

GOING UP WITH JOY

וְשָׁם נָשִׁיר שִׁיר חָדָשׁ וּבִרְנָנָה נַעֲלֶה

V'sham nashir shir chadash uvir'nanah na'aleh.
And there we will sing a new song; with joy we will go up.
(from *Tzur Mishelo*)

These words are from the last stanza of *Tzur Mishelo*, a Shabbat hymn that was composed and compiled between the eleventh and sixteenth centuries under the guidance of Rabbis Isaac Luria and Israel Najara. It is a reflection upon and praise of Shabbat and is thought to be an introduction to *Birkat Hamazon* (Grace after Meals), on which the first three stanzas are clearly based. Some believe this Shabbat table song to have originated with the *Tannaim*, the Rabbinic sages whose views are recorded in the Mishnah, from approximately 70–200 CE.

This is a practice of letting the joy in our voices raise us up into sacred space.

Scripture

KNOWING BEAUTY AND
FINDING THE UNIVERSE

אֶת־הַכֹּל עָשָׂה יָפֶה בְעִתּוֹ גַּם אֶת־הָעֹלָם נָתַן בְּלִבָּם

Et hakol asah yafeh v'ito, gam et ha'olam natan b'libam.
[God] makes everything beautiful in its time,
and also hides the universe in their hearts.
(Ecclesiastes 3:11)

Kohelet lays before us a profound spiritual challenge: "to completely enjoy what is before you" (Ecclesiastes 3:22), even through uncertainty, even though all our pleasures are temporary.

The practice we are given is to receive and comprehend the beauty of this changing world without grasping or attachment. The hint we are given that can help us is that everything that we perceive as outside of ourselves is actually hidden within our own hearts.

We look inward to find the whole universe hidden there, waiting to be discovered. There we find that everything is beautiful in its time. When we can perceive the beauty of each and every phase of our existence, then we will recognize the Truth that was inside us all along.

159

AN OATH OF FRIENDSHIP

הִנֵּה יהוה בֵּינִי וּבֵינְךָ עַד־עוֹלָם

Hineih Yah beini uveincha, ad olam!
Here is God between me and you forever!
(1 Samuel 20:23)

This is the oath of friendship that Jonathan says to David. He invokes God's presence in the space between himself and his friend, as a way of sanctifying the relationship. We can use this chant to acknowledge the holiness of the space between, the miracle of the divine glue that connects us.

This chant can be done with movement as a two-part round facing a partner. It can also be done in two concentric circles, with each person in the inner circle facing out toward a partner. After each repetition, one circle steps to the right while the other stands still, so that you are facing a different partner. The movements: When you sing "*Hinei Yah* ...," with one hand's flowing gesture, create a figure eight between you and your partner. When you sing "*ad olam*," put your hands at your side facing forward, slowly lift them up as high as you can, and slowly lower them.

HOLY GROUND

אַדְמַת־קֹדֶשׁ הוּא

Admat kodesh hu!
It is holy ground!
(Exodus 3:5)

When Moses is called into prophecy at the burning bush, he is told to take off his shoes, "for the place on which you stand, it is holy ground!" (Exodus 3:5). As we prepare ourselves for prophecy, we are called into presence by the sudden knowledge that the ground on which we stand is holy. We are commanded to take off our shoes, for nothing must come between us and this sacred ground—the ground of this life, this world, this family, these circumstances. When we begin to apprehend the holiness of this ground beneath our feet, then the firmness of this holy ground becomes our dance floor; the fertile mystery of this holy ground invites us to till and to plant.

GO WITHIN US

יֵלֶךְ־נָא אֲדֹנָי בְּקִרְבֵּנוּ

Yeilech na Adonai b'kirbeinu.
Please, God, go within us.
(Exodus 34:9)

In the book of Exodus, which tells the story of our journey to freedom, Moses realizes that the only way to accomplish this journey and reach the Land of Promise is for God's presence to be within, between, and among us as we go. Even after all the trouble of the Golden Calf, the murmurings and rebellions ... Moses knows that it is only this "innerness" that makes our holy journey worth all the bother.

I address myself to You, God, the Great Mystery, with the knowledge that "I can't and don't want to do this without You!" In the silence after the chant, I make a place inside me for that Divine Presence to dwell.

ASCENDING

וְעַל בָּמוֹתַי יַדְרִכֵנִי

V'al bamotai yadricheini.
He prepares a path for me upon the high places.
(Habakkuk 3:19)

As I investigate my own vast inner spaces, I am shown pathways of exploration. The high places are my own capacities for love, forgiveness, courage, wisdom, compassion, perspective, curiosity, and humor. God prepares the pathways to those places through the beauty of my world, through the gifts of my inheritance, through the stories of those who have walked this path before me, even through the humbling power of my mistakes. I chant these words as a reminder that I am guided on this path. I chant these words to affirm my commitment to embrace the possibilities of the extraordinary.

OPENING TO THE SOURCE OF FLOW

וְנָהָר יֹצֵא מֵעֵדֶן לְהַשְׁקוֹת אֶת־הַגָּן

V'nahar yotzei mei'Eden, l'hashkot et hagan.
A river comes forth from Eden to water the garden.
(Genesis 2:10)

My friend and teacher Melila Hellner told me that this line from Genesis was the most quoted sacred phrase in the *Zohar*, one of the central texts of Kabbalah. I was intrigued and began chanting this phrase with the intention of opening to the Source of Flow. Chant these words until the chant begins to chant itself. In the silence after the chant, open to the flow.

As we delight in the garden of this moment, let us attune to the Source of its vitality and beauty.

BELOVED

אֲנִי לְדוֹדִי וְדוֹדִי לִי

Ani l'Dodi v'Dodi li.
I am my Beloved's and my Beloved is mine.
(Song of Songs 6:3)

God *as* this world holds me in Her loving embrace. I belong to the Whole. I am an integral aspect to Everything-that-is. I belong. And that wondrous mystery I call God is central to all I see, all I do, all I know, all I am. With this chant, I raise up my awareness and attune my vibration with the truth of being totally accepted, and totally beloved ... flowing with the divine will, lifted up into the arms of the Infinite.

HOW BEAUTIFUL!

הִנָּךְ יָפָה רַעְיָתִי הִנָּךְ יָפָה

Hinach yafah rayati, hinach yafah!
How beautiful You are, my Friend, how beautiful!
(Song of Songs 1:15)

This practice teaches me to cultivate generosity by acknowledging the beauty that God has placed before me as my life, as this world. I begin by chanting to that beauty and befriending this world as the manifestation of God's miraculous presence. I close my eyes, visualize, remember, and appreciate the splendor and magnificence of landscape and color, taste and fragrance, shape and texture.

In the second phase of the practice, I open my eyes and see, really see, the beauty before me. I see and appreciate the beautiful faces of the people in my chant circle; I receive the light that is shining out from those faces; I see and appreciate the setting, the space, the air between us ... everything. I let go of my argument with Reality. I befriend this very moment.

In the last phase of the practice, I close my eyes again. I imagine that God is chanting these words to me, acknowledging my unique beauty. I fully receive that divine acknowledgment and appreciation, letting all self-doubts dissolve in God's loving embrace and acceptance of my own distinct and inimitable beauty.

IN HIS SHADE

בְּצִלּוֹ חִמַּדְתִּי וְיָשַׁבְתִּי וּפִרְיוֹ מָתוֹק לְחִכִּי

B'tzilo chimadti v'yashavti, ufiryo matok l'chiki.
In His shade I delight to sit, tasting His sweet fruit.
(Song of Songs 2:3)

This is a practice of reconnecting with and remembering the essential beneficence of Reality. Sometimes when it feels as if the whole world is my enemy and I am struggling with my predicament, I can stop and rest in the blessing of pure Being. With this practice, I receive the gift of feeling held by Reality itself. Imagine leaning back against the trunk of a sturdy tree on a hot summer day. This is the Tree of Life, offering protection, inspiration, and unending generosity. At the end of the chant, tune into your breath as you receive the sweet fruit of Being. Let each breath nourish, delight, and renew.

COME, MY BELOVED

לְכָה דוֹדִי נֵצֵא הַשָּׂדֶה

L'cha Dodi neitzeih hasadeh.
Come, my beloved, let us go out to the field.
(Song of Songs 7:12)

These are the words that inspired kabbalist Shlomo Alkabetz to compose the hymn *L'cha Dodi*, which is sung in congregations around the world to welcome the Sabbath. The mystics of sixteenth-century S'fat would go out to the fields to watch the sun set and greet Shabbat as their bride.

For me, the image of the field represents the state of spaciousness that the practice of Shabbat gives us. I do this chant as a practice of "sacred mingling." I divide the congregation into three groups, each chanting a different melody and rhythm. I give the following instruction: When you begin to feel comfortable in your part, stand up and gently walk around the room. Find someone who is chanting something different from you and engage in a holy encounter. Notice the contrasts and harmonies that you create together. Receive the gift of that relationship ... then move on and find someone else. The holiness of each encounter requires that you fully hold your own part while listening and appreciating the other and what the two of you can create together.

At the end of the chant, I instruct everyone to stop and stay perfectly still, feel their feet on the ground, and close their eyes. I ask them to breathe all of the beauty and complexity of the chant into their hearts and find there the image of a wide, spacious, green field. That field is wide enough that all of the congregation and all of your beloveds can rest there and receive the blessing of your loving breath.

This is the spaciousness of Shabbat, when our hearts can expand to receive and embrace all of our beloveds, with their unique and varied gifts.

LOVING "THIS"

זֶה דוֹדִי וְזֶה רֵעִי

Zeh Dodi v'zeh Rei'i.
This is my Beloved; this is my Friend.
(Song of Songs 5:16)

Meditation is the practice of opening to "this"—this very moment, this very place. Ordinarily I may have my judgments—things about this that I like or not. But in meditation I just say yes to whatever is before me. I accept it fully. I may not like it, but I surrender to "this." I fall in love, each moment, again and again. I make this moment my friend.

My friend and teacher Sylvia Boorstein has taught me a phrase of intention: "I greet this moment in friendship with an undefended heart."

This phrase from the Song of Songs helps me enter into meditation with a clear and vital intention of making each moment my Beloved.

AN APPETITE FOR HOLINESS

וּבָא בְּכָל־אַוַּת נַפְשׁוֹ אֶל־הַמָּקוֹם

U-va-a-a b'chol avat nafsho el HaMakom.
And he [the Levite] shall come with all the desire of his soul to the Place.
(Deuteronomy 18:6)

With this practice, we invite the Levite, the part of ourselves that is the artist for God, to come to the Center of Holiness and partake of the bounty that is rightly his. We welcome and respond to the hunger of that expressive aspect, by feeding her a fair and generous share of our attention and honor.

HOW AWESOME!

מַה־נּוֹרָא הַמָּקוֹם הַזֶּה

Mah nora HaMakom hazeh!
How awesome is this Place!
(Genesis 28:17)

On Jacob's mythic journey, he stops to rest and dreams of angels going up and down a ladder. He awakens with a realization, "God was in this place and I, I didn't even know it. This is none other than the house of God; this is the gate of heaven!" (Genesis 28:16–17). He realizes that this very moment is awesome. This present moment, wherever we find ourselves on the journey, *is* the house of God (the place we've been looking for), and this present moment *is* the gate of heaven (the doorway to all the mysteries of the beyond). This is a practice of remembering that God is waiting for us right here in this present moment. Becoming fully present is knowing God's presence in *this*.

LISTENING TO THE VOICE OF WISDOM #1

הֲלֹא־חָכְמָה תִקְרָא וּתְבוּנָה תִּתֵּן קוֹלָה

Halo chochmah tikra, ut'vunah titein kolah!

Isn't it Wisdom calling and Understanding raising her voice!

(Proverbs 8:1)

LISTENING TO THE VOICE OF WISDOM #2

אַשְׁרֵי אָדָם שֹׁמֵעַ לִי

Ashrei adam shomei'a li.

Happy is the one who listens to me.

(Proverbs 8:34)

In *Mishlei*, the book of Proverbs, we are introduced to a great and powerful feminine archetype whose name is *Chochmah*, Wisdom. She was there when the earth was created, and she speaks to us through the majesty of Creation. She is the Great Mother who delights in our existence, yet also warns us that when we sin against her, we destroy our own souls. She asks for our love and daily attention.

These two chants are designed to help us open to the voice of *Chochmah*, to become attentive to her presence and message every day as she speaks through the natural world.

SOUL LIGHT

נֵר יהוה נִשְׁמַת אָדָם חֹפֵשׂ כָּל חַדְרֵי בָטֶן

Neir Adonai nishmat adam chofeis kol chadrei vaten.

My soul is the flame of God that searches the inner chambers.

(Proverbs 20:27)

This practice from Proverbs defines the soul as an aspect of God that is pure awareness, which can be activated as a force of holy curiosity as we explore the inner landscape. This chant can be sung as a four-part round to build the energy and intention for inner search and inquiry.

THE REWARDS OF OUR ATTENTION

נֹצֵר תְּאֵנָה יֹאכַל פִּרְיָהּ

Notzeir t'einah yochal piryah.
Those who guard the truth will be nourished by her fruit.
(Proverbs 27:18)

The literal meaning of this verse is "Those who guard a fig tree will eat its fruit." But since this is from the book of Proverbs, I receive its meaning figuratively rather than literally. When I can bring my attention to the fullness of this moment, in all its complexity, beauty, poignancy, and meaning, then I will be nourished by its fruit. When I become fully present, attentive, reverent, and receptive to the holiness and truth of each moment, then I will receive the bounty of my experience.

AWAKENING COMPASSION

מִי יָכִין לָעֹרֵב צֵידוֹ כִּי־יְלָדָו אֶל־אֵל יְשַׁוֵּעוּ

Mi yachin la'oreiv tzeido ki y'ladav el El y'shavei'u?
Who prepares nourishment for the raven
when its young ones call out to God?
(Job 38:41)

This practice calls forth from each of us the divine quality of compassion for all creatures who are calling out in hunger, yearning, or despair. We also open to the parts of ourselves that are calling out for tender consideration and care.

PLANTING AND HARVEST

וְנָטְעוּ כְרָמִים וְשָׁתוּ אֶת־יֵינָם
וְעָשׂוּ גַנּוֹת וְאָכְלוּ אֶת־פְּרִיהֶם

V'nat'u ch'ramim v'shatu et yeinam,
v'asu ganot v'achlu et p'rihem.

And they will plant vineyards and drink the wine thereof,
And they shall make gardens and eat the fruit of them.

(Amos 9:14)

The prophet Amos gives us a vision of what it feels like to harvest the rewards of our intentions, love, and work, to drink the wine and eat the fruit of what we have planted. Now, what would it mean if with this out-breath, I planted a vineyard, and with the very next in-breath, I drank the wine thereof? And with this out-breath, I made a garden, and with the very next in-breath, I am nurtured by the fruit of that garden? This is the practice that Amos gives me. As I exhale, I direct my presence and love into the world. As I inhale the very next breath, I harvest my life's bounty, drinking in its wine and integrating its fruit.

Once you have mastered this breathing pattern, reverse it. Allow the vineyard that you are to be planted by God on the inhale. Breathe out the wine of your life in generous response. Let the garden of your life be planted on the inhale. And as you exhale, give the world your fruits.

Let the chant inspire you in this practice.

PRAISE: THE FORCE OF HEALING AND SALVATION

רְפָאֵנִי יהוה וְאֵרָפֵא הוֹשִׁיעֵנִי וְאִוָּשֵׁעָה כִּי תְהִלָּתִי אָתָּה

R'fa'eini Yah v'eirafei; hoshi'eini v'ivashei'ah ki t'hilati atah.

Heal me, God, and I will be healed; save me and I will be saved ...
for my praise is You.

(Jeremiah17:14)

I cry out from the depths of my suffering, and in the moment
when my cry reverberates, I know that I am healed, made whole,
embraced in the arms of Love. I call out from the apprehension of
being lost, and in my calling, I hear the truth of how connected I
have always been and always will be. My prayer of longing becomes
praise. My asking becomes receiving. In my prayer I know God as
the Transforming Force that moves through me. My praise *is* that
Force.

A NEW COVENANT

נָתַתִּי אֶת־תּוֹרָתִי בְּקִרְבָּם וְעַל־לִבָּם אֶכְתֲּבֶנָּה

Natati et Torati b'kirbam, v'al libam echtavenah.

I will put my Torah into their inmost being
and inscribe it upon their hearts.

(Jeremiah 31:33)

Through the prophet Jeremiah, God promises to make a new covenant. It will be different. You will find this one inside you. A covenant
is always a two-way agreement ... so when I chant these words, I am
expressing my own commitment, so that I can stand up in partnership
with the divine force of Love.

CRYING OUT TO GOD

אִם־כֵּן לָמָּה זֶּה אָנֹכִי

Im kein, lamah zeh anochi?
If this is the way it is, why am I?
(Genesis 25:22)

When Rebecca is suffering through a very difficult pregnancy, she cries out to God and then engages in the process of inquiry. By inquiring of God, Rebecca's suffering is given meaning.

I live with this hypothesis: Every narrow place is a birth canal.

As I chant these words and cry out to God, I hold this question in my heart: "What am I birthing?"

RUTH

עַמֵּךְ עַמִּי וֵאלֹהַיִךְ אֱלֹהָי

Ameich ami veilohayich Elohai.
Your people are my people, and your God is my God.
(Ruth 1:16)

On Shavuot, we read the book of Ruth, which recounts the story of love and loyalty. As we chant Ruth's vow to Naomi, we can each find our own love and loyalty. Though Ruth was a Moabite (Moab was an enemy of Israel), she became the honored ancestor of King David, whose bloodline produces the Messiah. Through her steadfast devotion to Naomi, her people, and her God, Ruth found her own way. So too may we find a sense of belonging and birth *mashiach* (messianic) consciousness into the world.

I chant these words as a practice of belonging. Each repetition allows me to address wider and wider circles of relations, letting that sense of belonging expand. I begin by chanting these words to my family, my students, my close friends. As I chant, I am filled with the joy of connection and kinship. After chanting to all the people I love, I begin to chant these words to everyone else, to people I don't yet know, to people who might seem different than me, to people who I don't even like or I might consider my enemies. "Oh, you are also my people. We come from the same root in God." When I run out of people, I chant these words to all the animals, to the plants, to the rocks. And as I chant, I am glorying in the truth that "we are all related; we all come from the same root in God." I chant these words of power to the stars and know myself as one of them, shining, belonging to the cosmos. I am attuning myself to this truth.

FIRE ON THE ALTAR

אֵשׁ תָּמִיד תּוּקַד עַל־הַמִּזְבֵּחַ לֹא תִכְבֶּה

Aish tamid tukad al hamizbayach; lo tichbeh.
Fire always shall be kept burning on the altar; it shall not go out.
(Leviticus 6:6)

Inside our hearts is a flame that must be kept burning. That fire is our passion for Life, our yearning for God, our curiosity about the mysteries, our sparkle of humor, our enthusiasm for the Work. We keep that fire burning by engaging in spiritual practice, by surrounding ourselves with beauty, by giving and receiving love and support, and by fully connecting with what (and whom) we love.

It is crucial to bring attention to that flame on the altar of the heart—to feed that fire and to guard it with loving vigilance.

(I composed this chant during the last days of Chanukah as I lit the candles and took their flames inside me.)

Psalms

MY CUP

כּוֹסִי רְוָיָה

Kosi r'vayah.
My cup overflows.
(Psalm 23:5)

Though I walk through the valley of the deepest darkness, I will not fear evil, for You, God are with me. How do you manifest Yourself to me? I have come face-to-face with my own demons across the lavish table that You spread before me. And on that table is a cup that is overflowing.

In building the *kavanah*, the intention for this chant, I would invite the community to begin to become aware of two different dimensions of "cup." One cup is located in the heart. It is the connection to the source of life and love within us, and no matter what befalls us or what "enemy" faces us from across the table, that inner cup continues to flow and to overflow. The sound of the chant reconnects us to that flow. The other "cup" is the cup that is formed in community. The sound of our voices and the strength of our shared intention create that cup, which both contains the divine flow and serves as a vehicle for our nourishment. As we form the cup of community, we enable each person to access exactly what he or she needs, to drink individually from the flow that we create together.

This chant is composed of three parts, which through different rhythmic patterns evoke the feeling of rivulets flowing mellifluously together and apart. At the end of the chant, we can breathe into the heart and look for an image of a cup. Stay with that image as it gets clearer and clearer with each breath. Imagine touching the cup, drinking from it, being filled with its contents.

And then raise the eyes of your heart to see who (or what) it is that sits across from you at that table—your enemy or demon. Know that the cup contains exactly what you need in order to do that facing. Complete the practice by drinking again from your cup.

CALLING FORTH THE HIDDEN POWER

קוּמָה יהוה הוֹשִׁיעֵנִי אֱלֹהַי

Kumah Adonai, hoshi'eini Elohai.
Rise up, YHVH; save me, my God.
(Psalm 3:8)

With this practice, I call forth the hidden power. I sing to the force that is hidden in my depths and in the secret places of this world. I sing with a bold demand and with a humble plea for that force to reveal itself. As I chant, I dedicate myself as a vessel for that power. I pray to be saved from the traps of superficiality. I pray to have access to depths of meaning and purpose rather than be a prisoner to the surface of things.

INVITING OUR FUTURE SELVES

הוֹדִיעֵנִי יהוה קִצִּי וּמִדַּת יָמַי מַה־הִיא

Hodi'eiani Yah kitzi, umidat yamai mah hi?
O God, show me my end, and what is the measure of my days?
(Psalm 39:5)

With this chant we can pray for a vision of who we are becoming. At the end of the chant, open up to receive a visit from your future self. Let your imagination lead you to your vision and trust what comes. Receive the gift, wisdom, guidance, or blessing of your future self.

PREPARATION FOR RECONNECTING

חָנֵּנִי יהוה כִּי אֻמְלַל אָנִי

Choneini Yah ki umlal ani.
Grace me, Yah, for I am withered [disconnected].
(Psalm 6:3)

In order to connect with God, our Source, we have to acknowledge how disconnected we sometimes get. That disconnection manifests as weariness, irritability, loneliness, emptiness, or a feeling of being scattered or lost.

Reconnecting requires that we acknowledge the price of that disconnection and then open in yearning and hopefulness to the mystery of God's grace.

EVEN IN THE DARKNESS

זָרַח בַּחֹשֶׁךְ אוֹר לַיְשָׁרִים חַנּוּן וְרַחוּם וְצַדִּיק

Zarach bachoshech or lay'sharim, chanun v'rachum v'tzadik.
Even in the darkness a light shines for the upright,
gracious, compassionate, and just.
(Psalm 112:4)

The light that we shine sustains us through the darkness, through difficult times. That light awakens in us (and in others) the qualities of grace, compassion, and a passion for justice. This three-part round is a practice of affirming and strengthening that shining inner light as we face hard challenges and scary times.

SUPPORTED

סָמוּךְ לִבּוֹ לֹא יִירָא

Samuch libo lo yira.

סָמוּךְ לִבָּהּ לֹא תִּירָא

Samuch liba lo tira.
Heart supported, fearless.
(Psalm 112:8)

Samuch libo lo yira. We sing this in the feminine as *Samuch liba lo tira*, "Heart supported, fearless." This practice opens up a new way of approaching the cultivation of courage. What if we became fearless by allowing our heart to feel completely supported? Can you imagine what that would feel like? The courage that emerges from the heart that feels and receives the full support of the universe is a courage that is steady, deep, and abiding. When I chant this in a group, we all place our right hand on our own heart and our left hand on the back of the heart of the person standing beside us. We turn slightly to the left and get very close so that we can sway and feel what it's like to be supported, to know that someone has "got our back." We connect the chant to this sensation and let it become a body-memory that we will be able to call on whenever we feel "unsupported." At the end of the chant, breathe into the sensation of "heart supported," and imagine your courage arising from the center of that support.

EFR—ENERGY FIELD RECHARGE

This practice can be used for protection, for clearing, and for strengthening the energy field.

אֱלֹהִים יְחָנֵּנוּ וִיבָרְכֵנוּ יָאֵר פָּנָיו אִתָּנוּ סֶלָה

Elohim y'choneinu vivarcheinu ya'eir panav itanu selah.

God, grace us, bless us; may its light shine among us, selah.

(Psalm 67:2)

First Phase: Visualization and Energy Patterning

1. Find a point of light deep in your belly and bring it up through the body, out the top of your head until it's about a foot above your head.
2. Weave an egg of light clockwise from the point above your head down the body until you reach a point at the bottom of the egg about a foot below your feet.
3. Pull that point of light up through your perineum back to the beginning point in your belly.
4. Connect the point in your belly to a point within your heart.
5. Radiate out from the heart, filling the entire egg with a white/golden light.
6. End by rooting your attention back in the belly.

Second Phase: Visualization, Energy Patterning, and Breath Concentration

1. *On the inhalation*: Find a point of light deep in your belly and bring it up through the body, out the top of your head until it's about a foot above your head.
2. *On the exhalation*: Weave an egg of light clockwise from the point above your head down the body until you reach a point at the bottom of the egg about a foot below your feet.
3. *On a partial inhalation*: Pull that point of light up through your perineum back to the beginning point in your belly.
4. *Continue the inhalation*: Connect the point in your belly to a point within your heart.
5. *Breathing in and out from the heart*: Radiate out from the heart, filling the entire egg with a white/golden light. End by directing the breath into the belly.

Third Phase: Chant, Visualization, and Energy Patterning

1. *Elohim*: Find a point of light deep in your belly and bring it up through the body, out the top of your head until it's about a foot above your head.
2. *Y'choneinu*: Weave an egg of light clockwise from the point above your head down the body until you reach a point at the bottom of the egg about a foot below your feet.
3. *Vivarchei*: Pull that point of light up through your perineum back to the beginning point in your belly.
4. *Nu*: Connect the point in your belly to a point within your heart.
5. *Ya'eir panav itanu selah*: Radiate out from the heart, filling the entire egg with a white/golden light. End by rooting your attention back in the belly on the word *selah*.

Fourth Phase: Silent Chant

Chant silently with breath concentration.

GIVING MY "SELF" IN SERVICE

אָנָּה יהוה כִּי־אֲנִי עַבְדֶּךָ אֲנִי עַבְדֶּךָ

Anah Yah ki ani avdecha; ani avd'cha.
Please, God, for I am your servant; I am your servant.
(Psalm 116:16)

With this practice, I am asking God to please take my small self and connect me with the larger whole so that everything that I have imagined, constructed, developed, and refined as my separate self can be reconnected and be given in service to the whole of life.

I am saying, "Please use me," as I give myself to the Greatest Intelligence and Deepest Mystery of Oneness. With each repetition of the chant, I find more of my "self" to give away in dedication to my higher purpose of service.

JUSTICE IN PEACE

יִפְרַח בְּיָמָיו צַדִּיק וְרֹב שָׁלוֹם

Yifrach b'yamav tzadik, v'rov shalom!
O justice, O justice ... in the fullness of peace!
O, justice shall flourish in its time, and the fullness of peace.
(Psalm 72:7)

At the funeral of Senator Edward M. (Ted) Kennedy, his daughter Kara led the congregation in a version of Psalm 72. After each line, the congregation of dignitaries responded in refrain, "Justice shall flourish in its time, and the fullness of peace forever."

Senator Kennedy, may his memory be a blessing, understood that justice is the inner truth of peace. His legacy of making justice for the poor, for the disabled, for the disenfranchised people of this land, can be our inspiration as we all become makers of peace.

This practice marries justice with peace, affirming that the fullness of peace *is* justice. All our work for justice must have peace as its driving force, and as we work for peace, we must make justice our goal.

RE-PARENTED

כִּי אָבִי וְאִמִּי עֲזָבוּנִי
וַיהוה יַאַסְפֵנִי
הוֹרֵנִי יהוה דַּרְכֶּךָ

Ki avi v'imi azavuni (2x)
V'Adonai ya'asfeini (4x)
Horeini Yah darkecha. (4x)
Though my father and my mother have forsaken me,
God will gather me in.
Teach me Your way, O God.
(Psalm 27:10–11)

This three-part round is a three-part process of first admitting the ways that your parents may have "failed" you. They may not have been able to give you the exact safety, encouragement, nourishment, guidance, or embrace that you needed. From your grown-up perspective, now you can stop blaming them and instead cultivate compassion for their limitations and for yourself. They were really doing the best they could.

The second step is to turn to God, the Great Father/Mother, and allow yourself to be embraced, gathered in, and re-parented. Surrender into the arms of that Divine Parent, and let yourself be held, seen, known, and sent to your own truth.

And the third step is to open to guidance, internalizing that Divine Parent as you connect to wisdom in this very moment on your life path.

MORNING SONG

וַאֲנִי אָשִׁיר עֻזֶּךָ וַאֲרַנֵּן לַבֹּקֶר חַסְדֶּךָ

Va'ani ashir uzecha va'aranein labokeir chasdecha.
And I will sing Your glory and I will sing Your love to the morning.
(Psalm 59:17)

As my morning practice, I attune myself to the divine attributes, allowing God's strength, glory, and love to sing through me. I become the channel for God to address this new day.

HEALING CHANT

מַה יָּקָר חַסְדְּךָ אֱלֹהִים

Mah yakar chasd'cha Elohim.
How precious is Your love, God.
(Psalm 36:8)

Each of us is like a unique crystal through which the light and love of God might shine. This healing practice is done through the perception and amplification of that unique refraction of God-light. The person seeking healing lies down in the center of the circle and is instructed to shine her unique light. The circle of healers then bring all of their attention to that unique light and shine it back to her through this chant. A healing field is created, and the person seeking healing is connected up with her own "blueprint of perfection."

FROM THE DEPTHS

מִמַּעֲמַקִּים קְרָאתִיךָ יהוה,

Mima'amakim k'raticha Yah!
From the depths I call to You, O God. Hear my voice!
(Psalm 130:1)

For me the practice of chanting is about finding those depths from which to call, thereby unlocking the treasures of passion, longing, love, and wisdom at my core. Slavery is the state of being trapped on the surface. I find my freedom by opening to the possibilities of the infinite space within. Calling out to God is a practice of dropping down into those infinite depths and allowing my deepest and truest expression to emerge.

THE HEAVENS

הַשָּׁמַיִם מְסַפְּרִים כְּבוֹד־אֵל

Hashamayim m'saprim k'vod Eil.
The heavens open up and tell Your story,
Of sun and clouds and storm, of wind and glory.
(Psalm 19:2)

Where I live in New Mexico, the skies are my great entertainment and inspiration. With this practice, we watch the sky and receive from its wide expanse and changing colors the story of God's expanse and the Truth of Impermanence. You can try this practice lying back on a grassy field with your chant buddies, looking up at the sky and receiving the amazing story that the Heavens tell. (If you do this practice at night you can substitute "stars" for "sun.")

DAY AND NIGHT

יוֹם לְיוֹם יַבִּיעַ אֹמֶר וְלַיְלָה לְּלַיְלָה יְחַוֶּה־דָּעַת

Yom l'yom yabia omer, v'lailah l'lailah y'chaveh da'at.
Day after day pours forth speech,
night after night declares knowledge.
(Psalm 19:3)

God speaks through the movement of time. Through the cycles of day and night, meaning is expressed, wisdom is revealed. We chant these words in order to open our eyes to this mystery. We dance to the rhythms of night and day and allow the sacred word to move us and to pour out through us. True knowledge is made real as we dive again and again into night. Each day returns with new opportunities for the holy word to manifest in our lives.

RIVER OF BLISS

וְנַחַל עֲדָנֶיךָ תַשְׁקֵם

V'nachal adanecha tashkeim.
And from the river of Your bliss you will give them drink.

כִּי־עִמְּךָ מְקוֹר חַיִּים בְּאוֹרְךָ נִרְאֶה־אוֹר

Ki im'cha m'kor chayim; b'or'cha nireh or.
For with You is the source of life, in Your light we see light.
(Psalm 36:9–10)

The spiritual practice that I return to again and again is cultivating an awareness of the river that is constantly and continually flowing into me from the Source. The best way that I've found to drink from that "river of bliss" is to bring my attention to the breath. I use my imagination to attune to the reality of the divine flow which is pouring into this world. I imagine that river as light pouring in through the breath. When I am fully bathed in that supernal light, then I am able to perceive that light everywhere. On the inhale, I drink from the "river of bliss." On the exhale, I spread this awareness into the world, sharing the light.

ROSH HASHANAH CHANT

אַשְׁרֵי הָעָם יוֹדְעֵי תְרוּעָה יהוה בְּאוֹר־פָּנֶיךָ יְהַלֵּכוּן

Ashrei ha'am yodei t'ruah Adonai b'or panecha y'haleichun.
O God, happy are the people who know the blast of the shofar;
they walk in the light of Your presence.
(Psalm 89:16)

What kind of "happy" is this? Certainly not the happiness of superficial pleasure—a lifestyle of denial that masks a terrible truth—and not the la-di-da happiness that keeps life bland and safe.

This is the kind of "happy" that is a dynamic force waiting quietly at our center, the deep joy for existence itself. The blast of the shofar can break open the shell that imprisons that inner joy. When that joy is freed, it becomes a light that shines regardless of circumstance. And that joy is our power. It is the power that moves us as "we walk in the light of God's presence," as we walk with integrity, courage, commitment, as we walk in beauty.

May the blast of the shofar shatter the rigid walls that imprison our true joy.

May the wail of the shofar open our hearts and send us with compassion to profound forgiveness.

May the call of the shofar inspire each of us to respond with our unique love as we rise to the challenge that is set before us this year.

This practice can be done as a dance of stillness and movement. As you chant *"Ashrei ha'am yodei t'ruah Adonai,"* stand very still and listen, raising your arms to receive God's presence with the word *Adonai*. Then, with the words *"b'or panecha y'haleichun,"* do a mindful walking meditation around the circle. This practice can be done as a round with two concentric circles.

THE SEA LION'S QUESTION

מִי־הָאִישׁ הֶחָפֵץ חַיִּים אֹהֵב יָמִים לִרְאוֹת טוֹב

Mi ha'ish hechafeitz chayim, oheiv yamim lirot tov?
Who is the one that has a passion for life,
loving every day, seeing the good?
(Psalm 34:13)

During my pilgrimage to the Galapagos, I communed with a variety of animals who amazed me with their forthright presence, beauty, and intelligence. Many of the animals I saw exist nowhere else. Marine iguanas, Galapagos penguins, and blue-footed boobies astounded me. Everywhere were the reminders of the humor and creative genius of the Creator.

The climax of my Galapagos adventure was the opportunity to swim with the sea lions. We hiked across Floreana Island to their secret cove and jumped into the clear swirling tide. The sea lions immediately surrounded us, excited to play.

All afternoon we frolicked in delighted abandon with these sweet and bold teachers of the sea. When I got back on the boat, I was inspired to sing this line from Psalm 34:13: "Who is the one with a passion for life, loving each day, seeing the good?"

I imagined that through their play, the sea lions were asking me this question. And I answered without hesitation, "I will be that one. I promise."

PLANTING SEEDS OF JOY AND LIGHT

אוֹר זָרֻעַ לַצַּדִּיק וּלְיִשְׁרֵי לֵב שִׂמְחָה

Or zarua la tzadik, ul'yishrei leiv simchah.

Plant the seeds of joy and light;
tend them carefully day and night,
In this soil so dark and deep,
I plant the dreams that love will reap.

(Psalm 97:11)

I wrote this practice in honor of the winter solstice leading up to the passage of Chanukah. In preparation for this chant, recall the shining peak moments in your life that revealed to you a great joy or profound wisdom, moments of ecstasy or prophecy, delight or enchantment. Imagine those moments as seeds. Create an intention to plant those seeds and tend them with your loving attention as you grow a life of joy and light.

SINGING A NEW SONG

שִׁירוּ לַיהוה שִׁיר חָדָשׁ תְּהִלָּתוֹ בִּקְהַל חֲסִידִים

Halleluyah!

Shiru l'Adonai shir chadash; t'hilato bik'hal Chasidim.

Sing to God a new song;
God's praise is found in a community of lovers.

(Psalm 149:1)

How do we make every song we sing to God a "new" song? The secret to making my song new is the same secret to being a good lover. I forget everything I know about my Beloved and encounter God as a brand-new miracle. I let myself be surprised.

When we worship together as a community of lovers, encountering each other as surprising miracles, then our love for each other becomes an expression of praise for our Creator.

The kindness and generosity that we offer each other in community is our most precious gift to God. Our new song to God emerges from our connection to each other.

MIN HAMEITZAR

מִן־הַמֵּצַר קָרָאתִי יָהּ עָנָנִי בַמֶּרְחָב יָהּ

Min hameitzar karati Yah, anani vamerchav Yah.
From the narrow place I called out to God
who answered me with the divine expanse.
(Psalm 118:5)

With this chant, we can dedicate our own narrow places—the places of struggle, difficulty, suffering, or challenge in our lives. We can know and accept those narrow places as that which will make our "call" beautiful and compelling. When we can allow the force of our call to move through our narrow places, through what makes us all too human, then our call will be answered by God's divine expanse—a sense of spaciousness in which transformation can happen.

SURRENDER

בְּיָדְךָ אַפְקִיד רוּחִי, בְּעֵת אִישָׁן וְאָעִירָה
וְעִם רוּחִי גְּוִיָּתִי, יהוה לִי וְלֹא אִירָא

B'yad'cha af'kid ruchi, b'ayt ishan v'a-ira,
v'im ruchi g'vi-ati, Adonai li v'lo ira.
Into Your hand I entrust my spirit, when I sleep and when I awaken,
when spirit is with my body, God is with me; I will not fear.
(the last lines of *Adon Olam*, attributed to Solomon ibn Gavirol)

I created this practice in preparation for knee surgery. For the couple of months leading up to surgery, I was limping around somewhat nonchalantly, mostly preoccupied with getting a lot done. Then as the time approached I experienced the first stages of panic, realizing exactly what kind of power tools, screws, cadaver parts, and strange manipulations were waiting for me. The message that my soul whispered so very clearly was that I was required to surrender now. I had done all the work of setting up care for myself, learning what I needed, renting and buying the right devices for rehab, listening to the message that my knee was communicating to me so articulately. Now I could almost see the smoking trail of my good witch's broomstick in the sky: "Surrender, Shefa."

So, as a chanter I looked for a sacred phrase that might help me and chose Psalm 31:6, "Into Your hand I entrust my spirit." As the chant/practice developed, I began to become aware of God's hands manifesting *in and through the world*—through those that love me, through my doctors, through devices, through breath and color. With each repetition of the chant, I could release control and trust the Great Hand that held me. I could also become aware of just how much I had been holding on to control and see how much work was still before me.

The chant that accompanies this practice expands the practice to include phrasing from *Adom Olam*, which is why you'll find it in the Liturgy section within the musical notations section.

SINGING GOD'S LOVE

חַסְדֵי יהוה עוֹלָם אָשִׁירָה

Chasdei Adonai olam ashirah.
I will sing forth from the hidden infinite,
the loving-kindnesses of God.
(Psalm 89:1)

Chant is the practice of calling forth hidden truths and bringing them into awareness and manifestation through voice and intention. I don't sing about those truths ... I sing those truths *into being*. With the power of my voice and the wholeheartedness of my intention, I call forth the beauty that is hidden within existence. As that beauty sings itself through me, I open myself as a channel, as a vessel, as a vehicle for the awareness of God's presence in the world.

The word *olam* means the infinite both in time and in space. And it also means the hidden or concealed. Our song reaches through the cracks of time and space and calls forth the hidden dimension of the Infinite, which has been waiting all along.

The song opens our eyes to the manifestations of God's love that surround us—evidence of the Infinite pouring itself into and through our finite world.

TUNING IN TO THE CREATOR-FUNCTION

אֶשָּׂא עֵינַי אֶל־הֶהָרִים מֵאַיִן יָבֹא עֶזְרִי

Esa einai el heharim mei'ayin yavo ezri. (2x)
My help comes from the One (3x)
Creator of heaven and earth.
(Psalm 12:11)

I wrote this chant for a friend to use during labor. During the process of birthing, it seemed important to tune in to the Creator-function of God, to become partners with God in the work of Creation, and to turn toward that aspect of God that is continually creating through us.

Even if you are not literally "giving birth," this chant can be used to stimulate and celebrate the creative force that moves through us each day.

This is a two-part round.

EXPANDING INNER SPACE

אֵלֶיךָ יהוה אֶקְרָא

Eilecha Yah ekra.
To You, God, I call.
(Psalm 30:9)

With this practice we employ concentration on reaching vast inner distances from an anchored depth by projecting consciousness beyond the farthest horizon. We focus and direct emotional energy, absorbing and radiating divine energy.

The expanse of inner space determines the power of the voice.

Phase 1: Chanting and Visualization

1. *Eilecha Yah ekra*: Reach deep inside on the first note, ground, then move out, projecting your "call" wide and far past the farthest horizon you can imagine. Crescendo in emotion and volume.

2. *Eilecha Yah ekra*: Feel the voice returning to you from beyond the horizon, coming a great distance, as the words come to rest gently and deeply within you. Decrescendo in emotion and volume.

3. Same as 1.

4. Same as 2.

5. *Eilecha*: Focus your "call" on a point in the far distance. This call is refined and directed, like a laser beam from the third eye.

6. *Yah*: Let your call extend even further and dissolve into the "beyond-the-beyond."

7. *Ekra*: Feel as if you have seeded the clouds with your longing and are now opening to the gentle rain and receiving the divine flow into you.

Phase 2: Chanting and Movement

1–4. Bowing to each side (left, then right), generating energy, intensifying commitment.

5. *Eilecha*: Longing, lifting, reaching, with both hands, palms up.

6. *Yah*: Deep bow to center, surrendering to the vastness of God.

7. *Ekra*: Coming back to center with palms at the heart.

Phase 3: Silent Chanting on the Breath

1. *Eleicha Yah ekra*: Exhale toward the place beyond the wide horizon.

2. *Eleicha Yah ekra*: Inhale, receiving the call back from a great distance.

3. *Eleicha Yah ekra*: Exhale toward the place beyond the wide horizon.

4. *Eleicha Yah ekra*: Inhale, receiving the call back from a great distance.

5. *Eleicha*: Exhale, focusing on a distant point with refined breath.

6. *Yah*: Inhale simultaneously through the crown and the root into the heart.

7. *Ekra*: Exhale, radiating divine light in all directions like the sun.

8. Inhale in preparation, realignment, setting your intention.

PREPARATION FOR HEALING

אַתָּה עֻזִּי

אַתָּה חַיַּי

אַתָּה אוֹרִי

אַתָּה לְפָנַי

Atah Ozi

Atah Chayai

Atah Ori

Atah l'fanai

You are my Strength

You are my Life

You are my Light

Ever before me.

(inspired by Psalm 27)

In the practice of healing we leave the "small mind" place of fear and separation and enter into the "big mind" place of infinite possibility and gratefulness for the blessing that is already flowing. We take the journey from "small mind" to "big mind" by addressing God as "You." We must become calm enough and spacious enough to receive God's presence in response to our invocation. When we are filled with that presence, then we can open to the healing power that flows through us.

SOUL PERSPECTIVE

אֵלֶיךָ יהוה נַפְשִׁי אֶשָּׂא

Eilecha Yah nafshi esa.

To You, God, I lift up my soul.

(Psalm 25:1)

Sometimes it feels like I am a human who is in search of the expanse of my soul ... yet in my clearer moments I know that I am that expansive soul, enjoying and learning from the experience of being human. This practice of "Soul Perspective" lifts me up into that clarity. In difficult circumstances that don't make sense from my human perspective, I use my holy imagination to access the soul contract. For example, when I am involved in a serious conflict with someone, I imagine our two souls hanging out before birth, making a loving agreement. "Let's meet when we're in our twenties, OK? And we'll have this amazing attraction, and then we'll gradually find out how different we are and begin learning from those differences. I'll help you heal that old rigidity that you've been carrying so many lifetimes, and you can help me get rid of my fantasies about love so that I can eventually open to real Love."

This chant helps me remember that when I open to the soul perspective, even the most difficult encounters can be transformed into opportunities for soul growth. After chanting this, you might try writing an imaginary dialogue from the soul perspective between yourself and someone who triggers you. Let it begin from a premise that as souls, we come to love and serve each other, but that love and service often take forms that are difficult and troubling as forces of awakening.

ENCOUNTERING THE LIVING GOD

צָמְאָה נַפְשִׁי לֵאלֹהִים לְאֵל חָי

Tzam'ah nafshi l'Eilohim l'Eil Chai.
My soul thirsts for God, for the Living God.
(Psalm 42:3)

Deep inside of us there is a soul-thirst to know God, the underlying Unity, the Mystery within and between all the things of our world. The word *Elohim* is a God name that is in the plural, alluding to the many faces of the One—what Taoists might call "the ten thousand things." We enter through this world of multiplicity so that we might encounter the "Living God," *Eil Chai,* who can only be experienced with the wholeness of presence in this very moment. The God of the past, my own or other people's conceptions, beliefs, or expectations, will not suffice. They will not open the doors to the Living God. My soul thirsts for direct encounter with God/Reality in each moment.

TURNING

סוּר מֵרָע וַעֲשֵׂה־טוֹב בַּקֵּשׁ שָׁלוֹם וְרָדְפֵהוּ

Sur meira va'asei tov, bakeish shalom v'radfeihu.
Turn away from evil and do good;
Seek peace/wholeness and go after it.
(Psalm 34:15)

With a discerning heart, I see my life divided into two categories: that which drains my energy and separates me (which here is called evil), and that which gives me energy and connects me to the wholeness of life. My spiritual practice is to turn away from the seduction of evil, because I know its power to sap my strength and love, and then to counter the pull of "evil" with an action that brings goodness into the world—an act of kindness, a gesture of compassion, a deed of justice making. When I glimpse the possibility of *shalom* (peace or wholeness), then I must go after it, like a detective searching out clues, like a warrior facing the enemy within that is reflected in my world.

The practice is to first ask, "What is it that separates me or drains me of strength, love, or compassion?" It may be a habit or thought or something you do without ever questioning its place in your life. As you chant, use the power of the words to turn away from that which you have discerned to be the "evil" in your life. Let the chant strengthen your commitment toward good. At the end of the chant, make a commitment toward one specific action that represents "good." And do it.

SATISFACTION AND ITS FRUITS

שַׂבְּעֵנוּ בַבֹּקֶר חַסְדֶּךָ וּנְרַנְּנָה וְנִשְׂמְחָה בְּכָל־יָמֵינוּ

Sab'einu vaboker chasdecha;
Un'ran'nah v'nism'chah b'chol yameinu.
May Your loving-kindness satisfy us in the morning;
and we will sing out and we will rejoice for all our days.
(Psalm 90:14)

Satisfaction is a daily practice of opening to the flow of God's love and receiving that flow in gratefulness. Then we can let our lives be an expression of the wonder, surprise, appreciation, awe, and delight that comes from receiving the gift of our lives each day. The practice of satisfaction requires that I suspend my habitual complaint, create a space of inner stillness and receptivity, and then open my senses to the subtle flows of loving-kindness that are always flowing into our world. That flow may come through the color of the sky or the song of a bird or the touch of silk against my skin. That flow may come through the rhythm of my breath, through a sudden inspiration, or through the kindness of a friend. Our practice is to become attentive to that flow, be filled by it, and then let our lives become a response to this divine generosity.

LONGING

כֵּן נַפְשִׁי תַעֲרֹג אֵלֶיךָ אֱלֹהִים

Kein nafshi ta'arog eilecha Elohim.
Just as the deer longs for water by the riverbank,
So does my soul long for You, O God.
(Psalm 42:2)

The deer that we are recalling with this practice is standing at the riverbank. Her longing is for that water that is right there, right in front of her. Our longing for God, for truth, for the doorway into the sublime mystery is just like this. We long to know intimately the Reality that is right before us; we long to feel the earth that is beneath our feet, to taste the food that is in our mouths, to touch the life that is embracing us. We long for the power of presence to awaken us to the gift that is given in this very moment.

LET MY GLORY SING

יְזַמֶּרְךָ כָבוֹד וְלֹא יִדֹּם

Y'zamercha chavod v'lo yidom.
Let my glory sing to You and not be silenced.
(Psalm 30:13)

This is a practice of devotion, of finding the glory inside and pouring it out to God. Before you begin, examine what it is that silences that glory. Is it self-doubt, living in your head, being distracted, unforgiving, or drained of passion? Has your glory been silenced by grief, cynicism, or the fear of how you might sound or appear to others? Once you have made this discernment, look beneath the obstacle and find within you that glory that wants to be acknowledged and celebrated. As you chant, let the spark of God in you be fanned into glorious flame.

RE-MEMBERING

לַיהוה הָאָרֶץ וּמְלוֹאָהּ תֵּבֵל וְיֹשְׁבֵי בָהּ

L'Adonai ha'aretz um'loah, teiveil v'yosh'vei vah.
The earth and all that fills her, and all who dwell in her ...
all belong to God.
(Psalm 24:1)

With this practice we acknowledge everything and everyone as part
of the Divine Body. And we surrender to the One who encompasses
our very being. Our intention is to re-member, to acknowledge just
how integral we are to the Whole of God, to the community of all,
to each other.

TRUSTING

שַׁבְתִּי בְּבֵית־יהוה

Shavti b'veit Adonai.
I place myself in Your care.
(Psalm 23:6)

I place myself in the context of an intelligent, loving universe that
holds me in compassion and supports my work. I trust in the whole
and allow myself to be nurtured and embraced by a great mystery.

HEART WALK

אֶתְהַלֵּךְ בְּתָם־לְבָבִי בְּקֶרֶב בֵּיתִי

Et'haleich b'tom l'vavi, b'kerev beiti.
I will walk within my house in the integrity of my heart.
(Psalm 101:2)

To find the integrity of my heart is to return to its innocence, simplicity, and wholeness and then live my life from that place. When life
gets complicated, tangled up, and overwhelming, it's time to "go for
a walk."

Et'haleich is a reflexive verb (to take yourself for a walk) that
describes a way of living that is self-aware. I must take this walk within
my own house first, if I am to manifest that integrity in the world. My
own house might mean the workings of my inner life, or the life of my
family and intimate relationships, or the sacred realm of "Home."

This practice is a walking meditation.

PROTECTING OUR "INNER CHILD"

כִּי־חִזַּק בְּרִיחֵי שְׁעָרָיִךְ בֵּרַךְ בָּנַיִךְ בְּקִרְבֵּךְ

Ki chizak b'richei sh'arayich, beirach banayich b'kirbeich.
When your boundaries are strong, your inner child is blessed.
(Psalm 147:13)

There is a place inside each of us that is young and fragile and innocent. Part of our spiritual practice is to protect and honor that part
of ourselves. When we protect her from our own cynicism and from
the harshness of the world, she is nurtured from within and blessed
with the space to feel safe. When she doesn't feel that safety, the inner
child is apt to "act out."

WITH EVERY BREATH

כֹּל הַנְּשָׁמָה תְּהַלֵּל יָהּ הַלְלוּיָהּ

Kol han'shamah t'haleil Yah.
Every soul praises Yah with every breath,
From the moment of birth until death! *Halleluyah!*
(Psalm 150:6)

This is the very last line of the book of Psalms, and it pretty much sums it up. Can we know our very breath as praise?

WHOSE FACE?

אַל־תַּסְתֵּר פָּנֶיךָ מִמֶּנִּי

Al tasteir panecha mimeni.
Do not hide Your face from me.
(Psalm 27:9)

I begin chanting this prayer with insistence and passion because I long to see and know the face of God in all things, in all people, in all places, in all blessings, in all predicaments. After a while it feels as if God is chanting these words to me, saying, "I have been here all along; it is you who have been hiding. Show your face to Me." And then I enter the subtle state that I call "the holy confusion." Whose face? Mine? God's? Both? Neither? Or does God look out from my face? Or do I look out from God's face?

If I chant long enough, I may be able to rest in this holy confusion, bathe in its questions, and come to the state of un-knowing that leads to wisdom.

This is a three-part round.

PURE HEART

לֵב טָהוֹר בְּרָא־לִי אֱלֹהִים

Leiv tahor b'ra li Elohim.
Create for me a pure heart. [God] has created for me a pure heart.
O pure heart, create for me [the experience of] God.
The pure heart has created God for me.
(Psalm 51:12)

The heart, in our tradition, is the seat of holistic intelligence. The heart center mediates between the upper and lower worlds. And the heart center is the nexus point between the realms of the finite and the infinite. Since we receive divine guidance through the open heart, our spiritual practice is about purifying that channel ... or acknowledging its essential purity. I freely translate this phrase from Psalm 51 in three different ways. As you chant these words, notice which translation resonates for you.

Am I asking God to re-create my heart in purity? Am I affirming the essential purity within me? Am I calling on the power of my heart to allow me to access the Divine? Or am I affirming that access?

A SPIRIT OF "YES!"

וְרוּחַ נָכוֹן חַדֵּשׁ בְּקִרְבִּי

V'ruach nachon chadeish b'kirbi.
Renew within me a spirit of "Yes!"
(Psalm 51:12)

The *ruach nachon* that I'm in need of renewing is the remembrance of the "rightness" of the reality before me. When my spirit can fully agree to and accept "what is," then I am empowered to rest in the truth of this moment and walk through the doors of transformation that open. I need this renewal because I sometimes fight with the truth of "what is," and that is an exhausting and losing battle. (Inwardly I say, "Oh, no! I don't like what this is." And I can get stuck there in my "Oh, no!") When the spirit of "Yes" is renewed in me, I lean into the mystery of this moment and look for the doors of opportunity and transformation that open in response to my curiosity and in response to my agreement to accept the challenge of my life.

THE VALLEY OF DEATH

גַּם כִּי־אֵלֵךְ בְּגֵיא צַלְמָוֶת לֹא־אִירָא רָע

Gam ki eileich b'gei tzalmavet, lo ira ra.
Though I walk through the Valley of Death,
I will not fear,
Though I walk through the Valley of Death,
my God is near.
(Psalm 23:4)

I wrote this chant to help myself and others deal with a difficult
time of tragedy. When I encounter "evil" in the world—the pre-
mature death of a friend, the terrible suffering caused by madness
or terrorism, the injustice of innocents dying, the horrible suffering
that "shouldn't" have been—I may tremble inside, lose my way, or
become paralyzed. These words from Psalm 23 have helped me find
the steadiness of God's presence within me, to find the path of loving,
to move forward again in courage.

PURE

כָּל־מִשְׁבָּרֶיךָ וְגַלֶּיךָ עָלַי עָבָרוּ
טָהוֹר הוּא, טְהוֹרָה הִיא

Kol mishbarecha v'galecha alai avaru
Tahor hu, t'horah hi.
All of Your breakers and Your waves have swept over me.
He is pure; she is pure.
(Psalm 42:8)

Every moment can be received as a point of transition and an opening
into a whole new world. As I step into who I am becoming, I need

to be washed clean of prejudice, expectation, disappointment, and limited perspective.

This chant was written for *taharah* (preparing a body for burial), specifically the part of the ritual where water is poured over the body. It is also a wonderful chant for the practice of *mikvah* (ritual immersion) or any ritual of purification.

The "breakers" represent the forces of enlightenment that break the patterns of habit and conditioning, while the "waves" wash us clean.

The breakers and waves that cleanse us can also be understood as our life experience. Through living and learning, we are returned to our essential purity.

MY ROCK AND REDEEMER

אַתָּה צוּרִי וְגֹאֲלִי

Atah Tzuri v'Go'ali.
You are my Rock and my Redeemer.
(adapted from Psalm 19:15)

These two names of God describe the process of liberation. When I know God as "my Rock," I am feeling the loving support that holds me; I am leaning into a sense of basic trust in reality. From that sense of trust, I can receive God as "my Redeemer." I can allow the force of liberation to move me, to send me to new challenges and into the unknown. As I address myself to these two divine aspects, I can allow the feeling of support to send me toward liberation, toward opening, flowering, and self-realization. The steady rock beneath me allows me to take that necessary "leap of faith."

MY PROTECTION

מָגִנִּי עַל־אֱלֹהִים מוֹשִׁיעַ יִשְׁרֵי־לֵב

Magini al Elohim, moshia yishrei leiv.
My protection is all about the God-field;
that's what saves the upright heart.
(Psalm 7:11)

When the source for my own energy field is the *Shechinah*, that
indwelling Divine Presence, then I am protected, shielded, and ultimately safe. That sense of ultimate safety allows my heart to risk
being open and expansive no matter what the circumstance. My heart
stands up within me and takes the lead.

MY PRAYER AS INCENSE

תִּכּוֹן תְּפִלָּתִי קְטֹרֶת לְפָנֶיךָ

Tikon t'filati k'toret l'fanecha.
Let my prayer be incense before You.
(Psalm 141:2)

Our ancestors knew the secrets of fragrance. They carefully mixed
balsam, frankincense, myrrh, spikenard, cinnamon, and other precious spices with secret ingredients that would help the smoke
ascend. This powerful practice of incense helped focus our intentions
and create an atmosphere of holiness. The complex and beautiful
fragrance penetrated our consciousness directly and lifted us up into
mystery.

Our prayer can have this same power, lifting us up in beauty,
bringing us into an awareness of the Divine Presence.

WAITING ...

דּוֹם לַיהוה וְהִתְחוֹלֵל לוֹ

Dom l'Yah v'hitcholeil lo.
Be still and wait for God.
(Psalm 37:7)

When I chant the word *dom*, which is a cross between stillness and silence, I arrive at that still, silent place within me. And then I experience the waiting, which is full of movement and dynamic tension. The root of the word *v'hitcholeil*, translated as "wait," is *chol*, which suggests whirling, dancing, writhing, and birthing. And then I come back to stillness. This is the perfect description of my meditation practice. I find that point of stillness, and then my mind fills up with thoughts that take me on a wild ride ... and then I find my way back to stillness.

Each time I find my way back to stillness, I am spiraling deeper, offering up to God the whirling, dancing, writhing, birthing turbulence of my thoughts.

FROM WORLD TO WORLD

מֵעוֹלָם עַד־עוֹלָם אַתָּה אֵל

Mei'olam ad olam atah Eil.
From world to world, You are God.
(Psalm 90:2)

We spend our lives moving from world to world. I might walk into a convenience store and be waiting on line under bright fluorescent lights with three truck drivers and a harried mom. Can I remember God's presence there? In the forest? In the mall? Sitting in front of the computer doing e-mail? Stuck in the airport after my flight is cancelled? At home washing dishes? Walking through a littered, dirty neighborhood? Stepping into a luxury hotel? Driving on a busy freeway?

How do I maintain a loving awareness of God's presence through all the worlds I navigate?

This is a practice of establishing an intention for that unconditional awareness.

ALWAYS WITH YOU

וַאֲנִי תָּמִיד עִמָּךְ

Va'ani tamid imach.
I am always with You.
Though my heart is troubled and I'm filled with dread
I turn to face Your Mystery
Though I've been lost inside my head
I open to Eternity.
(Psalm 73:23)

The highest Jewish ideal is attaining a state of constant *d'veikut*, an uninterrupted awareness of God's presence, even as we are immersed in the experience of this precious world. My addictions and cravings, my doubts, fears, and worries, my plans and regrets often pull me away from that awareness—that *d'veikut*.

This practice is a vow, a commitment, and a rededication to the possibility of *d'veikut*. I chant directly to God, the great underlying and encompassing Mystery ... and through my bold address, I strengthen my commitment to turn again and again toward the divine expanse.

♪

The Daily Psalms

FROM THE PSALM FOR SUNDAY

Psalm 24:9

שְׂאוּ שְׁעָרִים רָאשֵׁיכֶם וּשְׂאוּ פִּתְחֵי עוֹלָם

S'u sh'arim rasheichem, us'u pitchei olam!
Lift up your head, O you gates; lift them up, you everlasting doors!

We are the gates; we are the doorways. God enters the world through us when we "lift up our heads"—when we raise our consciousness. We begin the week with an intention to listen for the call to awareness that lifts us up out of our small concerns into a wide perspective and compassionate responsiveness. By answering that call, we become everlasting doorways between the finite and infinite realms.

FROM THE PSALM FOR MONDAY

Psalm 48:10

דְּמִינוּ אֱלֹהִים חַסְדֶּךָ

Diminu Elohim chasdecha.
Our stillness/silence is Your love, God.

Coming into relationship with God and opening to divine love are perhaps the best ways of becoming authentic and of knowing the true

Self. As we come into this relationship and open to the force of love, God strips us of all artifice. We become naked to ourselves. In relationship to God, the Great Mystery, all the layers of defense fall away; all of our posturing dissolves.

FROM THE PSALM FOR TUESDAY

Psalm 82:8

קוּמָה אֱלֹהִים שָׁפְטָה הָאָרֶץ

Kumah Elohim shaftah ha'aretz.
Arise, God, and judge the land.

As we explore the inner landscape, we find places of shadow—corners of the heart that are unhealed or hidden in shame. We call on the God-force within us to rise up, to reveal the divine perspective so that the entirety of our inner landscape can be bathed in awareness.

FROM THE PSALM FOR WEDNESDAY

Psalm 94:19

בְּרֹב שַׂרְעַפַּי בְּקִרְבִּי תַּנְחוּמֶיךָ יְשַׁעַשְׁעוּ נַפְשִׁי

B'rov sarapai b'kirbi
Tanchumecha y'sha'ashu nafshi.
When worries multiply within me,
Your comfort soothes my soul.

When we become aware of the multitude of voices within and place those concerns into the context of a vast inner spaciousness, then our harried souls can be soothed, comforted, and allowed their freedom.

FROM THE PSALM FOR THURSDAY

Psalm 81:4–5

תִּקְעוּ בַחֹדֶשׁ שׁוֹפָר בַּכֵּסֶה לְיוֹם חַגֵּנוּ
כִּי חֹק לְיִשְׂרָאֵל הוּא מִשְׁפָּט לֵאלֹהֵי יַעֲקֹב

Tiku vachodesh shofar
Ba'keiseh l'yom chageinu
Ki chok l'Yisrael hu mishpat Elohei Ya'akov.

Sound a shofar at the new moon ... at the moment of concealment/
potential for our celebration day. It is a statute for Israel;
it is a rule for Jacob.

We live our lives in the holy cycles of exile and return, forgetting and
remembering, going out from ourselves and returning again to center.
We cycle between being Jacob, the ego struggling to manipulate the
world, to being Israel, the one who encounters God directly. Through
our calendar and festivals, we attune to the cycles of the moon, whose
waxing and waning reflects our own spiritual cycles. As awareness of
those cycles deepens, the circles of our lives become spirals, connecting the mysteries of the universe with our own center.

FROM THE PSALM FOR FRIDAY

Psalm 93:2

נָכוֹן כִּסְאֲךָ מֵאָז מֵעוֹלָם אָתָּה

Nachon kisacha mei'az, mei'olam atah!
Your throne was long ago secured; beyond eternity are You!

As we prepare for Shabbat, we gradually release our grip on personally
mastering this world. No matter how we have struggled, succeeded,

or failed during this past week, today we prepare ourselves now to let go of the illusion of control and surrender our cleverness to the vast Intelligence who has been in charge all along.

FROM THE PSALM FOR SHABBAT

Psalm 92:6

מַה־גָּדְלוּ מַעֲשֶׂיךָ יהוה מְאֹד עָמְקוּ מַחְשְׁבֹתֶיךָ

Mah gadlu ma'asecha Yah, m'od am'ku machsh'votecha!
How great is Your work, O God, how very deep are Your thoughts!

On Shabbat we step outside of the ordinary stream of time; we leave behind the structures of duality in order to drink from the extraordinary river of delight that flows directly from the Source. We set aside our struggles and worries in order to simply appreciate and celebrate life. Shabbat consciousness requires us to embrace a profound paradox. On the one hand, we see the amazing beauty of God's Creation, and in that same vision we encounter the unfathomable suffering and mystery of our world. On Shabbat we let go of our struggle to understand, explain, make excuses, or figure it out. We embrace and accept it all and celebrate existence itself.

Isaiah

THE MIRACLE

וַיָּשֶׂם מִדְבָּרָהּ כְּעֵדֶן וְעַרְבָתָהּ כְּגַן־יהוה

Vayasem midbarah k'eiden, v'arvatah k'gan Adonai.
He transforms her wilderness into delight,
her wasteland into a divine garden.
(Isaiah 51:3)

With this practice, I acknowledge and celebrate the miracle of transformation. Each time I have experienced devastation, it feels as if even the possibility of redemption is a cruel illusion. And then I find myself in Eden, surrounded by beauty, held in God's loving embrace.

DIVINE CONGRATULATIONS

כִּי מָלְאָה צְבָאָהּ

Ki malah tz'va'ah.
Her time of service is fulfilled.
(Isaiah 40:2)

Sometimes I can feel oppressed by the feeling that I'm never finished. I feel the weight of everything that is left undone, and that weight can keep me from receiving the joy of this present moment, which is always complete in itself. This practice allows me to rest in the satisfaction of having completed my whole life up until now. God is congratulating me for my achievements. This is a practice of receiving these divine accolades so that I can rest in fulfillment and be renewed.

AWAKENING THE HEART

הִתְעוֹרְרִי הִתְעוֹרְרִי קוּמִי יְרוּשָׁלַיִם

Hitor'ri, hitor'ri, kumi Y'rushalayim!
Awake, awake, arise Jerusalem!
(Isaiah 51:17)

Sometimes, layers of despair can blanket the heart, and we feel numb. Then the heart must be awakened. This is a practice of igniting the spark of wakefulness at the center of our hearts, the place that is called Jerusalem. With each repetition, we welcome our core vitality and invite that aliveness to shine out into our lives.

BREAKTHROUGH

עִבְרוּ עִבְרוּ בַּשְּׁעָרִים פַּנּוּ דֶּרֶךְ הָעָם

Ivru, ivru bash'arim, panu derech ha'am!
Go through, go through the gates, clear the way of the people!
(Isaiah 62:10)

As I move forward on my spiritual journey, I sometimes encounter thresholds that require my clear will and concerted effort. These are moments where I must be mindful of my old habits and resistances as I call forth my outer allies and inner strength to help me through the gates of transition into my truer self.

COME FOR WATER!

הוֹי כָּל־צָמֵא לְכוּ לַמַּיִם

Hoy! Kol tzamei l'chu lamayim!
All who are thirsty, come for water!
(Isaiah 55:1)

Our spiritual challenge is first to acknowledge our thirst for love, wisdom, comfort, nurturance, and pleasure ... and then to "come for water." Isaiah tells us that even if you feel that you have no money or worth, still you can come and buy this wine and this milk. The wine represents the power of transformation, and the milk is that which nurtures our deepest yearnings. He warns us not to waste our life's energy trying to buy something that in the end won't nurture us. We chant these words to acknowledge our thirst and then to move us toward the true "water," which is as intoxicating as wine and as nurturing as breast milk.

GETTING PERSPECTIVE

עַל הַר־גָּבֹהַּ עֲלִי־לָךְ

Al har gavo'ah ali lach.
Get yourself up upon the high mountain.
(Isaiah 40:9)

Sometimes it's necessary to step out of our narrow dilemmas and climb up upon the high mountain. There we can get a better perspective on our difficulties. From that wider perspective we can also learn to cultivate compassion for ourselves. From the high mountain we can bless the valleys of struggle. Sometimes our new perspective can even spark a sense of humor about our lives. We can return to those valleys inspired, encouraged, and renewed.

PALMISTRY

הֵן עַל־כַּפַּיִם חַקֹּתִיךְ

Hein al kapayim chakotich.
You are engraved on the palm of My hand.
(Isaiah 49:16)

When God says that I am engraved on the palm of the divine hand, I receive this truth as a metaphor for my interconnectedness with all of Creation. My life matters. It is written indelibly on the cosmic map. I am seen by the eyes of Beauty. I am known by the Great Intelligence. I am loved and acknowledged.

FOR IN JOY

כִּי־בְשִׂמְחָה תֵצֵאוּ וּבְשָׁלוֹם תּוּבָלוּן

Ki v'simchah teitzei'u,
Uv'shalom tuvalun.
For in joy will you go out,
In peace be led across the Land,
Mountains and hills will burst into song,
And the trees of the field will clap their hands.
(Clap!)
(Isaiah 55:12)

This is a practice that sends me to my life! It is joy that moves me into the world, and it is joy that opens my ears to the song that Creation is singing.

SHINING

קוּמִי אוֹרִי כִּי־בָא אוֹרֵךְ וּכְבוֹד יהוה עָלַיִךְ זָרָח

Kumi ori ki va oreich uch'vod Adonai alayich zarach.
Arise and shine for your light has come,
and the Glory of God is shining upon you.
(Isaiah 60:1)

I chant these words at sunrise, letting the slanted rays of the sun awaken my own hidden light. The sun becomes my teacher, as I learn to shine. In awakening my own light, I am better able to see and call forth the light in others and to celebrate their light. At the end of the chant, I bring my attention to the breath and imagine breathing into the center of my heart, imagining there a flame. With each breath, I let the flame glow brighter. The light fills my inner spaces and then shines out into the world. How far can you shine your inner radiance? With practice, your light can radiate out forever, while still being anchored in the light source at your core.

SPACIOUSNESS

הַרְחִיבִי מָקוֹם אָהֳלֵךְ

Harchivi m'kom ohaleich.
Enlarge the place of your tent.
(Isaiah 54:2)

In dealing with emotional or physical pain, I have noticed a pattern of contraction. I become overwhelmed because the pain takes up the entire space of my awareness. I have found that even when I can't "make the pain stop," it is possible to create a spaciousness around the sensation, so that in that very large space of my awareness, the pain can be experienced as just a small part of who I am. When I can become spacious, "enlarging the place of my tent," then the pain becomes manageable and I am not overwhelmed. With this practice of spaciousness, I experience the vastness of my true Being. Instead of contracting around the pain, I expand my awareness into that spaciousness. The expansive harmonies really help.

PEACE LIKE A RIVER

הִנְנִי נֹטֶה־אֵלֶיהָ כְּנָהָר שָׁלוֹם

Hin'ni, noteh eileha k'nahar shalom.
Here I am, extending peace to her like a river.
(Isaiah 66:12)

This is a practice of receiving through our receptive presence ("Here I am") the divine flow, and then immediately giving that gift to the world that is before us. The gift that pours through us is given with "no strings attached." We become an extension of the divine river, flowing unself-consciously into our world. In becoming fully present, we find our true generosity. Peace, a sense of wholeness, is received and given at once.

DELIGHT

אָז תִּתְעַנַּג עַל־יהוה

Az titanag al Havayah.
Then you will delight in God (being itself!).
(Isaiah 58:14)

The prophet Isaiah admonishes us to live a life of justice and love. He warns us that our complacency and complicity in the injustice of our time will obstruct the divine flow. Then he tells us about the treasures of delight that await us:

"If only you would truly celebrate Shabbat, and put down your business, your buying and selling and bargaining and scheming with the resources that were never yours to begin with, if you would delight in the restful sanity of Pure Being, then you are delighting in Me, participating in the holiness of God. Then I will set you on the high places, so you can get some perspective, so you can truly enjoy the precious inheritance of the life I have given you."

I chant these words (using *Havayah*, a word that points us toward Being itself, to stand for the unpronounceable *YodHeiVavHei*) and let waves of delight wash me up onto the highest shores, where I can celebrate the persistent radiance of Being that shines out through the ever-changing content of my life.

HERALDS OF PEACE

מַה־נָּאווּ עַל־הֶהָרִים רַגְלֵי מְבַשֵּׂר מַשְׁמִיעַ שָׁלוֹם

Mah navu al heharim raglei m'vaseir mashmia shalom.
Oh, how lovely—our footsteps on the mountain;
we are messengers;
we are heralds of peace.
(Isaiah 52:7)

This chant came to me as I opened to an intention for pilgrimage to the Holy Land. As I chanted these words from Isaiah, I felt a definite shift from being a victim of circumstance to being a "messenger"— empowered, deployed, inspired, and open to the flow of Mystery. With each step on the mountain, I plant blessing (the goodness that is in me); and with each step, I receive the blessing of "the Place," that I might take that blessing home and share it with all.

THROUGH THE WATERS

כִּי־תַעֲבֹר בַּמַּיִם אִתְּךָ־אָנִי וּבַנְּהָרוֹת לֹא יִשְׁטְפוּךָ

Ki ta'avor bamayim it'cha ani, uvan'harot lo yisht'fucha.
When you pass through the waters,
I am with you, yes, I am with you.
I won't let the rivers overwhelm you,
I will be with you.
(Isaiah 43:2)

The waters represent the times of transition, as we pass from slavery to freedom, from womb through birth into our lives, from life through death into the sea of Oneness or into the embrace of the Beloved. The important thing is not to fear, to know that God's presence is and has always been with you ... through every transition, through every transformation.

COMFORT

נַחֲמוּ נַחֲמוּ עַמִּי

Nachamu, nachamu ami!
Comfort, comfort my people!
(Isaiah 40:1)

These words become the channel for the healing flow of comfort. As I chant them, I can direct that flow in ways that open my heart profoundly. I begin by sending comfort out into the world, imagining those in need receiving and benefiting from this flow. As the power of the chant builds, I begin chanting to specific people who are in need of comfort. Though my intention is to channel divine love, in the process, the space of my own heart is softening, expanding, and healing. If we are chanting this in a group, at some point I ask us to open our eyes and chant this to each other. And finally, in the last phase of the chant, we close our eyes and allow our voices to become the vehicle for God's chant to us. We open our hearts to receive this gift. In the silence afterward, we can continue the practice by breathing the energy of comfort into our hearts and directing this flow to exactly the places of wounding, fear, hardness, or shame that lie buried within us.

GARMENTS OF SALVATION

שׂוֹשׂ אָשִׂישׂ בַּיהוה תָּגֵל נַפְשִׁי בֵּאלֹהַי
כִּי הִלְבִּישַׁנִי בִּגְדֵי־יֶשַׁע

Sos asis badonai tageil nafshi beilohai,
ki hilbishani bigdei yesha.
I will rejoice in God, who has dressed me
in the garments of salvation.
(Isaiah 61:10)

The prophet Isaiah compares us to the bridegroom and the bride, decked out in our finery, bejeweled and shining in glory. What if each morning we claimed our rightful place of dignity, splendor, and brilliance? This is a practice of rejoicing in our inheritance. This is a practice of matching up our outer countenance with our royal inner radiance.

MINDFULNESS

שִׁמְעוּ שָׁמוֹעַ אֵלַי וְאִכְלוּ־טוֹב

Shim'u shamo'a eilai, v'ichlu tov.
If you really listen to Me, then you will eat what is good.
(And your souls will delight in richness.)
(Isaiah 55:2)

In the language of Judaism, listening to God (really listening!) means letting go of distraction, quieting your inner tumult, tuning in to the "still, small voice," opening to the Divine Presence in this very moment. In the language of Buddhism, this is called "mindfulness."

So many of us experience anxiety around food. If it's plentiful and good, "Will I eat too much?" If it's scarce, "Will there be enough?" If it's not what we prefer, "Will I be nourished and satisfied?" To bring a calm clarity in regard to what we eat, but also what we consume in general (what we buy and how we use our precious resources), is at the heart of a holy life.

Isaiah reminds us to listen, to really pay attention, to come into a state of expansive, receptive calm. Only then will we consume in just the right measure and be delighted in the richness of our lives.

SEND ME!

אֶת־מִי אֶשְׁלַח וּמִי יֵלֶךְ־לָנוּ הִנְנִי שְׁלָחֵנִי

Et mi eshlach umi yeilech lanu?
Hin'ni sh'lacheini.
Whom shall I send, and who shall go for us?
Here I am. Send me.
(Isaiah 6:8)

This is a practice of listening to "the call" and responding. When I hear the question, "Who shall go for *us?*" I wonder who that "*us*" might be. As I step forth to fulfill my unique mission, I am doing this first for myself (because I must) and then for all those who need to hear my voice, for all those who have not yet found their voice, for all those who do not feel heard and have not found their way into the great conversation. I come into the fullness of my presence and then go forth for all of us. We depend on each other. My going forth will inspire others to also find their own voice, mission, power, and destiny.

As you develop this practice, I suggest you begin by just chanting the question, allowing the answer to well up within you. Then let your willingness to be present and be deployed burst forth in response to "the call."

A Few More Practices

ELEMENTS, DIRECTIONS, SPIRIT BUDDIES

PURIFICATION BREATH PRACTICE

This practice was taught to me by Paul Ray and comes out of the Western Sufi Tradition of Hazrat Inayat Khan.

Earth

Breath pattern: inhale through nose, exhale through nose.

As you exhale, breathe all impurities down into the earth, which uses them as compost. Trace the energy with your hands reaching down, sending all your excess tension, worry, or impurities into the earth. On the inhale, reach into the earth and pull up delicious earth energy through your body. Trace the flow up until you reach the top of your head, filling with the strength and vitality of earth.

Water

Breath pattern: inhale through nose, exhale through mouth.

Imagine a powerful waterfall that you've actually experienced (I remember myself on the *Maid of the Mist* at Niagara Falls). Reach up into the waterfall, and as you let the force of water enter you, inhale and pull it down. When your hands get to shoulder height, begin the exhale, making a water sound. Continue pushing your hands down on the exhale, imagining that the downward flow continues all the way through your body. Hold the breath out and reach up again into the waterfall.

Fire

Breath pattern: inhale through mouth, exhale through nose.

Begin by rubbing your hands together to make a fire. Place the fire in your hands on each chakra, charging it up, igniting the fire in each energy center with quick small inhales until you reach the crown. You can imagine colors at each chakra, brightening and becoming vivid as the fire lights it up. On the exhale, send your hands up and then out to your sides, imagining that you are radiating the light of the sun.

Air

Breath pattern: inhale through mouth, exhale through mouth.

Inhale holding your fingertips at the heart. Exhale opening your arms wide to each side, imagining the space between all your molecules expanding, sending your essence out to the edges of the universe. Inhale back to the center.

THE FOUR DIRECTIONS

As you face each direction, it is good to bring to mind the qualities of that direction and breathe them into your body, as well as welcoming the four archangels. The following are the qualities I associate with each of the directions and the angels:

East

ELEMENT: AIR

Qualities: the rising sun, birth, new beginnings, spring, the mind, thoughts and ideals, all winged creatures, the power of wind, communication, breath, voice, poetry, inspiration, boundaries, song, vision and visualization, fragrance

ARCHANGEL: URIEL
Qualities: light, vision, direction

South

ELEMENT: FIRE
Qualities: energy, spirit, heat, the will, summer, healing and destroy-ing, purification, the power of the sun, passion, relationships, courage and daring, children, desire, focus, transformation, burning incense

ARCHANGEL: MICHA'EL
Qualities: love, trust

West

ELEMENT: WATER
Qualities: emotions, sexuality, feeling and feelings, intuition, setting sun, dreamtime and trance journeys, the flow of life and emotional flow, menstruation, joy and sorrow, tears, laughter, the womb, the unconscious, source of all life, divination, the twilight, autumn, all creatures of the water, connection with the moon as it affects the waters of the world

ARCHANGEL: RAFA'EL
Qualities: healing, wisdom, compassion

North

ELEMENT: EARTH
Qualities: the things that are manifest on the earth, food and all things we eat, the body, sensation, growth, nature, knowledge, dark-ness, secrecy, the treasures of the earth, money, abundance, rocks and crystals, reproduction, winter, midnight, death, our ancestors, sleep, drums and dancing, animals, the shelter and the home, being grounded

ARCHANGEL: GAVRI'EL
Qualities: strength of God, spiritual warrior

SPIRIT BUDDIES

The Kabbalists of S'fat began their prayer with the following intention: "For the sake of the union of the Blessed Holy One with the *Shechinah*, I stand here, ready to take upon myself the *mitzvah*, 'You shall love your fellow human being as yourself,' and by this merit may I open my mouth."

This intention formed the foundation and measure for all practices. Our practice of Spirit Buddies is the concrete embodiment of this abstract intention. The daily practice of kindness, compassion, and service to each other helps keep us from the dangers of inflation, isolation, delusion, or greediness. We get to check in with our own souls in the presence of a discerning friend. We can also dedicate the energy that we receive from our practice to our partners. This gesture of dedicating energy in service has the effect of opening our channels further for more and finer energy to flow.

The practice of Spirit Buddies requires us to search beneath the layers of personality and invite the pure soul/essence of our partner to be revealed. We do this through the practice of presence. This means letting go of judgment, letting go of the need to "fix" our partner or offer solutions. It means co-creating the safe and sacred space in which healing, self-realization, and transformation can occur. It means "trusting the process."

Spirit buddies
    ... become anchors and grounding for one another
    ... create the container for practice for each other
    ... pray for each other
    ... offer one another as windows into the infinite divine expanse

Through our spirit buddies we are loved unconditionally by the "Great Love."

Our spirit buddies listen with warm delighted attention, witnessing our dreams and commitments, taking us seriously, and holding us accountable to our promises. In this relationship we experience "safe space," making possible the leap into the unknown. We see the strength, essence, and potential of our spirit buddies and share our vision with them; sending them with confidence and joy to the work before them.

May this *mitzvah* of love be fulfilled for the sake of the unification within ourselves, between us, and through all the worlds.

Spirit Buddy Guidelines

SACRED SPACE = SAFE SPACE

- Create sacred space between you with a chant, meditation, blessing, or rhythm that moves you from thinking/figuring-it-out mind to heart space.

- Listen to your spirit buddy with respect and openness, delighting in his uniqueness.

- Encourage your spirit buddy to say what's in her heart.

- Honor confidentiality.

- Remember that you can't judge and serve at the same time. So since we're here to serve one another, continue to let go of all judgment.

- Don't interrupt or give advice or try to fix things. Don't say, "That reminds me of ..." and then tell your own story.

- Allow for silence to deepen between you. Tune in to the breath of your spirit buddy.

- Make sure each of you gets equal time for expression.

- Before you go to sleep each night, pray for your spirit buddies. Your prayer can be as simple as visualizing them shining with their particular and beautiful light or calling on God, the Great Mystery, to let the very best unfold for them for the period of time you are together.

- Before the end of your time together, express your intention for deepening or expanding your spiritual practice (prayer, meditation, *tikkun olam* work, and study), inspired by what you've been doing. Witness each other's commitments.

THE
MUSICAL
NOTATIONS

Introduction to the Musical Notations

I have been blessed to be the channel for an abundant flow of melodies, which have found their way across the world. Sometimes I get letters from travelers who write and say, "Shefa, I heard your song being sung in Moscow! In Havana! In Uruguay!" Or I travel somewhere and hear a chant I composed twenty years ago and the community is sure that it is *"miSinai"* (brought down from Mount Sinai with the Torah) ... and they'll even tell me I'm singing it wrong! Or sitting in a pew at B'nai Jeshurun in New York City, I join over one thousand worshipers in singing my chant *Mah Gadlu*.

I love it ... and yet, there is a deep yearning in me to dedicate the power of these melodies as spiritual practices that can evolve over a lifetime and keep taking us deeper and deeper. The words and melody are powerful by themselves, but they are just the surface.

I am so grateful to be able to present these melodies to you in the context of a book about the magic of Hebrew chant. I hope that you will use them as incantations or as vehicles for transport as you explore the far reaches of consciousness and the depths of the heart.

You can think of each of these melodies as a *Mishkan*, a place where the Divine Presence can be invited to enter. In building the *Mishkan*, we must gather up all of our talent, power, intuition, skills, vision, imagination, and musicality and dedicate all of the beauty and force of the chant to the possibility of creating a home for *Shechinah*.

The *Mishkan* is portable; we carry it with us through the wilderness of our lives so that we will always have access to the inner mysteries.

God says, "*V'asu li mikdash v'shachanti b'tocham*. Make for me a holy place so that I can dwell among, between, and within you" (Exodus 25:8). In the book of Exodus, we find detailed instruction for the building of the *Mishkan*. Only those with willing, generous hearts are allowed to contribute to this endeavor. We bring the most exquisite colors, jewels, fragrance ... all of our finest artistry to this project, and then all of this beauty is dedicated as a nexus between human and Divine, between heaven and earth. In the end, the important part is not the outer form, but what is inside, for that is where God speaks to us. The farther within you get, the more holy is the space.

As you learn these melodies, you can use their outer forms to send you to that holy innerness.

These exquisitely detailed *Mishkan* texts of Exodus are interrupted by a story that is meant as a warning for our ancestors and for us. The people get nervous when Moses is up on the mountain for such a long time, and they ask Aaron to make them a golden calf, so they can worship. This turns out to be a big mistake with dire consequences.

The Golden Calf became synonymous with idolatry. And idolatry is understood by our tradition as the root of all our mistakes.

Well, when you think about it, what is the difference between a *Mishkan* and a Golden Calf? While the *Mishkan* is meant to send us to the beyond that is within, the Golden Calf is solid, existing of and for itself. We supply the gold, but then the Calf seems to take on a life of its own. Aaron describes the process, saying, "I cast the gold into the fire and out came this calf!" (Exodus 32:24). The Calf has no interior space. It glorifies itself. It is "full of itself." It represents the most dangerous hindrance in the life of spiritual practice: that of worshiping and staying attached to the forms, rather than allowing those forms to send us inward to the essence, as is their purpose.

The difference between building a *Mishkan* and building a Golden Calf is sometimes very subtle. Sometimes I really think I'm building a *Mishkan*, but then my habitual egoic manipulations ... my ambitions, attachments, pride, vanity, or arrogance seep in. Quite suddenly I find myself in the presence of a very beautiful and seductive Golden Calf. When I realize this, I can usually find my way back to *Mishkan* and again be sent to the infinite mystery within.

As you learn these chants, or create your own, just remember to keep asking, "Am I building a *Mishkan* or a Golden Calf?"

In composing a chant, I don't take a text and put it to music. I become intimate with a text, and the music is born out of this intimacy. I hope that when you chant these sacred words, these simple melodies, you too will be drawn into an intimate relationship with the text, with the ancestors who left these words for us as gifts to unwrap, with your own deepest desires, and with God, the Great Mystery, who is waiting for us with open arms.

As you learn these melodies, let them live inside you. The notes are just the bare bones. It's up to you to give them flesh and blood and spirit, so feel free to interpret them as you wish. (If you'd like to hear my interpretation, you can find most of these on my website: www.RabbiShefaGold.com). It will be your responsibility to learn the notes carefully before you decide to improvise. What is sometimes called "folk process" is often just carelessness.

Once someone asked Reb Schlomo Carlebach if it was OK to change a melody he had composed. After all, what did it matter? Reb Schlomo answered with a story:

> A young man went to a party and met the most beautiful woman he had ever encountered. She was perfect—sweet and smart, sexy and loving. She gave him her telephone number. When the young man got home he looked at the number and said, "Hmmm, I don't like this number so much ... I think I'll change this '3' to a '4.' I think this number is better."

May these melodies connect you to the Beloved. May they become the vehicles for the best in you to be carried into the world.

Liturgy

AWAKENING
מוֹדֶה אֲנִי לְפָנֶיךָ
Modeh ani l'fanecha.
I gratefully acknowledge Your face.
(from the morning liturgy)

Shefa Gold

CLEARING THE WAY
אָנָּא, בְּכֹחַ גְּדֻלַּת יְמִינְךָ, תַּתִּיר צְרוּרָה
Ana b'choach g'dulat y'min'cha tatir tz'rurah.
Please, with the strength of your right hand, untie our tangles.

Shefa Gold

BETROTHAL:
THE SEVEN CHANNELS OF COMMITMENT

וְאֵרַשְׂתִּיךְ לִי לְעוֹלָם

וְאֵרַשְׂתִּיךְ לִי בְּצֶדֶק

וּבְמִשְׁפָּט

וּבְחֶסֶד

וּבְרַחֲמִים

וְאֵרַשְׂתִּיךְ לִי בֶּאֱמוּנָה

וְיָדַעַתְּ אֶת־יהוה

V'eirastich li l'olam, v'eirastich li b'tzedek, uv'mishpat, uv'chesed,
uv'rachamim. V'eirastich li be'emunah, v'yada'at et Yah.

I will betroth you to Me forever, I will betroth you to Me with justice,
and with impeccability, and with love, and with compassion.
I will betroth you to Me in faith. And then you will know
[be intimate with] God.
(Hosea 2:21–22)

Shefa Gold

GRATEFULNESS

אוֹדְךָ בְּעוֹד תִּהְיֶה נִשְׁמַת אֱלוֹהַּ בִּי

Odach b'od t'h'yeh nishmat Eloha bi.

I will thank You as long as the divine breath is in me.

(Solomon ibn Gabirol, eleventh-century Spanish poet and philosopher)

Shefa Gold

O WONDROUS HEALER

רוֹפֵא כָל בָּשָׂר וּמַפְלִיא לַעֲשׂוֹת

Rofei chol basar umafli la'asot!

O wondrous Healer of all flesh!

(from the morning liturgy)

MORNING BLESSINGS

O God, who sets the captive free, who opens the eyes of the blind to see,
who heals the lame and loves the just. I will praise Yah with my life!
(Psalm 146:7–8, 146:2)

אֲהַלְלָה יהוה בְּחַיָּי

Ahal'lah Yah b'chayai!
I will praise Yah with my life!
(Psalm 146:2)

יהוה מַתִּיר אֲסוּרִים

יהוה   פֹּקֵחַ עִוְרִים

יהוה זֹקֵף כְּפוּפִים

יהוה אֹהֵב צַדִּיקִים

Adonai matir asurim, Adonai pokei'ach ivrim,
Adonai zokeif k'fufim, Adonai oheiv tzadikim.

HOLY SPEECH

בָּרוּךְ שֶׁאָמַר וְהָיָה הָעוֹלָם

Baruch she'amar v'hayah ha'olam.

Blessed is the One who speaks the world into being.

Shefa Gold

GATHERING IN

וַהֲבִיאֵנוּ לְשָׁלוֹם מֵאַרְבַּע כַּנְפוֹת הָאָרֶץ

V'havi'einu l'shalom mei'arba kanfot ha'aretz.

(Bring us in peace from the four corners of the earth.)

Uriel! Micha'el! Rafa'el! Gavri'el!

Shefa Gold

ASHREI

אַשְׁרֵי יוֹשְׁבֵי בֵיתֶךָ עוֹד יְהַלְלוּךָ

Ashrei yosh'vei veitecha od y'hal'lucha.

Happy are those who dwell in Your house; they keep on praising.

(Psalm 84:5)

Shefa Gold

MANIFESTING TORAH

לִלְמֹד וּלְלַמֵּד, לִשְׁמֹר וְלַעֲשׂוֹת וּלְקַיֵּם

Lilmod ul'lameid lishmor v'la'asot ul'kayeim.

To learn and to teach, to uphold and to practice and to manifest.

Shefa Gold

GOODNESS

הוֹדוּ לַיהוה כִּי־טוֹב כִּי לְעוֹלָם חַסְדּוֹ

Hodu ladonai ki tov, ki l'olam chasdo.

Give thanks to God for essential goodness; His kindness endures forever.

(Psalm 136:1)

SIM SHALOM

שִׂים שָׁלוֹם טוֹבָה וּבְרָכָה, חֵן וָחֶסֶד וְרַחֲמִים

Sim shalom tovah uv'rachah chein vachesed v'rachamim!

Grant us peace, goodness, grace, love, and compassion!

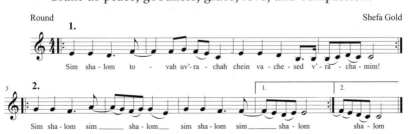

EYES, HEARTS, AND HANDS

וְהָאֵר עֵינֵינוּ בְּתוֹרָתֶךָ, וְדַבֵּק לִבֵּנוּ בְּמִצְוֹתֶיךָ

V'ha'eir eineinu b'Toratecha, v'dabeik libeinu b'mitzvotecha.

Enlighten our eyes with Your Torah,

and connect our hearts to Your *mitzvot.*

Shefa Gold

SHEHECHEYANU:
A MEDITATION ON THIS MOMENT
שֶׁהֶחֱיָנוּ וְקִיְּמָנוּ וְהִגִּיעָנוּ לַזְּמַן הַזֶּה

Shehecheyanu, v'kiy'manu, v'higianu laz'man hazeh.

O Mystery, Grace unfolding, O Miracle, it's You alone,

O Mystery, Grace unfolding, O Miracle, who brings us Home.

UNIFYING THE HEART
וְיַחֵד לְבָבֵנוּ לְאַהֲבָה וּלְיִרְאָה אֶת שְׁמֶךָ

V'yacheid l'vaveinu l'ahavah ul'yirah et sh'mecha.

Unify our hearts to love and to be in awe of Your name/essence.

O PURE SOUL

אֱלֹהַי, נְשָׁמָה שֶׁנָּתַתָּ בִּי טְהוֹרָה הִיא

Elohai n'shamah shenatata bi t'horah hi.

O pure soul, in you I see endless possibility!

(liturgy)

Shefa Gold

INCANTATION FOR HOPEFULNESS

לִישׁוּעָתְךָ קִוִּיתִי יהוה; קִוִּיתִי יהוה לִישׁוּעָתְךָ;

יהוה לִישׁוּעָתְךָ קִוִּיתִי

Lishuatcha kiviti Yah; kiviti Yah lishuatcha; Yah lishuatcha kiviti.

I wait/hope for Your salvation.

(Genesis 49:18; bedtime liturgy)

Shefa Gold

UNDER THE WINGS

וַאֲנִי מָצָאתִי מְנוּחָה מִתַּחַת כַּנְפֵי הַשְּׁכִינָה

Va'ani matzati m'nuchah mitachat kanfei HaShechinah.

Under the wings of *Shechinah* I have found my rest.

Shefa Gold

CHANUKAH CHANT

Let the flame be kindled within me, let Your love burn bright,
I hunger for Your light, I hunger for Your light.

Shefa Gold

FREEDOM AND HOMECOMING:
A CHANT FOR ROSH HASHANAH

תְּקַע בְּשׁוֹפָר גָּדוֹל לְחֵרוּתֵנוּ, וְשָׂא נֵס לְקַבֵּץ גָּלֻיּוֹתֵינוּ

T'ka b'shofar gadol l'cheiruteinu, v'sa neis l'kabeitz galuyoteinu.

Sound the great shofar for our freedom,

and raise the banner as we all come home.

Shefa Gold

PILGRIMAGE

לִירוּשָׁלַיִם עִירְךָ בְּרַחֲמִים תָּשׁוּב

Li'Y'rushalayim ircha, b'rachamim tashuv.

To Jerusalem Your city, with compassion you will return.

(from the daily *Amidah*)

Shefa Gold

ALL IS ONE

אַתָּה אֶחָד וְשִׁמְךָ אֶחָד

Atah Echad v'shimcha Echad.

You are One and Your name/essence is One.

מְנוּחַת אַהֲבָה וּנְדָבָה

M'nuchat ahavah un'davah.

Rest of love and generosity.

מְנוּחַת אֱמֶת וֶאֱמוּנָה

M'nuchat emet ve'emunah.

Rest of truth and faith.

מְנוּחַת שָׁלוֹם וְשַׁלְוָה

M'nuchat shalom v'shalvah.

Rest of peace and serenity.

מְנוּחָה שְׁלֵמָה שֶׁאַתָּה רוֹצֶה בָּה

M'nuchat sh'leimah she'atah rotzeh bah.

A perfect rest in which You find favor.

Shefa Gold

Verse 3: *M'nuchat emet ve'emunah.* All is One.
Verse 4: *M'nuchat shalom v'shalvah.* All is One.
Verse 5: *M'nuchat sh'leimah she'atah rotzeh bah.* All is One.
Verse 6: *Atah Echad v'shimcha Echad.* All is One.

ROLLING

גּוֹלֵל אוֹר מִפְּנֵי חֹשֶׁךְ, וְחֹשֶׁךְ מִפְּנֵי אוֹר

Goleil or mipnei choshech, v'choshech mipnei or.

Rolling away light before darkness, darkness before light.

(from the evening liturgy)

Shefa Gold

USHPIZIN

תִּיבוּ תִּיבוּ אוּשְׁפִּיזִין עִלָּאִין,

תִּיבוּ תִּיבוּ אוּשְׁפִּיזִין קַדִּישִׁין

Tivu tivu ushpizin ila'in, tivu tivu ushpizin kadishin.

Sit down, sit down, exalted guests; sit down, sit down, holy guests!

Round   Shefa Gold

LIFE AND DEATH

כִּי אַתָּה מְחַיֵּה הַמֵּתִים וּמֵמִית חַיִּים

Ki atah m'chayeih hameitim, umeimit chayim.

For You revive the dead and bring death to the living.

(from the *Taharah* liturgy)

Shefa Gold

BALANCING WILL AND SURRENDER

עָזִּי וְזִמְרָת יָהּ וַיְהִי־לִי לִישׁוּעָה

Ozi v'zimrat Yah vay'hi li lishuah.

My strength (balanced) with the song of God will be my salvation.

(Psalm 118:14; Exodus 15:2)

Shefa Gold

THE MEDICINE FOR OVERWHELM: *TACHANUN*

וְהוּא רַחוּם

V'hu rachum.

It is compassionate.

נִבְהֲלָה נַפְשֵׁנוּ מֵרֹב עִצְבוֹנֵנוּ,

Nivhalah nafsheinu meirov itzvoneinu. (2x)

אַל תִּשְׁכָּחֵנוּ נֶצַח

Al tishkacheinu netzach. (2x)

קוּמָה וְהוֹשִׁיעֵנוּ, כִּי חָסִינוּ בָךְ

Kumah v'hoshi'einu ki chasinu vach! (2x)

Our soul trembles, overwhelmed by sadness,

do not forget us, arise and save us, for we take shelter in You!

Shefa Gold

THE SAVING POWER OF GOD-CONSCIOUSNESS

שִׁירוּ לַיהוה כָּל־הָאָרֶץ
בַּשְּׂרוּ מִיּוֹם־אֶל־יוֹם יְשׁוּעָתוֹ

Shiru l'Adonai kol ha'aretz, bas'ru miyom el yom y'shuato!
Shiru la'Shechinah kol ha'aretz, bas'ru miyom el yom y'shuata!
Hallelu, Hallelu, Hallelu, Hallelu, Hallelu, HalleluYah!
Sing to the Lord, everyone on earth, announce His salvation daily!
Sing to the indwelling Divine Presence, announce Her salvation daily!
Praise Yah!
(1 Chronicles 16:23; Psalm 96:2)

Shefa Gold

STANDING BEFORE THE MYSTERY

דַּע לִפְנֵי מִי אַתָּה עוֹמֵד

Da lifnei mi atah omeid!
Know before whom you stand!
(adapted from Talmud, *B'rachot* 28b)

Shefa Gold

SUKKAT SHALOM

הַשְׁכִּיבֵנוּ יהוה אֱלֹהֵינוּ לְשָׁלוֹם,

וְהַעֲמִידֵנוּ מַלְכֵּנוּ לְחַיִּים טוֹבִים וּלְשָׁלוֹם,

וּפְרוֹשׁ עָלֵינוּ סֻכַּת שְׁלוֹמֶךָ

Hashkiveinu Adonai Eloheinu l'shalom.

V'ha'amideinu Malkeinu, l'chayim tovim ul'shalom.

Uf'ros Aleinu sukkat sh'lomecha.

O Lord, our God, let us lie down in peace.

Our Sovereign, raise us up again to good life and peace.

Spread over us a shelter of peace.

(liturgy)

Shefa Gold

THE MAJESTY OF NURTURE
לְתַקֵּן עוֹלָם בְּמַלְכוּת שַׁדַּי
L'takein olam b'malchut Shaddai.
Healing the world through the Majesty of Nurture.
(liturgy)

Shefa Gold

BLESSING OF MY SOUL
בָּרְכִי נַפְשִׁי אֶת יהוה, הַלְלוּיָהּ
Bar'chi nafshi et Adonai, halleluyah!
Bless the place of Sovereignty, O my soul!

Round   Shefa Gold

BEINI UVEIN

בֵּינִי וּבֵין בְּנֵי יִשְׂרָאֵל אוֹת הִוא לְעֹלָם
כִּי־שֵׁשֶׁת יָמִים עָשָׂה יהוה אֶת־הַשָּׁמַיִם
וְאֶת־הָאָרֶץ וּבַיּוֹם הַשְּׁבִיעִי שָׁבַת וַיִּנָּפַשׁ

Beini uvein b'nei Yisrael ot hi l'olam ki sheishet yamim asah Adonai et
hashamayim v'et ha'aretz uvayom hash'vi'i shavat vayinafash!

Let it be a sign between us forever, for in six days I made everything
and on the seventh day I made Shabbat, I made Shabbat for my Soul!
(Exodus 31:17)

Shefa Gold

GOING UP WITH JOY

וְשָׁם נָשִׁיר שִׁיר חָדָשׁ וּבִרְנָנָה נַעֲלֶה

V'sham nashir shir chadash uvir'nanah na'aleh.

And there we will sing a new song; with joy we will go up.

(from *Tzur Mishelo*)

SURRENDER

בְּיָדְךָ אַפְקִיד רוּחִי, בְּעֵת אִישָׁן וְאָעִירָה
וְעִס רוּחִי גְּוִיָּתִי, יהוה לִי וְלֹא אִירָא

B'yad'cha af'kid ruchi, b'ayt ishan v'a-ira,
v'im ruchi g'vi-ati, Adonai li v'lo ira.

Into Your hand I entrust my spirit, when I sleep and when I awaken,
when spirit is with my body, God is with me; I will not fear.
(the last lines of *Adon Olam*, attributed to Solomon ibn Gavirol)

Scripture

KNOWING BEAUTY AND
FINDING THE UNIVERSE

אֶת־הַכֹּל עָשָׂה יָפֶה בְעִתּוֹ גַּם אֶת־הָעֹלָם נָתַן בְּלִבָּם

Et hakol asah yafeh v'ito, gam et ha'olam natan b'libam.

[God] makes everything beautiful in its time,
and also hides the universe in their hearts.

(Ecclesiastes 3:11)

AN OATH OF FRIENDSHIP

הִנֵּה יהוה בֵּינִי וּבֵינְךָ עַד־עוֹלָם

Hineih Yah beini uveincha, ad olam!

Here is God between me and you forever!

(1 Samuel 20:23)

HOLY GROUND

אַדְמַת־קֹדֶשׁ הוּא

Admat kodesh hu!

It is holy ground!

(Exodus 3:5)

GO WITHIN US

יֵלֶךְ־נָא אֲדֹנָי בְּקִרְבֵּנוּ

Yeilech na Adonai b'kirbeinu.

Please, God, go within us.

(Exodus 34:9)

ASCENDING

וְעַל בָּמוֹתַי יַדְרִכֵנִי

V'al bamotai yadricheini.

He prepares a path for me upon the high places.

(Habakkuk 3:19)

OPENING TO THE SOURCE OF FLOW

וְנָהָר יֹצֵא מֵעֵדֶן לְהַשְׁקוֹת אֶת־הַגָּן

V'nahar yotzei mei'Eden, l'hashkot et hagan.

A river comes forth from Eden to water the garden.

(Genesis 2:10)

Shefa Gold

BELOVED

אֲנִי לְדוֹדִי וְדוֹדִי לִי

Ani l'Dodi v'Dodi li.

I am my Beloved's and my Beloved is mine.

(Song of Songs 6:3)

Shefa Gold

HOW BEAUTIFUL!

הִנָּךְ יָפָה רַעְיָתִי הִנָּךְ יָפָה

Hinach yafah rayati, hinach yafah!

How beautiful You are, my Friend, how beautiful!

(Song of Songs 1:15)

IN HIS SHADE

בְּצִלּוֹ חִמַּדְתִּי וְיָשַׁבְתִּי וּפִרְיוֹ מָתוֹק לְחִכִּי

B'tzilo chimadti v'yashavti, ufiryo matok l'chiki.

In His shade I delight to sit, tasting His sweet fruit.

(Song of Songs 2:3)

COME, MY BELOVED
לְכָה דוֹדִי נֵצֵא הַשָּׂדֶה
L'cha Dodi neitzeih hasadeh.
Come, my Beloved, let us go out to the field.
(Song of Songs 7:12)

Shefa Gold

LOVING "THIS"

זֶה דוֹדִי וְזֶה רֵעִי

Zeh Dodi v'zeh Rei'i.

This is my Beloved; this is my Friend.

(Song of Songs 5:16)

Shefa Gold

AN APPETITE FOR HOLINESS

וּבָא בְּכָל־אַוַּת נַפְשׁוֹ אֶל־הַמָּקוֹם

U-va-a-a b'chol avat nafsho el HaMakom.

And he [the Levite] shall come with all the desire of his soul to the Place.

(Deuteronomy 18:6)

HOW AWESOME!

מַה־נּוֹרָא הַמָּקוֹם הַזֶּה

Mah nora HaMakom hazeh!

How awesome is this place!

(Genesis 28:17)

Shefa Gold

THE REWARDS OF OUR ATTENTION

נֹצֵר תְּאֵנָה יֹאכַל פִּרְיָהּ

Notzeir t'einah yochal piryah.

Those who guard the truth will be nourished by her fruit.

(Proverbs 27:18)

Shefa Gold

LISTENING TO THE VOICE OF WISDOM #1

הֲלֹא־חָכְמָה תִקְרָא וּתְבוּנָה תִּתֵּן קוֹלָהּ

Halo chochmah tikra, ut'vunah titein kolah!

Isn't it Wisdom calling and Understanding raising her voice!

(Proverbs 8:1)

Shefa Gold

LISTENING TO THE VOICE OF WISDOM #2

אַשְׁרֵי אָדָם שֹׁמֵעַ לִי

Ashrei adam shomei'a li.

Happy is the one who listens to me.

(Proverbs 8:34)

Shefa Gold

SOUL LIGHT

נֵר יהוה נִשְׁמַת אָדָם חֹפֵשׂ כָּל חַדְרֵי בָטֶן

Neir Adonai nishmat adam chofeis kol chadrei vaten.

My soul is the flame of God that searches the inner chambers.

(Proverbs 20:27)

AWAKENING COMPASSION

מִי יָכִין לָעֹרֵב צֵידוֹ כִּי־יְלָדָו אֶל־אֵל יְשַׁוֵּעוּ

Mi yachin la'oreiv tzeido ki y'ladav el El y'shavei'u?

Who prepares nourishment for the raven

when its young ones call out to God?

(Job 38:41)

PLANTING AND HARVEST

וְנָטְעוּ כְרָמִים וְשָׁתוּ אֶת־יֵינָם

וְעָשׂוּ גַנּוֹת וְאָכְלוּ אֶת־פְּרִיהֶם

V'nat'u ch'ramim v'shatu et yeinam,

v'asu ganot v'achlu et p'rihem.

And they will plant vineyards and drink the wine thereof,

And they shall make gardens and eat the fruit of them.

(Amos 9:14)

PRAISE: THE FORCE OF HEALING
AND SALVATION

רְפָאֵנִי יהוה וְאֵרָפֵא הוֹשִׁיעֵנִי וְאִוָּשֵׁעָה כִּי תְהִלָּתִי אָתָּה

R'fa'eini Yah v'eirafei; hoshi'eini v'ivashei'ah ki t'hilati atah.

Heal me, God, and I will be healed; save me and I will be saved …

for my praise is You.

(Jeremiah 17:14)

A NEW COVENANT

נָתַתִּי אֶת־תּוֹרָתִי בְּקִרְבָּם וְעַל־לִבָּם אֶכְתֲּבֶנָּה

Natati et Torati b'kirbam, v'al libam echtavenah.

I will put my Torah into their inmost being and
inscribe it upon their hearts.

(Jeremiah 31:33)

Shefa Gold

CRYING OUT TO GOD

אִם־כֵּן לָמָּה זֶּה אָנֹכִי

Im kein, lamah zeh anochi?

If this is the way it is, why am I?

(Genesis 25:22)

Shefa Gold

6 part round - new part enter at each measure

RUTH

עַמֵּךְ עַמִּי וֵאלֹהַיִךְ אֱלֹהָי

Ameich ami veilohayich Elohai.

Your people are my people, and your God is my God.

(Ruth 1:16)

Shefa Gold

FIRE ON THE ALTAR

אֵשׁ תָּמִיד תּוּקַד עַל־הַמִּזְבֵּחַ לֹא תִכְבֶּה

Aish tamid tukad al hamizbayach; lo tichbeh.

Fire always shall be kept burning on the altar; it shall not go out.

(Leviticus 6:6)

Shefa Gold

Psalms

INVITING OUR FUTURE SELVES

הוֹדִיעֵנִי יהוה קִצִּי וּמִדַּת יָמַי מַה־הִיא

Hodi'eiani Yah kitzi, umidat yamai mah hi?

O God, show me my end, and what is the measure of my days?

(Psalm 39:5)

Shefa Gold

MY CUP

כּוֹסִי רְוָיָה

Kosi r'vayah.

My cup overflows.

(Psalm 23:5)

Shefa Gold

PREPARATION FOR RECONNECTING

חָנֵּנִי יהוה כִּי אֻמְלַל אָנִי

Choneini Yah ki umlal ani.

Grace me, Yah, for I am withered [disconnected].

(Psalm 6:3)

Shefa Gold

CALLING FORTH THE HIDDEN POWER

קוּמָה יהוה הוֹשִׁיעֵנִי אֱלֹהַי

Kumah Adonai, hoshi'eini Elohai.

Rise up, YHVH; save me, my God.

(Psalm 3:8)

EVEN IN THE DARKNESS

זָרַח בַּחֹשֶׁךְ אוֹר לַיְשָׁרִים חַנּוּן וְרַחוּם וְצַדִּיק

Zarach bachoshech or lay'sharim, chanun v'rachum v'tzadik.

Even in the darkness a light shines for the upright,

gracious, compassionate, and just.

(Psalm 112:4)

SUPPORTED

סָמוּךְ לִבּוֹ לֹא יִירָא

Samuch libo lo yira.

סָמוּךְ לִבָּה לֹא תִירָא

Samuch liba lo tira.

Heart supported, fearless.
(Psalm 112:8)

Shefa Gold

GIVING MY "SELF" IN SERVICE

אָנָּה יהוה כִּי־אֲנִי עַבְדֶּךָ אֲנִי עַבְדֶּךָ

Anah Yah ki ani avdecha; ani avd'cha.

Please, God, for I am your servant; I am your servant.
(Psalm 116:16)

Shefa Gold

JUSTICE IN PEACE

יִפְרַח בְּיָמָיו צַדִּיק וְרֹב שָׁלוֹם

Yifrach b'yamav tzadik, v'rov shalom!

O justice, O justice … in the fullness of peace!

O, justice shall flourish in its time, and the fullness of peace.

(Psalm 72:7)

Shefa Gold

RE-PARENTED

כִּי אָבִי וְאִמִּי עֲזָבוּנִי
וַיהוה יַאַסְפֵנִי
הוֹרֵנִי יהוה דַּרְכֶּךְ

Ki avi v'imi azavuni (2x)

V'Adonai ya'asfeini (4x)

Horeini Yah darkecha. (4x)

Though my father and my mother have forsaken me,
God will gather me in.
Teach me Your way, O God.
(Psalm 27:10–11)

Round

Shefa Gold

Ki__ a - vi v' - i - mi a - za - vu - ni. Ki__ a-
vi v' - i - mi a - za - vu - ni. Va - a - do - nai ya' - as-
fei - ni. Va - a - do - nai ya' - as - fei - ni. Va - a - do - nai ya' - as - fei - ni. Va - a - do-
nai ya' - as - fei - ni. Ho - rei - ni Yah dar - ke - cha.__ Ho - rei - ni Yah dar-
ke - cha.__ Ho - rei - ni Yah dar - ke - cha.__ Ho - rei - ni Yah dar - ke - cha.__ Ki__ a-

MORNING SONG
וַאֲנִי אָשִׁיר עֻזֶּךָ וַאֲרַנֵּן לַבֹּקֶר חַסְדֶּךָ

Va'ani ashir uzecha va'aranein labokeir chasdecha.

And I will sing Your glory and I will sing Your love in the morning.

(Psalm 59:17)

Shefa Gold

EFR—ENERGY FIELD RECHARGE
אֱלֹהִים יְחָנֵּנוּ וִיבָרְכֵנוּ יָאֵר פָּנָיו אִתָּנוּ סֶלָה

Elohim y'choneinu vivarcheinu ya'eir panav itanu selah.

God, grace us, bless us; may its light shine among us, selah.

(Psalm 67:2)

Shefa Gold

HEALING CHANT

מַה יָּקָר חַסְדְּךָ אֱלֹהִים

Mah yakar chasd'cha Elohim.

How precious is Your love, God.

(Psalm 36:8)

Shefa Gold

TURNING

סוּר מֵרָע וַעֲשֵׂה־טוֹב בַּקֵּשׁ שָׁלוֹם וְרָדְפֵהוּ

Sur meira va'asei tov, bakeish shalom v'radfeihu.

Turn away from evil and do good;

Seek peace/wholeness and go after it.

(Psalm 34:15)

Shefa Gold

FROM THE DEPTHS

מִמַּעֲמַקִּים קְרָאתִיךָ יהוה

Mima'amakim k'raticha Yah!

From the depths I call to You, O God. Hear my voice!

(Psalm 130:1)

Shefa Gold

EXPANDING INNER SPACE

אֵלֶיךָ יהוה אֶקְרָא

Eilecha Yah ekra.

To You, God, I call.

(Psalm 30:9)

Shefa Gold

THE HEAVENS

הַשָּׁמַיִם מְסַפְּרִים כְּבוֹד־אֵל

Hashamayim m'saprim k'vod Eil.

The heavens open up and tell Your story,
of sun and clouds and storm, of wind and glory.

(Psalm 19:2)

Shefa Gold

DAY AND NIGHT

יוֹם לְיוֹם יַבִּיעַ אֹמֶר וְלַיְלָה לְלַיְלָה יְחַוֶּה־דָּעַת

Yom l'yom yabia omer, v'lailah l'lailah y'chaveh da'at.

Day after day pours forth speech, night after night declares knowledge.

(Psalm 19:3)

Round

Shefa Gold

RIVER OF BLISS

וְנַחַל עֲדָנֶיךָ תַשְׁקֵם

V'nachal adanecha tashkeim.

And from the river of Your bliss You will give them drink.

כִּי־עִמְּךָ מְקוֹר חַיִּים בְּאוֹרְךָ נִרְאֶה־אוֹר

Ki m'cha m'kor chayim; b'or'cha nireh or.

For with You is the source of life, in Your light we see light.

(Psalm 36:9–10)

Shefa Gold

ROSH HASHANAH CHANT

אַשְׁרֵי הָעָם יוֹדְעֵי תְרוּעָה יהוה בְּאוֹר־פָּנֶיךָ יְהַלֵּכוּן

Ashrei ha'am yodei t'ruah Adonai b'or panecha y'haleichun.

O God, happy are the people who know the blast of the shofar;
they walk in the light of Your presence.

(Psalm 89:16)

Round

Shefa Gold

THE SEA LION'S QUESTION

מִי־הָאִישׁ הֶחָפֵץ חַיִּים אֹהֵב יָמִים לִרְאוֹת טוֹב

Mi ha'ish hechafeitz chayim, oheiv yamim lirot tov?

Who is the one that has a passion for life,

loving every day, seeing the good?

(Psalm 34:13)

Shefa Gold

PLANTING SEEDS OF JOY AND LIGHT

אוֹר זָרֻעַ לַצַּדִיק וּלְיִשְׁרֵי לֵב שִׂמְחָה

Or zarua latzadik, ul'yishrei leiv simchah.

Plant the seeds of joy and light; tend them carefully day and night,
in this soil so dark and deep, I plant the dreams that love will reap.
(Psalm 97:11)

Shefa Gold

SINGING A NEW SONG

שִׁירוּ לַיהוה שִׁיר חָדָשׁ תְּהִלָּתוֹ בִּקְהַל חֲסִידִים

Halleluyah!

Shiru l'Adonai shir chadash; t'hilato bik'hal Chasidim.

Sing to God a new song;

God's praise is found in a community of lovers.

(Psalm 149:1)

Shefa Gold

MIN HAMEITZAR

מִן־הַמֵּצַר קָרָאתִי יָהּ עָנָנִי בַמֶּרְחָב יָהּ

Min hameitzar karati Yah, anani vamerchav Yah.
From the narrow place I called out to God
who answered me with the divine expanse.
(Psalm 118:5)

Shefa Gold

SINGING GOD'S LOVE
חַסְדֵי יהוה עוֹלָם אָשִׁירָה
Chasdei Adonai olam ashirah.
I will sing forth from the hidden infinite,
the loving-kindnesses of God.
(Psalm 89:1)

Shefa Gold

TUNING IN TO THE CREATOR-FUNCTION
אֶשָּׂא עֵינַי אֶל־הֶהָרִים מֵאַיִן יָבֹא עֶזְרִי
Esa einai el heharim mei'ayin yavo ezri. (2x)
My help comes from the One (3x)
Creator of heaven and earth.
(Psalm 12:11)

Shefa Gold

PREPARATION FOR HEALING

אַתָּה עֻזִּי
אַתָּה חַיָּי
אַתָּה אוֹרִי
אַתָּה לְפָנַי

Atah Ozi
Atah Chayai
Atah Ori
Atah l'fanai

You are my Strength
You are my Life
You are my Light
Ever before me.
(inspired by Psalm 27)

Shefa Gold

SOUL PERSPECTIVE

אֵלֶיךָ יהוה נַפְשִׁי אֶשָּׂא

Eilecha Yah nafshi esa.

To You, God, I lift up my soul.

(Psalm 25:1)

Shefa Gold

ENCOUNTERING THE LIVING GOD
צָמְאָה נַפְשִׁי לֵאלֹהִים לְאֵל חָי
Tzam'ah nafshi l'Eilohim l'Eil Chai.

My soul thirsts for God, for the Living God.
(Psalm 42:3)

LONGING
כֵּן נַפְשִׁי תַעֲרֹג אֵלֶיךָ אֱלֹהִים
Kein nafshi ta'arog eilecha Elohim.

Just as the deer longs for water by the riverbank,
so does my soul long for You, O God.
(Psalm 42:2)

SATISFACTION AND ITS FRUITS

שַׂבְּעֵנוּ בַבֹּקֶר חַסְדֶּךָ וּנְרַנְּנָה וְנִשְׂמְחָה בְּכָל־יָמֵינוּ

Sab'einu vaboker chasdecha;
Un'ran'nah v'nism'chah b'chol yameinu.

May Your loving-kindness satisfy us in the morning;
and we will sing out and we will rejoice for all our days.
(Psalm 90:14)

Shefa Gold

LET MY GLORY SING
יְזַמֶּרְךָ כָבוֹד וְלֹא יִדֹּם
Y'zamercha chavod v'lo yidom.
Let my glory sing to You and not be silenced.
(Psalm 30:13)

Part 1 alone, then both parts

Shefa Gold

RE-MEMBERING

לַיהוה הָאָרֶץ וּמְלוֹאָהּ תֵּבֵל וְיֹשְׁבֵי בָהּ

L'Adonai ha'aretz um'loah, teiveil v'yosh'vei vah.

The earth and all that fills her, and all who dwell in her ...

all belong to God.

(Psalm 24:1)

Shefa Gold

TRUSTING

שַׁבְתִּי בְּבֵית־יהוה

Shavti b'veit Adonai.

I place myself in Your care.

(Psalm 23:6)

Shefa Gold

HEART WALK

אֶתְהַלֵךְ בְּתָם־לְבָבִי בְּקֶרֶב בֵּיתִי

Et'haleich b'tom l'vavi, b'kerev beiti.

I will walk within my house in the integrity of my heart.

(Psalm 101:2)

Shefa Gold

PROTECTING OUR "INNER CHILD"

כִּי־חִזַּק בְּרִיחֵי שְׁעָרָיִךְ בֵּרַךְ בָּנַיִךְ בְּקִרְבֵּךְ

Ki chizak b'richei sh'arayich, beirach banayich b'kirbeich.

When your boundaries are strong, your inner child is blessed.

(Psalm 147:13)

Shefa Gold

PURE HEART

לֵב טָהוֹר בְּרָא־לִי אֱלֹהִים

Leiv tahor b'ra li Elohim.

Create for me a pure heart. [God] has created for me a pure heart.

O pure heart, create for me [the experience of] God.

The pure heart has created God for me.

(Psalm 51:12)

Shefa Gold

WITH EVERY BREATH

כֹּל הַנְּשָׁמָה תְּהַלֵּל יָהּ הַלְלוּיָהּ

Kol han'shamah t'haleil Yah.

Every soul praises Yah with every breath,
From the moment of birth until death! *Halleluyah!*
(Psalm 150:6)

Shefa Gold

WHOSE FACE?

אַל־תַּסְתֵּר פָּנֶיךָ מִמֶּנִּי

Al tasteir panecha mimeni.

Do not hide Your face from me.

(Psalm 27:9)

A SPIRIT OF "YES!"

וְרוּחַ נָכוֹן חַדֵּשׁ בְּקִרְבִּי

V'ruach nachon chadeish b'kirbi.

Renew within me a spirit of "Yes!"

(Psalm 51:12)

THE VALLEY OF DEATH

גַּם כִּי־אֵלֵךְ בְּגֵיא צַלְמָוֶת לֹא־אִירָא רָע

Gam ki eileich b'gei tzalmavet, lo ira ra.

Though I walk through the Valley of Death, I will not fear,
Though I walk through the Valley of Death, my God is near.
(Psalm 23:4)

Shefa Gold

PURE

כָּל־מִשְׁבָּרֶיךָ וְגַלֶּיךָ עָלַי עָבָרוּ
טָהוֹר הוּא, טְהוֹרָה הִיא

Kol mishbarecha v'galecha alai avaru
Tahor hu, t'horah hi.

All of Your breakers and Your waves have swept over me.
He is pure; she is pure.
(Psalm 42:8)

Shefa Gold

MY ROCK AND REDEEMER

אַתָּה צוּרִי וְגֹאֲלִי

Atah Tzuri v'Go'ali.

You are my Rock and my Redeemer.

(adapted from Psalm 19:15)

Shefa Gold

A - tah Tzu - ri —— v' - Go' - a - li A - li. A - tah Tzu -

ri —— v' - Go' - a - li. A - tah Tzu - ri —— v' - Go' - a - li.

MY PROTECTION

מָגִנִּי עַל־אֱלֹהִים מוֹשִׁיעַ יִשְׁרֵי־לֵב

Magini al Elohim, moshia yishrei leiv.

My protection is all about the God-field;

that's what saves the upright heart.

(Psalm 7:11)

Shefa Gold

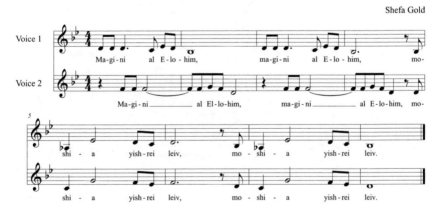

Voice 1: Ma - gi - ni　al E - lo - him,　ma - gi - ni　al E - lo - him,　mo-

Voice 2: Ma - gi - ni —— al El - lo - him,　ma - gi - ni —— al E - lo - him, mo-

shi - a　yish - rei　leiv,　mo - shi - a　yish - rei　leiv.

shi - a　yish - rei　leiv,　mo - shi - a　yish - rei　leiv.

MY PRAYER AS INCENSE

תִּכּוֹן תְּפִלָּתִי קְטֹרֶת לְפָנֶיךָ

Tikon t'filati k'toret l'fanecha.

Let my prayer be incense before You.

(Psalm 141:2)

Shefa Gold

WAITING ...

דּוֹם לַיהוה וְהִתְחוֹלֵל לוֹ

Dom l'Yah v'hitcholeil lo.

Be still and wait for God.

(Psalm 37:7)

Shefa Gold

FROM WORLD TO WORLD

מֵעוֹלָם עַד־עוֹלָם אַתָּה אֵל

Mei'olam ad olam atah Eil.

From world to world, You are God.

(Psalm 90:2)

Shefa Gold

ALWAYS WITH YOU

וַאֲנִי תָמִיד עִמָּךְ

Va'ani tamid imach.
I am always with You.
Though my heart is troubled and I'm filled with dread
I turn to face Your Mystery
Though I've been lost inside my head
I open to Eternity.
(Psalm 73:23)

Shefa Gold

The Daily Psalms

FROM THE PSALM FOR SUNDAY

Psalm 24:9

שְׂאוּ שְׁעָרִים רָאשֵׁיכֶם וּשְׂאוּ פִּתְחֵי עוֹלָם

S'u sh'arim rasheichem, us'u pitchei olam!

Lift up your head, O you gates; lift them up, you everlasting doors!

Round   Shefa Gold

FROM THE PSALM FOR MONDAY

Psalm 48:10

דְּמִינוּ אֱלֹהִים חַסְדֶּךָ

Diminu Elohim chasdecha.

Our stillness/silence is Your love, God.

Shefa Gold

FROM THE PSALM FOR TUESDAY

Psalm 82:8

קוּמָה אֱלֹהִים שָׁפְטָה הָאָרֶץ

Kumah Elohim shaftah ha'aretz.

Arise, God, and judge the land.

Shefa Gold

FROM THE PSALM FOR WEDNESDAY

Psalm 94:19

בְּרֹב שַׂרְעַפַּי בְּקִרְבִּי תַּנְחוּמֶיךָ יְשַׁעַשְׁעוּ נַפְשִׁי

B'rov sarapai b'kirbi,

Tanchumecha y'sha'ashu nafshi.

When worries multiply within me, Your comfort soothes my soul.

FROM THE PSALM FOR THURSDAY

Psalm 81:4–5

תִּקְעוּ בַחֹדֶשׁ שׁוֹפָר בַּכֶּסֶה לְיוֹם חַגֵּנוּ
כִּי חֹק לְיִשְׂרָאֵל הוּא מִשְׁפָּט לֵאלֹהֵי יַעֲקֹב

Tiku vachodesh shofar
Ba'keiseh l'yom chageinu
Ki chok l'Yisrael hu mishpat Elohei Ya'akov.

Sound a shofar at the new moon ... at the moment of concealment/
potential for our celebration day.
It is a statute for Israel; it is a rule for Jacob.

Shefa Gold

FROM THE PSALM FOR FRIDAY

Psalm 93:2

נָכוֹן כִּסְאֲךָ מֵאָז מֵעוֹלָם אָתָּה

Nachon kisacha mei'az, mei'olam atah!

Your throne was long ago secured; beyond eternity are You!

Shefa Gold

FROM THE PSALM FOR SHABBAT

Psalm 92:6

מַה־גָּדְלוּ מַעֲשֶׂיךָ יהוה מְאֹד עָמְקוּ מַחְשְׁבֹתֶיךָ

Mah gadlu ma'asecha Yah, m'od am'ku machsh'votecha!

How great is Your work, O God, how very deep are Your thoughts!

Shefa Gold

Isaiah

THE MIRACLE

וַיָּשֶׂם מִדְבָּרָהּ כְּעֵדֶן וְעַרְבָתָהּ כְּגַן־יהוה

Vayasem midbarah k'eiden, v'arvatah k'gan Adonai.

He transforms her wilderness into delight,
her wasteland into a divine garden.
(Isaiah 51:3)

Shefa Gold

DIVINE CONGRATULATIONS
כִּי מָלְאָה צְבָאָה
Ki malah tz'va'ah.
Her time of service is fulfilled.
(Isaiah 40:2)

AWAKENING THE HEART
הִתְעוֹרְרִי הִתְעוֹרְרִי קוּמִי יְרוּשָׁלַיִם
Hitor'ri, hitor'ri, kumi Y'rushalayim!
Awake, awake, arise Jerusalem!
(Isaiah 51:17)

BREAKTHROUGH

עִבְרוּ עִבְרוּ בַּשְּׁעָרִים פַּנּוּ דֶּרֶךְ הָעָם

Ivru, ivru bash'arim, panu derech ha'am!

Go through, go through the gates, clear the way of the people!

(Isaiah 62:10)

Shefa Gold

COME FOR WATER!

הוֹי כָּל־צָמֵא לְכוּ לַמַּיִם

Hoy! Kol tzamei l'chu lamayim!

All who are thirsty, come for water!

(Isaiah 55:1)

Shefa Gold

GETTING PERSPECTIVE

עַל הַר־גָּבֹהַ עֲלִי־לָךְ

Al har gavo'ah ali lach.

Get yourself up upon the high mountain.

(Isaiah 40:9)

Double Round

Shefa Gold

SHINING

קוּמִי אוֹרִי כִּי־בָא אוֹרֵךְ וּכְבוֹד יהוה עָלַיִךְ זָרָח

Kumi ori ki va oreich uch'vod Adonai alayich zarach.

Arise and shine for your light has come,

and the Glory of God is shining upon you.

(Isaiah 60:1)

Shefa Gold

FOR IN JOY

כִּי־בְשִׂמְחָה תֵצֵאוּ וּבְשָׁלוֹם תּוּבָלוּן

Ki v'simchah teitzei'u, uv'shalom tuvalun.

For in joy will you go out, in peace be led across the Land,

Mountains and hills will burst into song,

And the trees of the field will clap their hands. (Clap!)

(Isaiah 55:12)

Shefa Gold

PALMISTRY

הֵן עַל־כַּפַּיִם חַקֹּתִיךְ

Hein al kapayim chakotich.

You are engraved on the palm of My hand.

(Isaiah 49:16)

Shefa Gold

PEACE LIKE A RIVER
הִנְנִי נֹטֶה־אֵלֶיהָ כְּנָהָר שָׁלוֹם

Hin'ni, noteh eileha k'nahar shalom.

Here I am, extending peace to her like a river.

(Isaiah 66:12)

Shefa Gold

HERALDS OF PEACE
מַה־נָּאווּ עַל־הֶהָרִים רַגְלֵי מְבַשֵּׂר מַשְׁמִיעַ שָׁלוֹם

Mah navu al heharim raglei m'vaseir mashmia shalom.

Oh, how lovely—our footsteps on the mountain; we are messengers;
we are heralds of peace.

(Isaiah 52:7)

Shefa Gold

SPACIOUSNESS

הַרְחִיבִי מְקוֹם אָהֳלֵךְ

Harchivi m'kom ohaleich.

Enlarge the place of your tent.

(Isaiah 54:2)

COMFORT

נַחֲמוּ נַחֲמוּ עַמִּי

Nachamu, nachamu ami!

Comfort, comfort my people!

(Isaiah 40:1)

THROUGH THE WATERS

כִּי־תַעֲבֹר בַּמַּיִם אִתְּךָ־אָנִי וּבַנְּהָרוֹת לֹא יִשְׁטְפוּךָ

Ki ta'avor bamayim it'cha ani, uvan'harot lo yisht'fucha.

When you pass through the waters, I am with you, yes, I am with you.
I won't let the rivers overwhelm you, I will be with you.
(Isaiah 43:2)

Shefa Gold

DELIGHT

אָז תִּתְעַנַּג עַל־יהוה

Az titanag al Havayah.

Then you will delight in God (being itself!)
(Isaiah 58:14)

Round   Shefa Gold

GARMENTS OF SALVATION

שׁוֹשׂ אָשִׂישׂ בַּיהוה תָּגֵל נַפְשִׁי בֵּאלֹהָי
כִּי הִלְבִּישַׁנִי בִּגְדֵי־יֶשַׁע

Sos asis badonai tageil nafshi beilohai,
ki hilbishani bigdei yesha.

I will rejoice in God, who has dressed me in the garments of salvation.
(Isaiah 61:10)

SEND ME!

אֶת־מִי אֶשְׁלַח וּמִי יֵלֶךְ־לָנוּ
הִנְנִי שְׁלָחֵנִי

Et mi eshlach umi yeilech lanu?
Hin'ni sh'lacheini.

Whom shall I send, and who shall go for us?
Here I am. Send me.
(Isaiah 6:8)

Form: Part 1 alone (with repeat), Part 2 (with repeat), Part 1 (with repeat), thereafter both parts together

MINDFULNESS

שִׁמְעוּ שָׁמוֹעַ אֵלַי וְאִכְלוּ־טוֹב

Shim'u shamo'a eilai, v'ichlu tov.

If you really listen to Me, then you will eat what is good.

(And your souls will delight in richness.)

(Isaiah 55:2)

ACKNOWLEDGMENTS

I have dedicated this book to students and spirit buddies of Kol Zimra because you call the inspiration through me. We have fallen in love with "The Work" together, and you continue to be my partners in exploration and adventure.

Thank you!

… to my beloved Rachmiel for believing in me, sharing the journey, and loving me so well.

… to Rabbi Nadya Gross, Ruach Ha'Aretz, and Aleph: Alliance for Jewish Renewal for creating and maintaining the Mishkan for this work. Your dedication to the integrity and beauty of this container calls in the Divine Presence.

… to Judith Dack and Yaffah Schnitzer, the KZ Priestlets, for supporting the work of Kol Zimra and for bringing style and sparkle and playful love to the work.

… to Rabbi Phyllis Berman for listening so well, and teaching me about loyalty and the safety that allows us to take risks.

… to Reb Zalman Schachter-Shalomi for not settling for anything less than intimacy and ecstasy in his relationship to God.

… to Cantor Audrey Abrams for so lovingly, diligently, and skillfully notating the chants in this book. Your passion, joy, and musicality have penetrated each and every note that you have transcribed. Thank you to James Cooper who came to our rescue to help finish this monumental task.

Finally I acknowledge in gratefulness all of the angels, spirits, and guides who whisper to me persistently, and keep turning my face to receive the Great Mystery.

APPENDIX 1

1. The Empowerer

Dedicated to the group energy; channels energy through themselves to the center of the group so that everyone can be nurtured and empowered.

TASK: Building up group energy.

2. The Guide

Sees and holds to higher purpose of the group, builds structure and plan; sees and nurtures the potential of the whole and the capabilities of each part.

TASK: Perceiving guidance and steering the ship.

3. The Observer

Conscious attention on behalf of the group; maintains awareness of group's energies while still being a part of it; discriminates shifts without being judgmental.

TASK: Perceiving the energy of the whole.

4. The Container

Guardian of the group; creates safe/sacred space by containing the energy. Three methods—imaginal arms, heart, and voice; guards against outside intrusion.

TASK: Protecting and embracing the energy of the whole.

5. The Exalter

Raises up the spark of the Divine by seeing and celebrating it; lifts the group through joyful presence.

TASK: Loving whatever is Divine "in this"—exalting it and bringing it out still further.

6. The Foundation

Creates solidity; brings grounding; lays one's consciousness beneath what is happening as a dance floor that supports the group's energies.

TASK: Establishing the foundation for the group energy.

7. The Secret Heart

Is completely effaced in God/Devotion; the deepest part of the group, the least known part to outsiders and to the superficial; God in the silence.

TASK: Surrendering to the depths on behalf of the group, thus connecting the group with those depths.

8. The Bridge

Makes connections through interdisciplinary awareness; enlarges the meaning and the context for the group; bridges different states of consciousness and levels of meaning.

TASK: Holding paradox, cultivating stereoscopic mode.

SUGGESTIONS FOR
FURTHER READING

Almaas, A. H. *Facets of Unity: The Enneagram of Holy Ideas*. Boston: Shambhala, 2000.

Bahya ibn Pekuda. *Duties of the Heart*. Lanham, MD: Jason Aronson, 1996.

Buxbaum, Yitzhak. *Jewish Spiritual Practices*. Landham. MD: Jason Aronson, 1999.

Cousineau, Phil. *The Art of Pilgrimage: The Seeker's Guide to Making Travel Sacred*. San Francsico: Conari Press, 2000.

Dov Ber of Lubavitch. *Tract on Ecstasy*, translated by Louis Jacobs. Portland, OR: Vallentine Mitchell, 2006.

Gaynor, Mitchell. *The Healing Power of Sound: Recovery from Life-Threatening Illness Using Sound, Voice, and Music*. Boston: Shambhala Publications, 2002.

Gold, Shefa. *Torah Journeys: The Inner Path to the Promised Land*. Teaneck, NJ: Ben Yehuda Press, 2006.

Goldman, Jonathan. *Healing Sounds: The Power of Harmonics*. Rochester, VT: Healing Arts Press, 2002.

Heschel, Abraham Joshua. *The Prophets*. Peabody, MA: Hendrickson Publishers, 2007.

———. *The Sabbath*. New York: Farrar, Straus & Giroux, 2005.

Hirsch, Samson Raphael. *The Hirsch Psalms*. Nanuet, NY: Feldheim Publishers, 1997.

McClellan, Randall. *The Healing Forces of Music*. iUniverse, 2000.

McTaggart, Lynne. *The Bond: Connecting through the Space Between Us*. New York: Free Press, 2011.

———. *The Field: The Quest for the Secret Force of the Universe*. New York: Harper Perennial, 2008.

———. *The Intention Experiment: Using Your Thoughts to Change Your Life and the World*. New York: Free Press, 2008.

Roberts, Jane. *The Nature of Personal Reality: Specific, Practical Techniques for Solving Everyday Problems and Enriching the Life You Know*. San Rafael, CA: Amber-Allen Publishing, 1994.

Roth, Gabrielle. *Maps to Ecstasy: The Healing Power of Movement*. Novato, CA: Nataraj Publishing, 1998.

Steindl-Rast, David. *Gratefulness, the Heart of Prayer: An Approach to Life in Fullness*. Mahwah, NJ: Paulist Press, 1984.

Trugman, Avraham Arieh. *The Mystical Power of Music*. New York: Targum Press, 2005.

INDEX OF PRACTICES
AND NOTATIONS

INDEX OF FIRST LINES

Meditation

Jewish Meditation Practices for Everyday Life
Awakening Your Heart, Connecting with God *By Rabbi Jeff Roth*
Offers a fresh take on meditation that draws on life experience and living life with greater clarity as opposed to the traditional method of rigorous study.
6 x 9, 224 pp, Quality PB, 978-1-58023-397-2 **$18.99**

The Handbook of Jewish Meditation Practices
A Guide for Enriching the Sabbath and Other Days of Your Life
By Rabbi David A. Cooper Easy-to-learn meditation techniques.
6 x 9, 208 pp, Quality PB, 978-1-58023-102-2 **$16.95**

Discovering Jewish Meditation, 2nd Edition
Instruction & Guidance for Learning an Ancient Spiritual Practice
By Nan Fink Gefen, PhD 6 x 9, 208 pp, Quality PB, 978-1-58023-462-7 **$16.99**

Meditation from the Heart of Judaism
Today's Teachers Share Their Practices, Techniques, and Faith
Edited by Avram Davis 6 x 9, 256 pp, Quality PB, 978-1-58023-049-0 **$16.95**

Ritual / Sacred Practices

Davening: A Guide to Meaningful Jewish Prayer
By Rabbi Zalman Schachter-Shalomi with Joel Segel
A fresh approach to prayer for all who wish to join the age-old conversation that Jews have had with God. Winner, National Jewish Book Award.
6 x 9, 240 pp, Quality PB, 978-1-58023-627-0 **$18.99**

Jewish with Feeling: A Guide to Meaningful Jewish Practice
By Rabbi Zalman Schachter-Shalomi with Joel Segel
Taking off from basic questions like "Why be Jewish?" and whether the word *God* still speaks to us today, Reb Zalman lays out a vision for a whole-person Judaism.
6 x 9, 288 pp, Quality PB, 978-1-58023-691-1 **$19.99**

The Book of Jewish Sacred Practices: CLAL's Guide to Everyday &
Holiday Rituals & Blessings *Edited by Rabbi Irwin Kula and Vanessa L. Ochs, PhD*
6 x 9, 368 pp, Quality PB, 978-1-58023-152-7 **$18.95**

God in Your Body: Kabbalah, Mindfulness and Embodied Spiritual Practice
By Jay Michaelson 6 x 9, 272 pp, Quality PB, 978-1-58023-304-0 **$18.99**

The Jewish Dream Book: The Key to Opening the Inner Meaning of Your Dreams
By Vanessa L. Ochs, PhD, with Elizabeth Ochs; Illus. by Kristina Swarner
8 x 8, 128 pp, Full-color illus., Deluxe PB w/ flaps, 978-1-58023-132-9 **$16.95**

Jewish Ritual: A Brief Introduction for Christians
By Rabbi Kerry M. Olitzky and Rabbi Daniel Judson
5½ x 8½, 144 pp, Quality PB, 978-1-58023-210-4 **$14.99**

The Rituals & Practices of a Jewish Life: A Handbook for Personal Spiritual
Renewal *Edited by Rabbi Kerry M. Olitzky and Rabbi Daniel Judson*
6 x 9, 272 pp, Illus., Quality PB, 978-1-58023-169-5 **$18.95**

The Sacred Art of Lovingkindness: Preparing to Practice
By Rabbi Rami Shapiro 5½ x 8½, 176 pp, Quality PB, 978-1-59473-151-8 **$16.99**
(A book from SkyLight Paths, Jewish Lights' sister imprint)

See also Spirituality / Prayer.

Or phone, fax, mail or e-mail to: **JEWISH LIGHTS** Publishing
Sunset Farm Offices, Route 4 • P.O. Box 237 • Woodstock, Vermont 05091
Tel: (802) 457-4000 • Fax: (802) 457-4004 • www.jewishlights.com
Credit card orders: (800) 962-4544 (8:30AM–5:30PM EST Monday–Friday)
Generous discounts on quantity orders. SATISFACTION GUARANTEED. Prices subject to change.

Inspiration

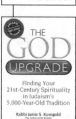

God of Me: Imagining God throughout Your Lifetime
By Rabbi David Lyon Helps you cut through preconceived ideas of God and dogmas that stifle your creativity when thinking about your personal relationship with God. 6 x 9, 176 pp, Quality PB, 978-1-58023-452-8 **$16.99**

The God Upgrade: Finding Your 21st-Century Spirituality in Judaism's 5,000-Year-Old Tradition *By Rabbi Jamie Korngold; Foreword by Rabbi Harold M. Schulweis* A provocative look at how our changing God concepts have shaped every aspect of Judaism. 6 x 9, 176 pp, Quality PB, 978-1-58023-443-6 **$15.99**

The Seven Questions You're Asked in Heaven: Reviewing and Renewing Your Life on Earth *By Dr. Ron Wolfson* An intriguing and entertaining resource for living a life that matters. 6 x 9, 176 pp, Quality PB, 978-1-58023-407-8 **$16.99**

Happiness and the Human Spirit: The Spirituality of Becoming the Best You Can Be *By Rabbi Abraham J. Twerski, MD*
Shows you that true happiness is attainable once you stop looking outside yourself for the source. 6 x 9, 176 pp, Quality PB, 978-1-58023-404-7 **$16.99**; HC, 978-1-58023-343-9 **$19.99**

A Formula for Proper Living: Practical Lessons from Life and Torah
By Rabbi Abraham J. Twerski, MD 6 x 9, 144 pp, HC, 978-1-58023-402-3 **$19.99**

The Bridge to Forgiveness: Stories and Prayers for Finding God and Restoring Wholeness *By Rabbi Karyn D. Kedar* 6 x 9, 176 pp, Quality PB, 978-1-58023-451-1 **$16.99**

The Empty Chair: Finding Hope and Joy—Timeless Wisdom from a Hasidic Master, Rebbe Nachman of Breslov *Adapted by Moshe Mykoff and the Breslov Research Institute* 4 x 6, 128 pp, Deluxe PB w/ flaps, 978-1-879045-67-5 **$9.99**

The Gentle Weapon: Prayers for Everyday and Not-So-Everyday Moments—Timeless Wisdom from the Teachings of the Hasidic Master, Rebbe Nachman of Breslov *Adapted by Moshe Mykoff and S. C. Mizrahi, together with the Breslov Research Institute* 4 x 6, 144 pp, Deluxe PB w/ flaps, 978-1-58023-022-3 **$9.99**

God Whispers: Stories of the Soul, Lessons of the Heart *By Rabbi Karyn D. Kedar* 6 x 9, 176 pp, Quality PB, 978-1-58023-088-9 **$15.95**

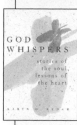

God's To-Do List: 103 Ways to Be an Angel and Do God's Work on Earth
By Dr. Ron Wolfson 6 x 9, 144 pp, Quality PB, 978-1-58023-301-9 **$16.99**

Jewish Stories from Heaven and Earth: Inspiring Tales to Nourish the Heart and Soul *Edited by Rabbi Dov Peretz Elkins* 6 x 9, 304 pp, Quality PB, 978-1-58023-363-7 **$16.99**

Life's Daily Blessings: Inspiring Reflections on Gratitude and Joy for Every Day, Based on Jewish Wisdom *By Rabbi Kerry M. Olitzky* 4½ x 6½, 368 pp, Quality PB, 978-1-58023-396-5 **$16.99**

Restful Reflections: Nighttime Inspiration to Calm the Soul, Based on Jewish Wisdom *By Rabbi Kerry M. Olitzky and Rabbi Lori Forman-Jacobi* 5 x 8, 352 pp, Quality PB, 978-1-58023-091-9 **$16.99**

Sacred Intentions: Morning Inspiration to Strengthen the Spirit, Based on Jewish Wisdom *By Rabbi Kerry M. Olitzky and Rabbi Lori Forman-Jacobi* 4½ x 6½, 448 pp, Quality PB, 978-1-58023-061-2 **$16.99**

Kabbalah / Mysticism

Jewish Mysticism and the Spiritual Life: Classical Texts, Contemporary Reflections *Edited by Dr. Lawrence Fine, Dr. Eitan Fishbane and Rabbi Or N. Rose* Inspirational and thought-provoking materials for contemplation, discussion and action. 6 x 9, 256 pp, HC, 978-1-58023-434-4 **$24.99**

Ehyeh: A Kabbalah for Tomorrow
By Rabbi Arthur Green, PhD 6 x 9, 224 pp, Quality PB, 978-1-58023-213-5 **$18.99**

The Gift of Kabbalah: Discovering the Secrets of Heaven, Renewing Your Life on Earth
By Tamar Frankiel, PhD 6 x 9, 256 pp, Quality PB, 978-1-58023-141-1 **$16.95**

Seek My Face: A Jewish Mystical Theology *By Rabbi Arthur Green, PhD*
6 x 9, 304 pp, Quality PB, 978-1-58023-130-5 **$19.95**

Zohar: Annotated & Explained *Translation & Annotation by Dr. Daniel C. Matt; Foreword by Andrew Harvey* 5½ x 8½, 176 pp, Quality PB, 978-1-893361-51-5 **$16.99**
(A book from SkyLight Paths, Jewish Lights' sister imprint)

See also *The Way Into Jewish Mystical Tradition* in Spirituality / Lawrence Kushner.

Holidays / Holy Days

Prayers of Awe Series

An exciting new series that examines the High Holy Day liturgy to enrich the praying experience of everyone—whether experienced worshipers or guests who encounter Jewish prayer for the very first time.

We Have Sinned—Sin and Confession in Judaism: *Ashamnu* and *Al Chet*
Edited by Rabbi Lawrence A. Hoffman, PhD
A varied and fascinating look at sin, confession and pardon in Judaism, as suggested by the centrality of *Ashamnu* and *Al Chet*, two prayers that people know so well, though understand so little. 6 x 9, 304 pp, HC, 978-1-58023-612-6 **$24.99**

Who by Fire, Who by Water—*Un'taneh Tokef*
Edited by Rabbi Lawrence A. Hoffman, PhD 6 x 9, 272 pp, HC, 978-1-58023-424-5 **$24.99**

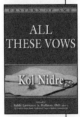

All These Vows—*Kol Nidre*
Edited by Rabbi Lawrence A. Hoffman, PhD 6 x 9, 288 pp, HC, 978-1-58023-430-6 **$24.99**

Rosh Hashanah Readings: Inspiration, Information and Contemplation
Yom Kippur Readings: Inspiration, Information and Contemplation
Edited by Rabbi Dov Peretz Elkins; Section Introductions from Arthur Green's These Are the Words
Rosh Hashanah: 6 x 9, 400 pp, Quality PB, 978-1-58023-437-5 **$19.99**
Yom Kippur: 6 x 9, 368 pp, Quality PB, 978-1-58023-438-2 **$19.99**; HC, 978-1-58023-271-5 **$24.99**

Reclaiming Judaism as a Spiritual Practice: Holy Days and Shabbat
By Rabbi Goldie Milgram 7 x 9, 272 pp, Quality PB, 978-1-58023-205-0 **$19.99**

The Sabbath Soul: Mystical Reflections on the Transformative Power of Holy Time
Selection, Translation and Commentary by Eitan Fishbane, PhD
6 x 9, 208 pp, Quality PB, 978-1-58023-459-7 **$18.99**

Shabbat, 2nd Edition: The Family Guide to Preparing for and Celebrating the Sabbath
By Dr. Ron Wolfson 7 x 9, 320 pp, Illus., Quality PB, 978-1-58023-164-0 **$19.99**

Hanukkah, 2nd Edition: The Family Guide to Spiritual Celebration
By Dr. Ron Wolfson 7 x 9, 240 pp, Illus., Quality PB, 978-1-58023-122-0 **$18.95**

Passover

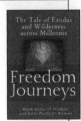

My People's Passover Haggadah
Traditional Texts, Modern Commentaries
Edited by Rabbi Lawrence A. Hoffman, PhD, and David Arnow, PhD
A diverse and exciting collection of commentaries on the traditional Passover Haggadah—in two volumes!
Vol. 1: 7 x 10, 304 pp, HC, 978-1-58023-354-5 **$24.99**
Vol. 2: 7 x 10, 320 pp, HC, 978-1-58023-346-0 **$24.99**

Freedom Journeys: The Tale of Exodus and Wilderness across Millennia
By Rabbi Arthur O. Waskow and Rabbi Phyllis O. Berman
Explores how the story of Exodus echoes in our own time, calling us to relearn and rethink the Passover story through social-justice, ecological, feminist and interfaith perspectives. 6 x 9, 288 pp, HC, 978-1-58023-445-0 **$24.99**

Leading the Passover Journey: The Seder's Meaning Revealed,
the Haggadah's Story Retold *By Rabbi Nathan Laufer*
Uncovers the hidden meaning of the Seder's rituals and customs.
6 x 9, 224 pp, Quality PB, 978-1-58023-399-6 **$18.99**

Creating Lively Passover Seders, 2nd Edition: A Sourcebook of Engaging Tales,
Texts & Activities *By David Arnow, PhD* 7 x 9, 464 pp, Quality PB, 978-1-58023-444-3 **$24.99**

Passover, 2nd Edition: The Family Guide to Spiritual Celebration
By Dr. Ron Wolfson with Joel Lurie Grishaver 7 x 9, 416 pp, Quality PB, 978-1-58023-174-9 **$19.95**

The Women's Passover Companion: Women's Reflections on the Festival of Freedom
Edited by Rabbi Sharon Cohen Anisfeld, Tara Mohr and Catherine Spector; Foreword by Paula E. Hyman
6 x 9, 352 pp, Quality PB, 978-1-58023-231-9 **$19.99**; HC, 978-1-58023-128-2 **$24.95**

The Women's Seder Sourcebook: Rituals & Readings for Use at the Passover Seder
Edited by Rabbi Sharon Cohen Anisfeld, Tara Mohr and Catherine Spector
6 x 9, 384 pp, Quality PB, 978-1-58023-232-6 **$19.99**

Spirituality

The Jewish Lights Spirituality Handbook: A Guide to Understanding, Exploring & Living a Spiritual Life *Edited by Stuart M. Matlins*
What exactly is "Jewish" about spirituality? How do I make it a part of my life? Fifty of today's foremost spiritual leaders share their ideas and experience with us.
6 x 9, 456 pp, Quality PB, 978-1-58023-093-3 **$19.99**

The Sabbath Soul: Mystical Reflections on the Transformative Power of Holy Time *Selection, Translation and Commentary by Eitan Fishbane, PhD*
Explores the writings of mystical masters of Hasidism. Provides translations and interpretations of a wide range of Hasidic sources previously unavailable in English that reflect the spiritual transformation that takes place on the seventh day.
6 x 9, 208 pp, Quality PB, 978-1-58023-459-7 **$18.99**

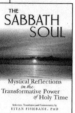

Repentance: The Meaning and Practice of *Teshuvah*
By Dr. Louis E. Newman; Foreword by Rabbi Harold M. Schulweis; Preface by Rabbi Karyn D. Kedar
Examines both the practical and philosophical dimensions of *teshuvah*, Judaism's core religious-moral teaching on repentance, and its value for us—Jews and non-Jews alike—today. 6 x 9, 256 pp, HC, 978-1-58023-426-9 **$24.99**

Aleph-Bet Yoga: Embodying the Hebrew Letters for Physical and Spiritual Well-Being
By Steven A. Rapp; Foreword by Tamar Frankiel, PhD, and Judy Greenfeld; Preface by Hart Lazer
7 x 10, 128 pp, b/w photos, Quality PB, Lay-flat binding, 978-1-58023-162-6 **$16.95**

A Book of Life: Embracing Judaism as a Spiritual Practice
By Rabbi Michael Strassfeld 6 x 9, 544 pp, Quality PB, 978-1-58023-247-0 **$19.99**

Bringing the Psalms to Life: How to Understand and Use the Book of Psalms
By Rabbi Daniel F. Polish, PhD 6 x 9, 208 pp, Quality PB, 978-1-58023-157-2 **$16.95**

Does the Soul Survive? A Jewish Journey to Belief in Afterlife, Past Lives & Living with Purpose *By Rabbi Elie Kaplan Spitz; Foreword by Brian L. Weiss, MD*
6 x 9, 288 pp, Quality PB, 978-1-58023-165-7 **$18.99**

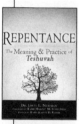

Entering the Temple of Dreams: Jewish Prayers, Movements and Meditations for the End of the Day *By Tamar Frankiel, PhD, and Judy Greenfeld*
7 x 10, 192 pp, illus., Quality PB, 978-1-58023-079-7 **$16.95**

First Steps to a New Jewish Spirit: Reb Zalman's Guide to Recapturing the Intimacy & Ecstasy in Your Relationship with God *By Rabbi Zalman M. Schachter-Shalomi with Donald Gropman* 6 x 9, 144 pp, Quality PB, 978-1-58023-182-4 **$16.95**

Foundations of Sephardic Spirituality: The Inner Life of Jews of the Ottoman Empire
By Rabbi Marc D. Angel, PhD 6 x 9, 224 pp, Quality PB, 978-1-58023-341-5 **$18.99**

God & the Big Bang: Discovering Harmony between Science & Spirituality
By Dr. Daniel C. Matt 6 x 9, 216 pp, Quality PB, 978-1-879045-89-7 **$18.99**

God in Our Relationships: Spirituality between People from the Teachings of Martin Buber *By Rabbi Dennis S. Ross* 5½ x 8½, 160 pp, Quality PB, 978-1-58023-147-3 **$16.95**

Judaism, Physics and God: Searching for Sacred Metaphors in a Post-Einstein World
By Rabbi David W. Nelson 6 x 9, 352 pp, Quality PB, inc. reader's discussion guide,
978-1-58023-306-4 **$18.99**; HC, 352 pp, 978-1-58023-252-4 **$24.99**

Meaning & Mitzvah: Daily Practices for Reclaiming Judaism through Prayer, God, Torah, Hebrew, Mitzvot and Peoplehood *By Rabbi Goldie Milgram*
7 x 9, 336 pp, Quality PB, 978-1-58023-256-2 **$19.99**

Minding the Temple of the Soul: Balancing Body, Mind, and Spirit through Traditional Jewish Prayer, Movement, and Meditation *By Tamar Frankiel, PhD, and Judy Greenfeld*
7 x 10, 184 pp, Illus., Quality PB, 978-1-879045-64-4 **$18.99**

One God Clapping: The Spiritual Path of a Zen Rabbi *By Rabbi Alan Lew with Sherril Jaffe*
5½ x 8¼, 336 pp, Quality PB, 978-1-58023-115-2 **$16.95**

The Soul of the Story: Meetings with Remarkable People
By Rabbi David Zeller 6 x 9, 288 pp, HC, 978-1-58023-272-2 **$21.99**

Tanya, the Masterpiece of Hasidic Wisdom: Selections Annotated & Explained
Translation & Annotation by Rabbi Rami Shapiro; Foreword by Rabbi Zalman M. Schachter-Shalomi
5½ x 8½, 240 pp, Quality PB, 978-1-59473-275-1 **$16.99**

These Are the Words, 2nd Edition: A Vocabulary of Jewish Spiritual Life
By Rabbi Arthur Green, PhD 6 x 9, 320 pp, Quality PB, 978-1-58023-494-8 **$19.99**

Spirituality / Prayer

Making Prayer Real: Leading Jewish Spiritual Voices on Why Prayer Is Difficult and What to Do about It *By Rabbi Mike Comins*
A new and different response to the challenges of Jewish prayer, with "best prayer practices" from Jewish spiritual leaders of all denominations.
6 x 9, 320 pp, Quality PB, 978-1-58023-417-7 **$18.99**

Witnesses to the One: The Spiritual History of the *Sh'ma*
By Rabbi Joseph B. Meszler; Foreword by Rabbi Elyse Goldstein
6 x 9, 176 pp, Quality PB, 978-1-58023-400-9 **$16.99**; HC, 978-1-58023-309-5 **$19.99**

My People's Prayer Book Series: Traditional Prayers, Modern Commentaries *Edited by Rabbi Lawrence A. Hoffman, PhD*
Provides diverse and exciting commentary to the traditional liturgy. Will help you find new wisdom in Jewish prayer, and bring liturgy into your life. Each book includes Hebrew text, modern translations and commentaries from all perspectives of the Jewish world.
Vol. 1—The *Sh'ma* and Its Blessings
  7 x 10, 168 pp, HC, 978-1-879045-79-8 **$29.99**
Vol. 2—The *Amidah* 7 x 10, 240 pp, HC, 978-1-879045-80-4 **$24.95**
Vol. 3—*P'sukei D'zimrah* (Morning Psalms)
  7 x 10, 240 pp, HC, 978-1-879045-81-1 **$29.99**
Vol. 4—*Seder K'riat Hatorah* (The Torah Service)
  7 x 10, 264 pp, HC, 978-1-879045-82-8 **$29.99**
Vol. 5—*Birkhot Hashachar* (Morning Blessings)
  7 x 10, 240 pp, HC, 978-1-879045-83-5 **$24.95**
Vol. 6—*Tachanun* and Concluding Prayers
  7 x 10, 240 pp, HC, 978-1-879045-84-2 **$24.95**
Vol. 7—Shabbat at Home 7 x 10, 240 pp, HC, 978-1-879045-85-9 **$24.95**
Vol. 8—*Kabbalat Shabbat* (Welcoming Shabbat in the Synagogue)
  7 x 10, 240 pp, HC, 978-1-58023-121-3 **$24.99**
Vol. 9—Welcoming the Night: *Minchah* and *Ma'ariv* (Afternoon and
  Evening Prayer) 7 x 10, 272 pp, HC, 978-1-58023-262-3 **$24.99**
Vol. 10—Shabbat Morning: *Shacharit* and *Musaf* (Morning and
  Additional Services) 7 x 10, 240 pp, HC, 978-1-58023-240-1 **$29.99**

Spirituality / Lawrence Kushner

I'm God; You're Not: Observations on Organized Religion & Other Disguises of the Ego
  6 x 9, 256 pp, Quality PB, 978-1-58023-513-6 **$18.99**; HC, 978-1-58023-441-2 **$21.99**

The Book of Letters: A Mystical Hebrew Alphabet
  Popular HC Edition, 6 x 9, 80 pp, 2-color text, 978-1-879045-00-2 **$24.95**
  Collector's Limited Edition, 9 x 12, 80 pp, gold-foil-embossed pages, w/ limited-edition silkscreened print, 978-1-879045-04-0 **$349.00**

The Book of Miracles: A Young Person's Guide to Jewish Spiritual Awareness
  6 x 9, 96 pp, 2-color illus., HC, 978-1-879045-78-1 **$16.95** *For ages 9–13*

The Book of Words: Talking Spiritual Life, Living Spiritual Talk
  6 x 9, 160 pp, Quality PB, 978-1-58023-020-9 **$18.99**

Eyes Remade for Wonder: A Lawrence Kushner Reader *Introduction by Thomas Moore*
  6 x 9, 240 pp, Quality PB, 978-1-58023-042-1 **$18.95**

God Was in This Place & I, i Did Not Know: Finding Self, Spirituality and
  Ultimate Meaning 6 x 9, 192 pp, Quality PB, 978-1-879045-33-0 **$16.95**

Honey from the Rock: An Introduction to Jewish Mysticism
  6 x 9, 176 pp, Quality PB, 978-1-58023-073-5 **$16.95**

Invisible Lines of Connection: Sacred Stories of the Ordinary
  5½ x 8½, 160 pp, Quality PB, 978-1-879045-98-9 **$16.99**

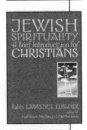

Jewish Spirituality: A Brief Introduction for Christians
  5½ x 8½, 112 pp, Quality PB, 978-1-58023-150-3 **$12.95**

The River of Light: Jewish Mystical Awareness
  6 x 9, 192 pp, Quality PB, 978-1-58023-096-4 **$18.99**

The Way Into Jewish Mystical Tradition
  6 x 9, 224 pp, Quality PB, 978-1-58023-200-5 **$18.99**; HC, 978-1-58023-029-2 **$21.95**

About Jewish Lights

People of all faiths and backgrounds yearn for books that attract, engage, educate, and spiritually inspire.

Our principal goal is to stimulate thought and help all people learn about who the Jewish People are, where they come from, and what the future can be made to hold. While people of our diverse Jewish heritage are the primary audience, our books speak to people in the Christian world as well and will broaden their understanding of Judaism and the roots of their own faith.

We bring to you authors who are at the forefront of spiritual thought and experience. While each has something different to say, they all say it in a voice that you can hear.

Our books are designed to welcome you and then to engage, stimulate, and inspire. We judge our success not only by whether or not our books are beautiful and commercially successful, but by whether or not they make a difference in your life.

For your information and convenience, at the back of this book we have provided a list of other Jewish Lights books you might find interesting and useful. They cover all the categories of your life:

Bar/Bat Mitzvah	Life Cycle
Bible Study / Midrash	Meditation
Children's Books	Men's Interest
Congregation Resources	Parenting
Current Events / History	Prayer / Ritual / Sacred Practice
Ecology / Environment	Social Justice
Fiction: Mystery, Science Fiction	Spirituality
Grief / Healing	Theology / Philosophy
Holidays / Holy Days	Travel
Inspiration	Twelve Steps
Kabbalah / Mysticism / Enneagram	Women's Interest

Stuart M. Matlins, Publisher

Or phone, fax, mail or e-mail to: **JEWISH LIGHTS Publishing**
Sunset Farm Offices, Route 4 • P.O. Box 237 • Woodstock, Vermont 05091
Tel: (802) 457-4000 • Fax: (802) 457-4004 • www.jewishlights.com
Credit card orders: **(800) 962-4544** (8:30AM–5:30PM EST Monday–Friday)
Generous discounts on quantity orders. SATISFACTION GUARANTEED. Prices subject to change.

**For more information about each book,
visit our website at www.jewishlights.com**